Open-Economy Macroeconomics for Developing Countries

Open-Economy Macroeconomics for Developing Countries

Akhtar Hossain

Akhtar Hossain

Senior Lecturer in Economics, University of Newcastle, Australia

Anis Chowdhury

Associate Professor of Economics, University of Western Sydney, Macarthur, Australia

Edward Elgar
Cheltenham, UK • Northampton, MA, USA

Published by
Edward Elgar Publishing Limited
8 Lansdown Place
Cheltenham
Glos GL50 2HU

Edward Elgar Publishing, Inc.
6 Market Street
Northampton
Massachusetts 01060
USA

A catalogue record for this book is available from the British Library

Library of Congress Cataloguing in Publication Data
Hossain, Akhtar.
    Open-economy macroeconomics for developing countries / Akhtar
Hossain, Anis Chowdhury.
    Includes bibliographical references and index.
    1. Fiscal policy—Developing countries.   2. Monetary policy—
Developing countries.   I. Chowdhury, Anis. 1954–   .   II. Title.
HJ1620.H67 1998
339.5'2'091724—dc21   97–50580
                                                                                          CIP

ISBN 1 85898 227 8

Typeset by Manton Typesetters, 5–7 Eastfield Road, Louth, Lincolnshire, LN11 7AJ, UK.
Printed and bound in England by MPG Books Ltd, Bodmin, Cornwall

Contents

Tables

Figures

Preface

The developing countries, having had nearly three decades of autarkic regimes, have embraced liberalization since the early 1980s. A number of factors were responsible for this shift, the foremost being those countries' inability to achieve the high economic growth necessary for breaking the vicious circle of poverty. This was despite the fact that the long-term growth objective always dominated their economic strategy, even if it meant the generation of macroeconomic instability. The crunch came when, ironically, the inward-looking economies found themselves in deeper trouble in the face of external shocks arising from sharp and sudden oil price rises than did a small number of open economies of North East Asia. There were at least two lessons to be learnt from the experience of successful North East Asian economies: first, macroeconomic stability is a prerequisite for high economic growth and, second, if economies are open then they must maintain macroeconomic stability. However maintaining macroeconomic stability is not an easy task as the achievement of internal balance often worsens the external balance and vice versa. Moreover open economies are more vulnerable to external shocks and international capital flows put a greater burden on traditional fiscal and monetary policies in achieving internal and external balance simultaneously.

This volume provides a comprehensive survey of developing countries' macroeconomic experience, such as the debt crisis and policy options, as they liberalize their economies. It also gives an overview of various institutional developments such as the IMF, WTO and UNCTAD. The volume brings together advanced theoretical and empirical research published in academic journals although the use of mathematics is kept at a minimum and the discussion is supplemented by diagrams and charts. This work will be found useful by advanced undergraduate/graduate students and policy makers who are interested in developing economies.

In writing an advanced macroeconomics text of this length, we quickly found ourselves running out of symbols. Thus, despite our best efforts to maintain consistency, we had to use the same symbol to express different concepts. Hence, the reader is reminded of the fact that symbols used in the book are chapter and topic specific.

In our research and writing we constantly benefited from discussions with our friends and colleagues, and our thanks go to everyone. We express our special gratitude to Professor Colm Kearney of the University of Technology, Sydney, Australia and Professor James Dean of Simon Fraser University, Vancouver, Canada, who have taken a lot of interest in our work and kindly read the manuscript. Their insightful comments have been immensely useful. Ahmad Assadzadeh of the University of Western Sydney, Macarthur, Australia has done an excellent job with diagrams – our thanks to him too. The Writing Fellowship from the University of Western Sydney, Macarthur (to the second author) has been extremely useful as the bloc of teaching-free time was crucial in producing the final draft without further delay.

Finally it is the family that takes the toll, especially when it is very young and growing, but they are happy to see the task accomplished. We dedicate this volume to our families.

1. Openness and macroeconomic performance

INTRODUCTION

> ...[for] less-developed nations ... macroeconomic problems and policies are not nearly as important as development plans and resources.

The above remark by Prachowny (1981:9) epitomizes the conventional wisdom that prevailed in developing countries until about the mid-1970s. The conventional wisdom with regard to macroeconomic policy or monetary stability and fiscal prudence in developing countries was directly related to the dirigistic regime that most of these countries had followed during the 1950s and 1960s, the main characteristics of which are as follows :

1. inward looking import substituting industrialization (ISI),
2. a repressed financial sector with interest rates set below the equilibrium level,
3. large government budget deficits financed by money creation,
4. a high inflation rate and
5. an overvalued real exchange rate.

The first three of these define the policy parameters while the last two are the consequences of these policies. Although with the benefit of hindsight any dirigistic regime is now found unsustainable, there were good political and economic reasons for these policies of newly independent former colonies. To begin with, the new nations wanted to break the dependence on their former colonial masters and ISI was regarded as the best possible route. This was backed by the initial success of the former Soviet Union in achieving accelerated industrialization through autarkic policies. The economic argument followed from the belief that the trade between developed nations (centres) and developing countries (peripheries) is characterized by unequal exchanges. This idea found its expression in the much celebrated Singer-Prebisch hypothesis, namely that the terms of trade of primary producing developing countries vis-à-vis industrial countries declines secularly, reducing their real purchasing power. Furthermore international commodity prices are more volatile than the world prices of manufactured goods and the commodity production depends on the vagaries of nature. The policy prescription that followed was that developing countries should start by substituting light consumer products for which there were domestic markets and then progressively substitute intermediate and capital goods. This was also believed to reduce pressure on their balance of payments.

How can rapid industrialization be achieved in capital scarce countries? There are two sides – demand and supply – to this problem. From the demand side it was argued that if left to the market the interest rate will be exorbitantly high, which will deter potential investors. What followed was the ceiling placed on the interest rate below the equilibrium level. This policy was seen to have an additional advantage in that when the interest rate is set below its equilibrium level, an excess demand for credit is created and that allows governments to ration (direct) credit to socially desirable sectors or projects.

The supply-side argument depends on the 'forced saving' hypothesis. According to this hypothesis investment can be increased autonomously by a government without prior savings through monetary expansion (Kalecki, 1976). Such an investment will generate its own savings in at least four ways. First, if resources are underemployed, monetary expansion will increase aggregate demand and hence output and savings. Second, if resources are fully employed or if there are supply rigidities, monetary expansion will generate inflation. Inflation lowers the real return on financial investment and thereby induces wealthholders to change their portfolio by investing in physical capital. The resultant rise in capital intensity increases output and hence savings (Tobin, 1965). Third, inflation increases savings by changing the income distribution in favour of profit earners with a higher propensity to save compared with that of wage earners (Kaldor, 1955–56). Fourth, inflation imposes tax on real money balances and thereby transfers resources to the government (Friedman, 1971), which can be used for financing investment.

In a world of fixed exchange rates under the Bretton Woods system, which existed until the early 1970s, high inflation meant an overvalued real exchange rate. The overvaluation of the exchange rate made the exports of developing countries uncompetitive in the international market. However this was not deemed inconsistent with the philosophy of ISI. The inability to earn foreign exchange through exports did not matter as the import needs were supposedly eliminated as the country attained self-sufficiency through ISI.

The above conventional wisdom was shattered in the 1970s by world events and both empirical and theoretical findings. The collapse of the Bretton Woods system in 1972–73 coincided with the unprecedented and sudden rise in the Organisation of Petroleum Exporting Countries (OPEC) oil prices. The oil price shock created a massive external imbalance and caused a decline in real incomes of oil-importing developing countries. It was found that those countries which relied on an export-oriented development strategy and hence had a more realistic exchange rate weathered the oil price shock much better than those following ISI. The open economies were also found to have a more stable macroeconomic environment and an enviable growth record. This is at least the experience of the newly industrializing economies (NIEs) of East and South East Asia.

The conventional wisdom was also challenged at the intellectual front by seminal publications of McKinnon and Shaw (McKinnon, 1973; Shaw, 1973). Both McKinnon and Shaw argued that low or negative real interest rates (a symptom of financial repression) have a number of growth-inhibiting effects. First, they encourage current consumption and induce people to hold their savings in real assets (gold, land) rather than financial assets, as they are a better hedge against inflation. Thus financial repression adversely affects both the volume and composition of savings. As a result the financial sector remains shallow, which inhibits the monetization of the economy and the efficiency of transactions. Second, low or negative real interest rates encourage inefficiency of investment as it costs so little. In the words of Fry (1991:30):

> Overtime, shift work and other measures that increase the effective utilization of plant and machinery are not worthwhile when keeping the capital stock idle is costless.

The negative or very low real interest rates also encourage capital intensive industrialization which is not in line with developing countries' comparative advantage. This has two adverse effects. First, employment does not grow at a sufficiently rapid rate with the result that the purchasing power and domestic market development suffer. Second, the trade balance deteriorates as import demands for capital goods outpace export growth. Thus both internal and external imbalance worsen with deleterious effects on economic growth.

In addition to the McKinnon-Shaw hypothesis, the intellectual challenge to the conventional wisdom also came from the works of Krueger (1978), Bhagwati (1978), and Bhagwati and Srinivasan (1975). The major theme of their argument is that when controls are imposed either on interest rates or the exchange rate (or for that matter on any other prices) or on imports, it creates excess demand, the net effect of which is the creation of monopoly rents or a scarcity premium. The presence of such rents can induce wasteful rent-seeking and lobbying activities. Even worse, a vicious circle may set in : an initial policy intervention creates monopoly elements which then become entrenched and oppose change and reform and, in fact, induce further policy interventions that create cumulative monopoly rents which retard economic development.

Lessons from East Asia

Table 1.1 presents some selected economic indicators of the North-East and South-East Asian NIEs. It also includes some African, Latin American and South Asian economies as comparators. Clearly North-East and South-East Asian economies are more open than the others as indicated by exports to GNP ratios. The open economies of North East and South East Asia stand out for their superior trade and macroeconomic performance. Starting from a very high base, exports from these economies (excluding Korea) grew by 15 to 21 per cent during the first half of the 1990s, as opposed to between 9 and 13 per cent in South Asia, between –2 and 9 per cent in Africa and between – 1.0 and 15 per cent in Latin America. The North- and South-East Asian economies grew at an average annual rate ranging from 6 to 10 per cent during the 1980s and the first half of the 1990s. By comparison the average annual growth rates varied between –1.4 and 4.4 per cent in Africa, between –0.3 and 7.6 per cent in Latin America and between 3.8 and 6.3 per cent in South Asia. The highest rate of inflation recorded in the North- and South-East Asian economies was about 9 per cent (Hong Kong), but was 11 per cent for South Asia (Pakistan), 42.4 per cent for Africa (Ghana) and 1231.5 per cent for Latin America (Brazil).

The spectacular success of the Asian NIEs begs two questions. Is there a link between openness and macroeconomic stability? What is the link between macroeconomic stability and economic growth?

The openness of an economy and macroeconomic stability are interlinked – they feed each other. For example, an export oriented economy must maintain its international competitiveness. This requires low inflation and a realistic real exchange rate. As summarised by Petrie (1993:14):

> Realistic exchange rates were a hallmark of East Asian macroeconomic policy. Several of miracles began with major exchange rate reforms, which included devaluations, the unification of multiple exchange rates, and the commitments to keeping real exchange rates competitive.... While these aggressive exchange rate policies were initially adopted to solve some balance of payments problems ... they proved so successful in generating export growth...

The experience of Asian NIEs also shows that if an economy is open, any policy mistake becomes obvious much earlier as its competitiveness suffers. To regain its position it must act quickly. Thus both recognition and reaction lags for an open economy are short (Chowdhury, 1996). Policy mistakes cannot extend too far, for too long. In other words, openness imposes an external constraint on macroeconomic mismanagement.

In operationalizing the hypothesis that 'sound macroeconomic policies' are systematically linked to good economic growth, Little *et al* (1993) adopt a

Table 1.1 Openness, macroeconomic performance and growth

Country	Export/GNP (%)		Export growth (%)		GDP growth (%)		Per capita GNP	Inflation rate (%)		Debt service ratio (%)	
	1980	1994	1980–90	1990–94	1980–90	1990–94	Growth 1985–94	1980–90	1990–94	1980	1994
Indonesia	33	25	5.3	21.3	6.1	7.6	6.0	8.5	7.4	13.9	32.4
Thailand	24	39	14.3	21.6	7.6	8.2	8.6	3.9	4.4	20.4	16.3
Malaysia	58	90	11.5	17.8	5.2	8.4	5.6	1.7	3.7	6.6	7.9
Korea	34	36	13.7	7.4	9.4	6.6	7.8	5.9	6.3	20.3	7.0
Hong Kong	90	139	15.4	15.3	6.9	5.7	5.3	7.7	8.9	na	na
Singapore	207	177	12.1	16.1	6.4	8.3	6.1	2.0	3.7	na	na
Bangladesh	6	12	7.5	12.7	4.3	4.2	2.0	9.5	4.1	25.6	15.8
India	7	12	6.3	7.0	5.8	3.8	2.9	8.0	10.1	10.0	26.9
Pakistan	12	16	9.5	8.8	6.3	4.6	1.3	6.7	10.8	18.1	35.1
Ghana	8	25	3.1	9.1	3.0	4.3	1.4	42.4	20.7	13.2	24.8
Burundi	9	14	7.4	-4.8	4.4	-1.4	-0.7	4.4	7.1	na	41.7
Niger	24	13	-6.4	-2.0	-1.1	-0.3	-2.1	2.9	4.7	22.7	26.1
Mexico	11	13	12.2	14.7	1.0	2.5	0.9	70.4	13.1	50.9	35.4
Argentina	5	7	3.1	-1.0	-0.3	7.6	2.0	389.1	27.6	42.3	35.1
Brazil	9	8	6.1	6.6	2.7	2.2	-0.4	284.5	1231.5	67.7	35.8

Note: na = not available.

Source: World Bank, World Development Report 1996

framework which is both tractable and intellectually appealing. Recognizing that economic growth reflects the confluence of a complex set of variables which may not be linked easily to macroeconomic policy, the Little *et al* study focuses on the behaviour of the average saving and investment ratios in terms of both their stability and productivity. The results of their study are summarised in Table 1.2. This reveals that the three Asia-Pacific economies had higher average investment and saving ratios than both the 'intermediate' and 'bad' performers and also achieved higher efficiency of investment.

Table 1.2   Impact of macroeconomic stability on growth, saving and investment, 1970–89

Economy	Growth in GNP capita (%)	Investment ratio (%)	Investment efficiency	Saving ratio (%)
Korea	6.5	29	21	25
Indonesia	4.2	26	16	26
Thailand	4.1	22	20	22
Group Average: 'Intermediate'	1.9	22	8	17
Group Average: 'Bad'	−2.3	20	2	16

Notes:
(1)   Group average 'intermediate' = average value for six intermediate performing countries (Brazil, Turkey, India, Morocco, Colombia, Kenya).
(2)   Group average 'bad' = average value for six badly performing countries (Mexico, Costa Rica, Chile, Côte d'Ivoire, Argentina, Nigeria).
(3)   Investment efficiency = growth in GNP per capita / investment ratio

Source: Little *et al*, 1993: Table 11.1

The focus on the behaviour of investment is justified on the ground that fiscal imbalances may 'crowd out' private investment. In addition, the macroeconomic experience of many developing economies tends to suggest that fiscal expansion through external financing is not a viable option for long-term sustained economic growth. For example, during the era of easy availability of external finance, the countries which engaged in a public-sector led investment boom were forced to undertake a drastic retrenchment once the macroeconomic crunch came in the early 1980s. In addition to the crippling debt crisis, the boom-bust cycle can undermine the confidence of the private sector and induce capital flight, exacerbating the external imbalance.

There is one other avenue through which a deficit financed boom-bust cycle may adversely affect economic growth. A public sector-led investment boom often leads to a choice of projects which do not satisfy strict cost-benefit analysis (Little and Mirless, 1991). High inflation due to money financed fiscal deficits in a repressed financial sector results in many cases in negative real interest rates. As mentioned earlier this encourages inefficient utilization of investment funds. As a result the portfolio of investments would be dominated by inefficient, poorly selected projects and the productivity of investment will suffer.

Reviewing the experience of the successful Asian countries, Leipziger and Thomas (1993:9) comment as follows on the central role of fiscal prudence in ensuring macroeconomic stability:

> East Asia's governments exercised macro-economic discipline, ensuring that fiscal and external deficits were kept in control ... Over the past quarter century the fiscal deficit and the current account deficit in developing East Asia were less than half the average for other developing countries.

Thus, there is a close association between openness, macroeconomic stability and growth performance, and the dichotomy between short-term macroeconomic management and long-term growth policies is an artificial one. In the words of Summers and Thomas (1993:248), 'Sound macroeconomic policies with sustainable fiscal deficits and realistic exchange rates are a prerequisite to progress'. There is now overwhelming evidence to support the view that high and variable inflation as well as unsustainable external imbalance adversely affect economic growth (Hossain and Chowdhury, 1996). The flow chart in Figure 1.1 shows the virtuous circle of openness, macroeconomic stability and economic growth.

Although the open economies perform better, they are not necessarily without problems. To begin with, the open economies face more policy dilemmas. For example in addition to traditional unemployment-inflation trade-off, they have to worry about external imbalance that may result from expansionary policies. While more policy targets require more policy instruments, the openness (especially capital flows) places more burden on traditional fiscal and monetary policies and reduces their effectiveness. The problem may compound as open economies are more vulnerable to external shocks (both demand and supply). The stagflation of the 1970s, following two oil price shocks, and the debt crises of the 1980s are stark reminders of the problems that open developing economies can face. This volume examines macroeconomic problems and policy dilemmas faced by open developing economies.

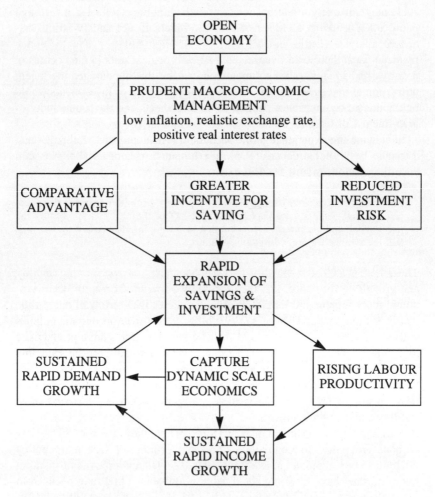

*Figure 1.1   Virtuous circle of openness, macroeconomic stability and
                growth*

A READER'S GUIDE

Chapter 2 deals with some important concepts such as the balance of payments accounts, exchange rates, purchasing power parity and the terms of trade. It then examines some of the problems and policy dilemmas faced by developing countries. Among the issues discussed are linkages between fiscal deficits, money supply and macroeconomic imbalances, and macroeconomic problems arising from external shocks and capital flows. This chapter also provides a brief overview of various institutional developments such as the IMF, GATT, WTO and UNCTAD.

Chapter 3 presents the salient features of some popular open macroeconomy models, with a view to highlighting the effectiveness of demand management and exchange rate policies. The models include the absorption and monetary approaches to the balance of payments, the Mundell-Fleming model, and the Swan-Salter-Corden traded-nontraded sectors model. The monetary approach to the balance of payments together with the traded-nontraded sectors model forms the basis of IMF/World Bank adjustment programmes designed for developing countries with a severe external imbalance.

Chapter 4 looks at foreign capital flows – both official and private. It examines the rationale for foreign capital within the two-gap model. A substantial part of the chapter is devoted to a discussion of the pros and cons of large short-run private capital inflows and macroeconomic management problems that they can present.

Chapter 5 revisits the debt crises of the 1930s and 1980s. It also analyses the reverse side of capital inflows, that is, capital flights. It argues that a stable financial and macroeconomic environment is a major requirement in preventing substantial capital flights.

Chapter 6 focuses on the link between budget deficits and macroeconomic imbalances. It examines various causes – economic and political – of large budget deficits. It shows that over-reliance on monetary expansion or on external borrowings for financing deficits carries the danger of causing both internal and external imbalances. It argues that although a one-off budget deficit may not create any major problem, a sustained large budget deficit can cause major macroeconomic imbalances when it is perceived by investors as unsustainable.

Chapter 7 is devoted to monetary policy. Having established the link between money supply growth and inflation, it argues that monetary policy should be targeted to price stability rather than output stabilization. It shows that a money supply growth rule can ensure intertemporal stability in inflation if a country follows a flexible exchange rate system and there is a stable money demand function.

Chapter 8 reviews key issues in exchange rate policy. It argues that a flexible or crawling-peg system is a better option for developing countries with stable or low inflation. However, for high inflationary countries it is argued that a fixed exchange rate can provide a credible nominal anchor.

Chapter 9 is the concluding chapter and reflects on the political economy of macroeconomic management and the need for institutional change. It reviews the sources of government failure and argues that the choice is not *laissez-faire* versus government intervention. Rather, the challenge is to pursue administrative and political reforms and design institutions which will minimize both market and government failures. It argues that an optimal mix of private and public sectors in an open economy can act as constraints on macroeconomic mismanagement.

2. Open-economy macroeconomics – concepts, issues and institutions

INTRODUCTION

Since the 1970s the world has witnessed a very rapid increase in the volume of international trade and capital flows. Both exports and imports grew at an annual rate of more than 20 per cent during the 1970s, as opposed to less than 10 per cent in the preceeding decade. What is significant is that developing countries outperformed developed market economies and recorded average annual growth rates of 25.9 per cent and 23.8 per cent for exports and imports respectively during 1970–1980. This implies that developing countries as a group have become more open since the 1970s and for many countries, especially in North and South East Asia, the share of world trade has increased manifoldly. These countries have also been attracting a huge flow of capital since the late 1980s, after a period of doubt in the international capital market resulting from the debt crisis in the early 1980s. Following the successful completion of the Uruguay Round of multilateral trade negotiations and the collapse of autarkic communist regimes, world trade is expected to grow further. The wave of trade and financial liberalization in developing countries since the early 1980s has accelerated their integration with the world economy and capital markets.

This increased interdependence among nations has major implications for national economies. The oil price shocks of the 1970s, subsequent recessions in industrialized countries and the debt crisis of developing countries in the early 1980s have revealed that economic disturbances can transmit across countries regardless of their level of development. It also revealed that, paradoxically, countries which were more open to international trade and capital adjusted to such external shocks relatively more easily and quickly than those which had followed autarkic policies (Balassa and McCarthy, 1984; Little *et al*, 1993). Their economies also grew at a faster rate than those of countries which had inward-looking policies.

Despite these revelations, scepticism still exists about the increased dependence of developing countries on world trade and finance. This chapter provides a brief overview of issues faced by developing countries in an interdependent world, beginning with a discussion of some relevant concepts. The chapter will end with a review of the historical development of institutions to deal with international transactions of goods, services and capital.

CONCEPTS

Balance of Payments

A nation's economic transactions with the rest of the world are recorded in its balance of payments and hence this is the primary point of focus for an open economy. It is also referred to as external accounts. There are two sides of the balance of payments or external accounts. The current account balance (CA) records the transactions of goods and services as well as interest payments on debt and remittances. The capital account balance (KA) records the flows of capital, both short-term (bank deposits and borrowings, known as portfolio investment) and long-term (foreign direct investment and equity). Foreign aid and grants are also recorded in the KA. The main components of the external accounts and their relationships are summarised in Table 2.1.

Table 2.1   External accounting relations

Merchandise Trade Balance				
				Net Portfolio Foreign Investment (Short-term capital flows)
Services Trade Balance	Current Account Balance	Capital Account Balance	Net Foreign Investment	
Property Income				
				Net Direct Foreign Investment (Long-term capital flows)
Labour and other Income				
Unrequited Transfers				

Note: Unrequited transfers are recorded whenever goods, services or financial assets (foreign aid, taxes, migrants' transfers) are transferred between residents and foreigners without anything of value being received by domestic residents in return.

By definition, the balance of payments always balances. That is, any deficit (surplus) in CA should be matched by a surplus (deficit) in KA. More capital inflows can be encouraged to match the deficit in CA by raising the domestic interest rate *vis-à-vis* the foreign interest rate. However if capital inflows are not sufficient, the adjustment happens through changes in the exchange rate. For example, if the deficit in CA exceeds the surplus in KA, the exchange rate depreciates making the country more competitive with the result that its exports increase and imports decrease. However if a country prevents adjustments in exchange rates (under a fixed or managed exchange rate system), any discrepancy between CA and KA will be matched by changes in official reserves of foreign currencies (OR). A country is said to suffer from a balance of payments crisis when deficits in CA are not matched by surpluses in KA and the country does not have enough foreign reserves, nor can it borrow any more, to fill the gap. It is at this point that developing countries approach the World Bank and/or the International Monetary Fund (IMF) for external adjustment loans.

Exchange Rates

The exchange rate is the relative price of one currency in terms of another. The bilateral nominal exchange rate (e) is the price of a unit of foreign currency (F$) in terms of domestic currency (D$). For example, the exchange rate of Bangladesh domestic currency is 40 Taka for one US dollar (e = D$/ F$). In simple terms the nominal exchange rate can be expressed as:

$$e = P_d/P_f$$

where P_d is the domestic price level and P_f is the foreign price level. It can also be defined as:

$$E = F\$/D\$ = P_f/P_d = 1/e$$

that is, the price of a unit of domestic currency in terms of foreign currency. In this book we will use the former definition (unless mentioned otherwise).

The multilateral exchange rate or nominal effective exchange rate (NEE) is a weighted average of a country's bilateral nominal exchange rate against the currencies of its trading partners. The weights are the country's trade shares with its major trading partners. When the nominal exchange rate is adjusted for domestic inflation, we obtain the real exchange rate as

$$R = e\ P_f/P_d.$$

Exchange rates can be fully market determined by the interaction of demand for and supply of foreign exchange. This is known as flexible exchange rates. The demand for foreign exchange arises from import demand (and capital outflows) while the supply of foreign exchange arises from exports (and capital inflows). If a country's imports exceed its exports and the country experiences an overall deficit in the balance of payments, the demand for foreign exchange will exceed its supply resulting in a rise in the price of foreign currency (depreciation of domestic currency – a rise in 'e').

In contrast to fully flexible exchange rates, there are fixed rates. When exchange rates are fixed, the central bank of a country must be ready to sell (buy) foreign currency whenever there is an excess demand (supply) of foreign currency at the official rate. Selling of foreign currencies is possible for a longer period of time if the country in question has sufficient reserves of foreign currencies. Furthermore selling and buying of foreign currencies by the central bank can have implications for the money supply.[1]

Until very recently most developing countries have followed a fixed exchange rate system or some variants of it known as managed pegs, meaning the currency is fixed in terms of either a weighted average of bilateral rates with a basket of currencies (usually of major trading partners) or special drawing rights (SDRs). SDRs are a 'paper' asset created by the IMF. However as developing countries are increasingly integrated with the world economy, their exchange rate system is moving towards a more flexible regime. Table 2.2 gives a summary picture of exchange rate systems of developing countries.

The exchange rate is claimed to be one of the most important variables for any economy which is highly integrated with the rest of the world, as it is a crucial determinant of that country's international competitiveness. The foreign demand for a country's product depends not only on the price expressed in its own currency but also on the conversion rate of foreign currency into its currency. Thus an index of competitiveness of a country is given by the real exchange rate, measured as:

$$R = eP_f/P_d \tag{2.1}$$

where P_d is the domestic price index and P_f is the foreign price index.

When the nominal effective exchange rate (that is, the rate weighted by bilateral trade shares) is used in (2.1) then the real exchange rate is called the effective exchange rate, expressed as:

$$REE = NEE \ (P_f/P_d) \tag{2.1a}$$

where NEE is the nominal effective exchange rate.

Table 2.2   Exchange rate systems of developing countries (30 June 1995)

Category	Countries	Number
Independently floating	Afghanistan, Bolivia, Costa Rica, El Salvador, Ethiopia, Gambia, Ghana, Guatemala, Guinea, Guyana, Haiti, India, Iran, Jamaica, Kenya, Lebanon, Madagascar, Malawi, Mexico, Mongolia, Mozambique, Papua New Guinea, Paraguay, Peru, Philippines, Rwanda, Sierra Leone, Somalia, Surinam, Tanzania, Trinidad and Tobago, Uganda, Zaire, Zambia, Zimbabwe	35
Other managed floating	Algeria, Angola, Brazil, Cambodia, People's Republic of China, Colombia, Dominican Republic, Egypt, Erithira, Guinea-Bissau, Honduras, Indonesia, Israel, Korea, Lao, Malaysia, Maldives, Mauritius, Pakistan, Singapore, Sri Lanka, Sudan, Tunisia, Turkey, Uruguay, Vietnam	26
Flexible according to a set of indicators	Chile, Ecuador, Nicaragua	3
Flexibility limited in terms of a single currency (US$)	Bahrain, Qatar, Saudi Arabia, United Arab Emirates	4
Pegged to other composite ('basket')	Bangladesh, Botswana, Burundi, Cape Verde, Cyprus, Fiji, Jordan, Kuwait, Malta, Mauritania, Morocco, Nepal, Solomon Islands, Thailand, Tonga, Vanuatu, Western Samoa	17
Pegged to SDR	Libya, Burma, Seychelles	3
Fixed to a single other Currency	Bhutan (to Indian rupee), Kiribati (to Australian dollar), Lesotho (to South African rand), Namibia (to South African rand), Swaziland (to South African rand)	5
Fixed to French franc	Benin, Burkina Faso, Cameroon, Central African Republic, Chad, Comoros, Congo, Côte d'Ivoire, Equatorial Guinea, Gabon, Mali, Niger, Senegal, Togo	14
Fixed to US dollar	Antigua and Bermuda, Argentina, Bahamas, Barbados, Belize, Djibouti, Dominica, Grenada, Iraq, Liberia, Nigeria, Oman, Panama, Sudan, Syria, Venezuela, Yemen	17

Note: The list does not include former Soviet Republics and East European transitional economies.

Source: IMF, International Financial Statistics Yearbook, 1995 : 18

A decline in REE means an improvement in international competitiveness. REE reflects two possible sources of changes in overall competitiveness. First, the competitiveness improves if the domestic rate of inflation is lower than the foreign rate for a given NEE. Second, if the NEE depreciates for a given ratio of domestic and foreign price levels, competitiveness improves. This also means that movements in the NEE and the P_f/P_d ratio in opposite directions can offset each other with a neutralizing effect on competitiveness. Therefore when a country allows its NEE to depreciate with a view to improving its competitiveness, it must resist an offsetting rise in the domestic price level.

Movements in exchange rates are also important due to their effects on debt servicing. If the value of domestic currency declines then the cost of servicing the debt increases even if the total debt, denominated in foreign currency, does not.

Purchasing Power Parity

The purchasing power parity (PPP) links nominal exchange rate movements to changes in national price levels or inflation rates. There are two versions of PPP – absolute and relative PPP. The absolute PPP is derived from the 'law of one price' which depends on commodity price arbitrage – buying from low price sources and selling to high price locations in order to take profit from price differentials among different locations. This process ensures that prices of homogeneous products are eventually equalized across countries. In a macroeconomic sense, the national price levels will tend to equalize due to arbitrage so that the absolute PPP relation becomes

$$e = P_d/ P_f \qquad (2.2)$$

where e is the nominal exchange rate. Equation (2.2) states that if the domestic inflation rate is higher than the trading partner's inflation rate, the exchange rate depreciates against the currency of the trading partner.

The relative PPP is an alternative specification and is expressed as

$$e^* = P_d^* - P_f^* \qquad (2.3)$$

where * indicates percentage changes. Equation (2.3) states that the percentage depreciation of the nominal exchange rate is equal to the inflation rate differential between two countries.

Edwards (1989:118) has examined the PPP relationship for 28 developing countries and concluded that '... the strong absolute version of PPP fails miserably'. There are several reasons which may prevent the strict holding of PPP, namely:

1. different weights used in calculating national price indices,
2. differentiated products instead of homogeneous products,
3. trade restrictions,
4. non-tradability of some goods and services and
5. transport costs.

However when the PPP holds, the real exchange rate ($R = eP_f/P_d$) will always be unity, so that any rise (fall) in the foreign price level would be fully offset by an appreciation (depreciation) of the nominal exchange rate (e).

If R falls below one, a country's competitiveness declines, suggesting that the current nominal exchange rate is overvalued. This can be offset by a nominal depreciation (a rise in 'e'). Typically, developing countries' nominal exchange rates are found to be overvalued and this is the basis for the World Bank/IMF prescription for currency devaluation when a country faces a serious balance of payments problem.

Terms of Trade

The terms of trade (TOT) is the ratio of the price of exports to the price of imports, that is:

$$TOT = P_x/P_m \tag{2.4}$$

where P_x is the export price index and P_m is the import price index. The TOT is a major vehicle through which external shocks are transmitted to small open economies. A country is said to be small if it is a price-taker in the international market. Except for a few countries, most developing countries do not have market powers and are small. The TOT may not matter much in a macroeconomic sense if a country exports and imports the same products. However the structure of exports and imports of most small developing countries is vastly different. As a result, these countries are susceptible to external shocks as the international factors affecting the prices of their exports are different from those affecting the prices of their imports.

The TOT effectively measures the purchasing power of a country's GDP. For example, if export prices rise at a faster rate than import prices (a rise in the TOT), a country is able to buy more imports with its export earnings. On the other hand if the TOT declines, the purchasing power of a country's GDP declines (that is, a drop in real GDP) . Therefore it is essential that the GDPs of open economies are adjusted for TOT changes. This can be done as follows:

GDP at constant prices – Exports (X) at constant prices
+ X deflated by the import price index (P_m).

Table 2.3 Real GDP and terms of trade adjusted GDP of selected developing countries (1973–1993)

All figures in 1987 US$ bn	1973	1975	1977	1979	1981	1983	1985	1987	1989	1991	1993
Colombia	20.7	22.3	24.4	27.9	29.6	30.4	32.5	36.4	39.2	41.5	45.5
	20.4	21.5	24.8	26.5	29.0	29.9	31.8	36.4	38.6	39.8	43.3
India	140.0	155.0	169.0	169.0	192.0	214.0	234.0	257.0	301.0	319.0	343.0
	142.0	154.0	171.0	168.0	191.0	213.0	233.0	257.0	302.0	318.0	340.0
Indonesia	32.9	37.3	43.4	49.6	57.6	62.5	68.4	75.9	86.3	98.6	112.0
	25.2	31.9	37.4	50.8	62.2	65.2	72.2	75.9	83.2	95.0	106.0
Kenya	4.3	4.6	5.1	5.8	6.4	6.6	7.0	8.0	8.9	9.4	9.4
	5.1	5.1	6.3	4.4	6.6	6.5	6.9	8.0	8.8	9.5	9.0
Korea	42.1	49.4	62.3	76.5	79.3	93.6	109.0	136.0	162.0	193.0	214.0
	43.0	47.8	62.8	74.2	76.6	91.4	107.0	136.0	167.0	198.0	212.0
Malaysia	14.0	15.3	18.4	21.5	24.7	27.8	29.6	31.6	37.6	44.8	52.4
	13.6	14.0	18.4	22.4	24.8	28.0	30.3	31.6	36.9	44.0	53.6
Mexico	83.7	93.8	101.0	119.0	141.0	134.0	143.0	140.0	147.0	158.0	164.0
	84.4	95.3	102.0	124.0	140.0	141.0	145.0	140.0	147.0	162.0	166.0
Pakistan	14.7	15.8	17.3	19.4	23.1	26.3	29.7	33.4	37.7	41.5	45.6
	15.7	16.0	17.9	18.3	23.2	26.1	29.0	33.4	37.0	40.3	44.3
Philippines	22.5	24.5	28.1	31.2	34.0	35.8	30.8	33.2	37.6	38.6	39.4
	23.5	24.6	27.8	28.4	33.1	34.3	30.4	33.0	36.7	38.1	38.6
Sri Lanka	3.4	3.8	4.2	4.7	5.2	5.9	6.5	7.0	7.1	7.9	8.8
	3.3	3.4	4.4	3.7	5.0	6.0	6.0	6.5	7.0	7.6	8.6
Thailand	21.0	23.0	27.5	32.0	35.5	39.5	43.7	51.5	64.2	77.5	89.9
	23.4	24.0	28.4	31.3	35.9	39.9	43.0	50.5	64.3	76.7	90.2

Note: The two figures shown for each country represent GDP and terms of trade adjusted GDP respectively. Terms of trade 1987 = 100.

Source: World Bank, World Tables 1995

18

Table 2.3 gives both real GDP and TOT-adjusted real GDP for selected developing countries. It can be seen that for most of these countries TOT-adjusted real GDP fell below unadjusted real GDP in 1979. This means that these countries experienced an adverse TOT due to the second oil price shock. Furthermore the trend shows that their TOT is generally declining, reducing their purchasing power in the international market.

PROBLEMS AND ISSUES

The fundamental macroeconomic question facing an open economy is how to maintain both internal and external balance. Internal balance is taken to mean full or 'high' employment and zero or 'low' inflation, and external balance means zero or 'sustainable' current account deficit. For a developing country, a sustained high rate of growth is essential to break the vicious circle of poverty and to provide jobs for a growing labour force. The conventional demand management policies (fiscal and monetary) are inadequate for tackling these problems. For example when demand expands in a situation where supply responds with a lag, at least two side effects emerge. First, as V.K.R.V. Rao (1952) pointed out more than forty years ago, expansionary policies will cause inflation so that the Keynesian multiplier will work only in nominal terms. Second, as demand cannot be filled with domestic supply, the current account deficit will widen. Therefore the demand management policies must be accompanied by supply-side policies designed to enhance growth and structural change so that the tradable sector of the economy expands at a faster rate (Corden, 1981).

The next chapter will examine some of the models designed to deal with internal and external balance. In this chapter the focus will be on some of the problems that are alleged to arise particularly from the openness of a developing economy. These problems are generally referred to as 'external shocks', sub-categorized into demand shocks, inflation shocks and terms of trade shocks. In addition, natural resource rich countries may suffer from what is known as the 'Dutch Disease' syndrome.

Demand Shocks

'Demand shocks' refers to the vulnerability of small open economies to recessions in the world economy or in major trading partners. The problem can easily be demonstrated by using the familiar national income and expenditure identity:

$$Y = C + I + G + X - M$$

where Y is gross national product (GNP), C is aggregate consumption, I is aggregate gross investment, G is government expenditure, X is exports and M is imports.

As exports are a component of aggregate demand, recessions in the economies of trading partners can be transmitted to an open economy if its export structure is not sufficiently diversified. In fact recessions in industrialized economies in the 1970s and early 1980s have been a major cause of slowdown in developing economies. In his Nobel lecture Arthur Lewis (1980:556) made the following assessment regarding the link between the growth in industrialized countries and developing countries' exports:

> The growth rate of world trade in primary products over the period of 1873 to 1913 was 0.87 times the growth rate of industrial production in the developed countries, and just about the same relationship, about 0.87, also ruled in the two decades to 1973... We need no elaborate statistical proof that trade depends on prosperity in the industrial countries.

While exports are the main vehicle through which recessions in industrialized countries may adversely affect developing economies, the other components of aggregate demand can also be vulnerable to slowdowns in industrialized economies. For example, to the extent government budget, especially development expenditure, is dependent on foreign aid, recessions in industrialized economies will adversely affect domestic activity in developing economies. This happens as foreign aid is found to be procyclical, tending to fall during recessions.

For most developing countries, imports are essential both for consumption and for industrial raw materials. This means that the recessionary impact of falling exports does not result in an equivalent reduction in imports, causing the current account of the balance of payments to worsen. Thus what emerges are both internal and external imbalances.

Inflation Shocks

The other side of the transmission of recessions is the transmission of inflation. If the major trading partners follow expansionary fiscal and monetary policies, there will be an increase in export demand. The increased export demand can create inflationary pressure if the exporting country does not have excess capacity or has substantial supply lags. Inflation can also occur if exports expand and the balance of payments position turns into a surplus. This happens under the fixed exchange rate system when increased inflows of foreign exchange, if unsterilized, lead to monetary expansion. The action of offsetting the effect of the balance of payments developments on money supply is known as sterilization (see notes 1 and 2). Bhalla (1982), in his cross-country study of 30 developing countries for the period 1956 to 1972, found that most countries failed to sterilize foreign exchange inflows.[2]

The above also means that open economies are able to export some of their inflation to their trading partners (Triffin and Grubel, 1962; Whitman, 1969). Iyoha (1973) extended the work of Triffin and Grubel and Whitman to developing countries and in a cross-country econometric study of 33 countries found that the more open economies had a lower rate of price inflation as some of the excess demand was met by imports financed by capital inflows.

However Iyoha's work was criticized on the ground that his assumptions of the existence of import surplus financed by capital flows and a high income elasticity of import demand do not hold in developing countries (Kirkpatrick and Nixson, 1977). It is argued that most developing countries' ability to import is constrained by the availability of foreign exchange. They are heavily dependent on imported capital goods and raw materials for which domestic substitutes are not available, and hence developing country imports are price inelastic. According to Kirkpatrick and Nixson (1977:150):

> The economy's increased dependence on imported inputs increases the likelihood of inflation being imported through rising international prices of essential capital and intermediate goods.

Otto Sunkel (1960) called it 'exogenous inflationary pressures'. (See the appendix for an explanation within an input-output framework).

According to the PPP relationship described earlier, if the foreign price rises relative to domestic price the exchange rate adjusts to offset the price differential. However as most developing countries follow either a fixed exchange rate or a managed float system, the exchange rate is prevented from necessary adjustments. As a result, the higher import price is passed on to domestic consumers. This can be shown simply by expressing the PPP relation as:

$$P_d = eP_f \qquad (2.5)$$

This shows that if the foreign price (P_f) rises and the exchange rate does not appreciate (a fall in 'e'), the domestic price (P_d) will rise proportionately. The domestic price of imports can also rise if the exchange rate depreciates ('e' rises). In fact, the acceleration of inflation in many developing countries in 1971–72 was largely ascribed to 'the extraordinary inflation of import prices in terms of local currencies, attributable in part to the December 1971 realignment of exchange rates' (IMF, 1973).

Terms of Trade Shocks

There is an ongoing pessimism about the benefits of openness which is rooted in the much celebrated 'Singer-Prebisch' thesis of declining terms of trade of developing countries and, in its more extreme version, of the dependency school. It is claimed that since most developing countries are exporters of primary products whose prices do not rise as much as industrial country exports, they experience a secular decline in their terms of trade. This pushes developing countries' production possibility frontier progressively inward resulting in a decline in their economic growth. The dependency school takes this hypothesis further to claim that developed industrial countries (centres) prosper at the expense of developing countries (peripheries). The terms of trade adjusted GDP as reported in Table 2.3 lends some support to this contention.

The impact of declining terms of trade (falling price of exports *vis-à-vis* price of imports) on a country's GDP can be illustrated by using Figure 2.1.[3]

Importables

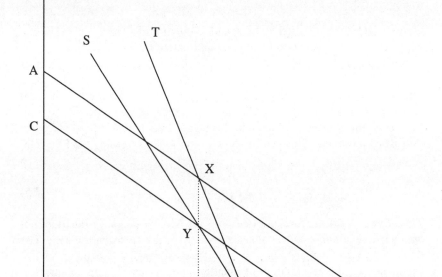

Figure 2.1   Effect of a decline in the terms of trade

AA' denotes the production possibility frontier of the economy. Let us assume that the terms of trade (price ratio at which exports can be converted into imports) is denoted by TT' which intersects AA' at X. At X, the country consumes OB amount of exportables and converts BT' amounts into BX amount of importables.[4] The GDP is thus given by point X. When the terms of trade declines to ST', the conversion of BT' amount of exportables yields only BY (<BX) amount of importables, giving GDP at Y which is below X. This is analogous to an inward shift of the production possibility frontier from AA' to CC'. Thus the terms of trade can be regarded as a shift parameter in the aggregate production function:

$$Y = \alpha\beta \, Y(L, K_0) \tag{2.6}$$

where Y is aggregate output, α is the terms of trade, β is technology, L is labour and K_0 is a given amount of capital stock.

A country can also experience a terms of trade shock due to a sudden rise in the price of imported raw materials. The classic example of such a shock is the increase in oil prices in the 1970s. A rise in import price shifts the aggregate supply curve to the left and causes prices to rise. The impact of such external shocks can be illustrated by using the aggregate production function.[5] In this case the production function can be expressed as:

$$Y = Y(f(L; K_0), \text{oil}) \tag{2.7}$$

As capital and oil are largely complementary, a rise in oil price resulting in the reduction in oil imports would mean some of the capital stock will remain idle. This is analogous to a reduction in the capital stock which shifts the production function downwards.

Both types of the terms of trade shock (declines in export price and increases in import price) can be analysed by combining the two production functions as:

$$Y = \alpha Y[\beta f(L, K_0), \delta] \tag{2.8}$$

where δ is the shift parameter for the rise in imported raw materials price (such as oil price shocks). When the production function shifts downward the aggregate supply curve shifts to the left, causing a decline in output and a rise in price (a situation of stagflation).

So far we have looked at the supply-side effect of terms of trade shocks. However terms of trade also affects the demand side. When the terms of trade decline, the income of exporters declines, given the exchange rate. For most primary exporting countries this may mean a substantial decline in income

Price

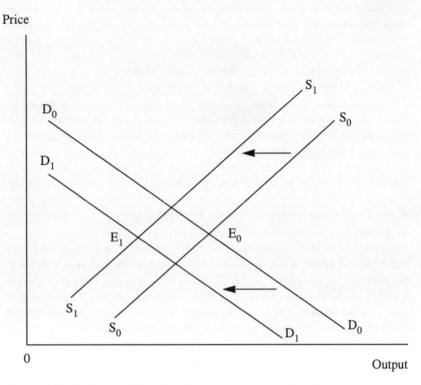

*Figure 2.2   Leftward shifts of both aggregate demand and aggregate supply
curves*

and aggregate demand with adverse impacts on output and employment. As
can be seen from Figure 2.2, when both aggregate demand (AD) and aggregate supply (AS) curves shift to the left, the decline in output is substantial.

The decline in terms of trade also causes external imbalance, as imports
are both price and income inelastic. Recall that most imports of developing
countries are essential and non-competitive in nature. As the balance of
payments position worsens, the country's debt burden rises and more resources (export earnings) are spent in debt repayments. This has a detrimental effect on the long-term growth potential of an economy.

Table 2.4 presents estimates of terms of trade shocks for selected developing countries following the dramatic oil price rises in both 1974 and 1979.
The sample of countries also includes two oil exporters – Indonesia and
Nigeria. The extent of adverse impact on GDP varies with the extent of
dependence of a particular country on oil imports. In India for example,
which is roughly self-sufficient in oil, the shock was not dramatic.

Table 2.4   Terms of trade shocks after oil price increases

	Terms of Trade Effect on GDP$_{t-1}$ (%)				Inflation Rate (%) (CPI)			
	1974	1975	1979	1980	1974	1975	1979	1980
Chile	−12.4	−5.1	na	−3.85	504.7	374.7	33.4	35.1
Cameroon	−3.8	−3.7	−3.06	−2.04	17.3	13.6	6.6	9.3
Costa Rica	−5.1	−1.0	−0.75	−2.79	30.1	17.4	9.2	18.1
Brazil	−2.6	−0.5	−1.40	−2.40	27.6	29.0	52.7	82.8
India	−0.9	0.0	−0.33	−0.46	27.7	5.6	6.4	11.4
Kenya	−4.1	−3.0	na	−2.42	17.9	19.1	8.0	13.8
Korea	−4.0	0.9	−0.81	−5.38	24.3	25.3	18.3	28.7
Sri Lanka	−3.1	−0.6	−2.82	−3.85	12.3	6.7	10.8	26.2
Thailand	−0.8	−3.0	−1.08	−1.75	24.4	5.3	9.9	19.7
Indonesia	17.0	−3.0	4.20	5.13	40.5	19.1	21.9	18.5
Nigeria	23.1	−2.6	4.29	7.56	12.5	33.7	11.1	11.4

Note: The formula used for the terms of trade effect in year t is : $\text{TOTE}_t = X_t \{(PI_{t-1}/PI_t)/(PE_{t-1}/PE_t)\}$, where X_t is the dollar value of exports, PI and PE are unit value indices for imports and exports respectively. TOTE_t is expressed as a percentage of GDP$_{t-1}$.

Sources: Terms of trade effects : Little *et al* (1993): Tables 3.1, 4.2
Inflation rate : IMF, International Financial Statistics, 1984

The Debt Crisis

As mentioned earlier, an adverse terms of trade shock worsens the debt burden as the countries cannot reduce expenditure to match the reduction in their real income. The decline in a country's real income (ΔY) due to an adverse terms of trade shock is equal to the change in the terms of trade (ΔTOT) multiplied by the initial level of exports, that is:

$$\Delta Y = \Delta TOT(Q_0 - C_0),$$

where Q_0 is the initial level of domestic output and C_0 is initial domestic absorption. If the domestic absorption (consumption) remains at the pre-shock level then the balance of payments will deteriorate and the foreign borrowing will increase by ΔY.

Whether a country should adjust expenditure or borrow to smooth out consumption depends on whether the shock is permanent or temporary in nature. If the shock is temporary 'then it makes sense to borrow from abroad

to cushion the short-run effects on domestic expenditure' (Gavin, 1993:179).
On the other hand, if the shock is permanent, 'the best response is for
consumption to decline immediately to the new, lower level of national
income; only such a policy maintains a smooth path for consumption while
still respecting the lifetime budget constraint' (Gavin, 1993:179). This policy

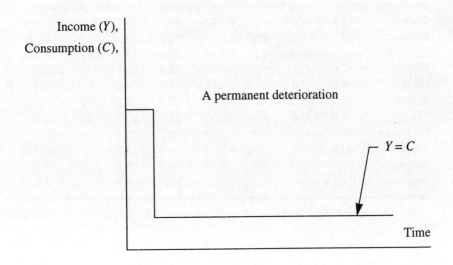

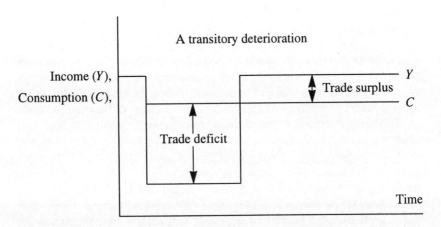

Source: Gavin (1993)

*Figure 2.3   Income, expenditure and current account responses to a change
in the terms of trade*

conclusion follows from the permanent income hypothesis of consumption. The consumption smoothing response to declines in real income due to a terms of trade shock is depicted in Figure 2.3.

A downward adjustment of domestic absorption requires tighter fiscal and monetary policies which are often very difficult to follow from the political perspective, especially when the unemployment rate is high. Thus, following the oil price shocks, many countries took the easier option of overseas borrowing instead of adjusting their expenditure pattern. This was possible because more money was available as the oil exporting countries began investing their surplus funds in the international money market (particularly in banks). Countries such as South Korea, which used international borrowings judiciously in investment for the expansion of the tradable sector, rather than maintaining the current consumption level, successfully weathered the shock. For other countries however it led to the debt crisis of the early 1980s, following the sharp rise in interest rates.

Ironically, some countries such as Nigeria, which experienced positive terms of trade shocks, also faced the debt crisis as the rise in their income was perceived to be permanent and, as a result, there was a huge increase in consumption expenditure. In particular government recurrent expenditure (as well as expenditure on 'prestige' projects) rose dramatically. However when the oil price dropped these countries could not adjust their expenditure downward. Rather they maintained their current expenditure level by borrowing in anticipation that there would soon be another windfall.[6] On the other hand countries such as Indonesia used their newly-found wealth in infrastructure investment and for the expansion of export-oriented manufacturing activities.

The experience of Korea, Nigeria and Indonesia shows that terms of trade shocks require financial as well as production responses. The financial response will depend on their intertemporal choice between present and future consumption. Countries which enjoy terms of trade gains can choose to either consume or save the increased income. If countries such as Indonesia save (and invest) the increased income due to terms of trade gain then their future consumption level will rise. Countries facing adverse terms of trade shocks can postpone the necessary reduction in consumption to match the decline in real income by dissaving or borrowing, which carries the risk of a debt crisis. On the other hand countries, such as Korea, which borrow to finance the expansion of the tradable sector will enjoy higher future income and consumption.

However while the optimal adjustment entails both financial and production responses, adjustments are not costless. To begin with one has to be reasonably certain as to whether the shock is temporary or permanent:

> In reality, of course, nobody knows whether a change in the terms of trade will be reversed, will persist, or will deteriorate even more (Gavin, 1993:176).

The uncertainty dictates that the saving rate must be higher than would otherwise have been required (precautionary saving). This also means that investment decisions must be delayed and long-term projects must be avoided.

Second, adjustment of production requires a shifting of resources and in the process there will be gainers and losers. If the gainers cannot adequately compensate the losers, adjustment may be blocked due to the lack of political support. Third, expenditure reduction through tighter fiscal and monetary policies is likely to affect the poorer section of the population more adversely and this may trigger political unrest.

The Dutch Disease

The 'Dutch Disease' syndrome arises when the export price of primary products or natural resources rises. As the balance of payments improves with the rise in export earnings, the exchange rate appreciates ('e' falls). That is, foreigners pay more in their currency for a unit of the resource exporting country's currency. This development has detrimental effects on the manufacturing sector of the resource exporting country. The manufacturing exports become uncompetitive in the international market as their dollar (export) price rises. This slows down the structural transformation of the resource rich countries and makes them vulnerable to commodity price fluctuations.

A similar problem arises if countries fail to devalue to maintain the real exchange rate when their domestic inflation rate exceeds the foreign inflation rate. As a result the pegged rate becomes overvalued and the prices of traded goods in domestic currency are held down relative to the prices of non-traded goods. This encourages domestic demand to switch from the non-traded sector to the traded sector while resources move away from the traded to the non-traded sector. The end result of this development is a chronic balance of payments problem (Krueger, 1978).

Capital Flows and Macroeconomic Instability

In recent times there has been a massive increase in the flows of capital to developing countries (Dooley *et al*, 1996; Fernandez-Arias and Montiel, 1996). What is more significant is the size of capital which is short-term in nature usually referred to as 'hot money'. This has caused concerns. To begin with there are questions as to the sustainability of this surge and the danger of another debt crisis. At the analytical level there are several problems. First, for countries following some sort of fixed or pegged exchange rates regime, the increased inflow of capital, unless sterilized, leads to monetary expansion and hence inflation. This will cause real appreciation of domestic currency, producing the Dutch Disease syndrome. The real appreciation can also pose a serious problem for the liberalizing countries as it effectively negates the impact of nominal devaluation which is an important element of the liberalization programme.

On the other hand sterilization has its costs and limits if the financial sector is not well developed. If the sterilization is carried out through open market operations, the central bank is forced to invest in low-yield foreign reserves, while at the same time issuing domestic debt at high enough yields to attract commercial banks and private citizens away from private loans and investments. The differential between the domestic and foreign yields, known as 'quasi-fiscal' cost, is estimated at almost one-half of one per cent of GDP in Latin America (Kiguel and Leiderman, 1993). Furthermore sterilization does not allow domestic interest rates to equalize with the foreign rate and thereby prolongs capital inflows. If the sterilization is carried out by raising the reserve requirement, the quasi-fiscal cost is transferred to the customers of commercial banks as the spread between loan and deposit rates widens.

When the capital account drives the current account developments then large capital flows can lead to an unsustainable current account deficit. This is particularly so if the inflow is in response to a consumption boom, as was the case in Nigeria discussed earlier.

Finally, the short-term capital flows (hot money) are volatile and the receiving country's currency can come under speculative attacks. Moreno (1995) has identified 126 episodes of speculative attacks on currencies of Asia-Pacific economies in the sense that there were pressures to either appreciate or depreciate which were not related to economic fundamentals. The most recent episode of speculative attack on South East Asian currencies (Thailand, Malaysia, Indonesia and the Philippines) happened in July 1997 and forced Thailand to move away from the peg (to a basket of currencies) system to a floating system. The move resulted in a 25 per cent devaluation of the Thai Baht. Furthermore rapid reversals of these flows can cause domestic liquidity problems and large increases in inflows may jeopardize the safety of the banking system as it rushes to expand credit.

Currency Substitution and Capital Flight

Currency substitution and capital flight reduce a government's ability to finance budget deficits by borrowing from the central bank and creating inflation. Capital flight and currency substitution have received substantial attention in recent times. Currency substitution, or dollarization, means the use of foreign currencies instead of the domestic currency for domestic transactions. This reduces the demand for domestic money and hence the government's ability to collect the inflation tax.[7]

Table 2.5 A summary of capital inflow experiences

	Capital inflow surges	Non-bank sterilization	Bank sector sterilization	Real exchange rate impact	1986–1993 Average annual change in banking asset ratio (%)
Indonesia	1986–87, 1990–91	–	Increased regulatory restrictions, Decreased public sector assets in commercial banks	Moderate real exchange rate appreciation	5.99
Korea	1991, 1992	Used 'money stabilizations' in open market operations	Increased reserve requirements	Large real exchange rate appreciation	–3.41
Malaysia	1991–93	Used government and pension fund securities in open market operations	Increased reserve requirements, increased regulatory restrictions	Moderate real exchange rate appreciation	6.24
Philippines	1988–93	Increased foreign debt service	Increased reserve requirements	Moderate real exchange rate depreciation	4.26

Singapore	1987, 1990, 1992–93	Used pension funds in open market operations	–	Moderate real exchange rate appreciation	–0.24
Taiwan	1986–87	–	Required commercial banks to directly purchase treasury bills and central bank certificates of deposit; decreased public sector assets in commercial banks	Moderate real exchange rate appreciation	–0.14
Thailand	1988–92	Increased foreign debt service; eased restrictions on capital outflows	–	Moderate real exchange rate depreciation	1.75

Source: Spiegel (1995).

Capital flight occurs when the residents of a country convert the domestic currency into foreign currencies and invest overseas. The incidence of capital flight increases when a country liberalizes its capital account (allowing the outward transfer of capital) in the presence of substantial macroeconomic imbalances. If the home country's economic situation worsens and a major devaluation of the currency is expected, people engaged in capital flights can profit by taking the currency out and bringing it back when devalued. It is a cause of concern for several reasons. First, it becomes self-fulfilling with regard to devaluation: as capital moves out, a country's balance of payments worsens further, forcing a deeper devaluation than was necessary. Second, a lot of capital flight happens outside the official sector, thereby escaping regulation and taxation. Third, the country is forced to borrow more from overseas to finance current account deficits, exacerbating the debt situation.

Deppler and Williamson's (1987) estimates show that during 1975–85 there were capital flights totalling $28.5 billion from Africa, $18.3 billion from Asia and $106.6 billion from Latin America. Governments of the countries facing massive capital flights must make a strategic decision: should they contain the flight by raising domestic interest rates on domestic financial assets; should they create foreign-currency linked domestic assets; or should they continue restrictions on the capital account?

Both high interest rates and foreign-currency linked domestic assets create an easily accessible domestic substitute for assets that yield seigniorage.[8] The resulting sophistication of the financial sector increases the inflationary effect of a given budget deficit. Dornbusch and Reynoso (1993) show this as follows:

$$\mu = \alpha\beta(\rho + \gamma\pi) \tag{2.9}$$

where μ is the growth rate of high-powered money, ρ and γ are parameters of the velocity equation and π is the rate of inflation.

Equation (2.9) gives a relationship between the growth rate of high-powered money (μ) and the budget deficit which is a fraction (α) of real income, and where the demand for high-powered money is a linear and increasing function of inflation.[9] It states that a fraction (β) of budget deficit $\alpha(\rho + \gamma\pi)$ is financed by creating money.

In a steady state, with output growth rate (g_y) and income elasticity of demand for money equal to one, an inflation rate can be obtained:

$$\pi = (\beta\rho\alpha - g_y)/(1 - \beta\Delta\alpha) \tag{2.10}$$

This equation shows that the relationship between the budget deficit and inflation is highly non-linear. Furthermore as ρ and γ rise with the sophistication of the financial structure, a given budget deficit will be associated with higher inflation. This occurs as more and more people substitute domestic currency with foreign currencies, the demand for domestic money declines and the government's ability to collect inflation tax or seigniorage declines, forcing the government to create more inflation.

In addition to the decline in seigniorage and higher inflationary impacts of a given deficit, domestic dollar deposits also carry the risk that if a major depreciation is required, the banking system is likely to suffer. This may create a tendency to overvalue the exchange rate.

Therefore the costs and benefits of capital flights and currency substitution (dollarization) need to be weighed. It is claimed that the decline in seigniorage is lower with capital flights than with dollarization. This is because capital flights involve large transaction costs which may deter capital flights. Therefore countries should accept some capital flights rather than institutionalize dollarization. This also means that countries should not revert back to capital controls as people will find ways and means to transfer capital.[10] Obviously the best solution is to tackle the root problem, macroeconomic instability arising from large budget deficits.

POLICY GOALS AND INSTRUMENTS: DILEMMAS AND INTERDEPENDENCE[11]

As mentioned earlier, from the perspective of macroeconomic stabilization the two goals are the maintenance of internal and external balance. These balances can be seriously disturbed, either by unanticipated exogenous shocks or policy-induced errors. These shocks shift the aggregate demand curve to the right (demand shocks) or the aggregate supply curve to the left (supply shocks) such that an unsustainable excess demand emerges. The vulnerability of open economies to external shocks and their nature have been explained in the previous section. An example of policy-induced errors is macroeconomic populism, whereby governments run unsustainable budget deficits to meet politically determined social objectives (Dornbusch and Edwards, 1990).

As referred to in the previous section, the extent to which the conventional fiscal and monetary policies should be applied to restore internal and external balance depends on whether the shock is temporary and reversible (for example, natural calamities) or permanent and irreversible (such as oil price rises). If the shocks are temporary then there is no scope for conventional demand management policies. Any attempt to ride out the temporary decline in output and employment with expansionary fiscal and/or monetary policies will end up accelerating the inflation rate and worsening the external balance. The best response to temporary supply shocks is consumption smoothing by drawing down on past stocks of food and foreign reserves (Gavin, 1993; Hossain and Chowdhury, 1996; Joshi and Little, 1994). In the case of a permanent shock, the application of contractionary fiscal and/or monetary policies to restore external balance will result in higher unemployment. There-fore a stabilization package (for permanent shocks) must include some de-gree of conventional demand management policies, the adjustment of the exchange rate and the wages or incomes policy. While demand management policies reduce domestic absorption, exchange rate depreciation switches expenditure away from the tradable sector to the non-tradable sector and resources from the non-tradable to the tradable sector, so that the overall demand and hence employment do not fall.[12] The wages policy must ensure that the impact of depreciation on international competitiveness is not eroded by rising wage costs and hence domestic inflation. This means that the restoration of external balance without adversely affecting the internal bal-ance can only be achieved by accepting the harsh reality of structural adjust-ment (shift from non-tradable to tradable) and falling real wage. (This is discussed further in the following chapter.)

While the above prescription appears simple and straightforward, a number of complications need to be highlighted. First, policy makers often ignore some well known rules: there must be as many effective policy instruments as there are objectives and the assignment of instruments to objectives should maximize the effectiveness of the instruments employed.[13] It is quite com-mon to find the use of one policy instrument to achieve multiple and conflicting objectives. Second, monetary, fiscal and exchange rate policies are closely interlinked. This interlinkage is particularly important in the presence of capital mobility, also when the capital market is not well developed and the government's ability to raise revenue is limited.

The interlinkage of policy instruments can be illustrated by using some macroeconomic identities. For example following Bruno (1993) the total money supply (M) can be written as:

$$M = \text{Domestic Credit (DC)} + \text{Net Foreign Assets (NFA)} \qquad (2.11)$$

where DC = central bank credit to government (CG) + commercial bank credit to public (CP).

Equation (2.11) shows the direct link between government budget deficit financed by borrowing from the central bank and the money supply. Evidence suggests that approximately 50 per cent of the public deficit in developing countries is financed through the banking system, making the monetary policy subservient to the needs of the fiscal authorities (Little *et al*, 1993). The inclusion of NFA signifies the fact that when a country runs a fixed exchange rate system, its balance of payments position and capital flows (either private or public borrowings) affect money supply unless these flows are sterilized by corresponding changes in the components of DC.

The link between fiscal policy and external balance can be shown by using the following identity:

$$\text{Current account deficit (CAD)} = \text{Private savings (S)}$$
$$- \text{ Private investment (I)} + \text{Fiscal deficit (FD)} \qquad (2.12)$$

Equation (2.12) is derived from the national income identity and $S - I$ is sometimes referred to as the 'private sector balance' (PB). The equation shows that for a given PB there is a direct relationship between FD and CAD and this is known as the 'twin deficit' hypothesis. FD leads to CAD through two channels. First, the rise in domestic expenditure following a fiscal stimulus sucks in more imports. Second, the rise in the domestic interest rate due to government borrowing induces capital inflows causing an appreciation of domestic currency. This crowds out exports. If, however, the country follows a fixed exchange rate system, the capital inflow will cause money supply to rise. This in turn will cause inflation and a reduction in international competitiveness. Thus the end effect on net export will be the same, regardless of the exchange rate policy.

Finally, inflationary expectations or the political atmosphere can generate wage claims which either reduce or completely eliminate the effectiveness of demand management and exchange rate policies. It is alleged that the real wage in developing countries is already too low and no further reduction in real wage is possible without seriously affecting the social fabric. The violent riots that followed the introduction of IMF austerity measures in many developing countries bear testimony to this claim. It is now generally agreed that political instability adversely affects economic growth thus reducing a country's ability to achieve internal and external balance. On the other hand, macroeconomic stability is vital for sustained high economic growth.

Thus a fundamental issue which policymakers must address is how to avoid political instability in the process of attaining the necessary macroeconomic stability which will ensure economic growth. If one considers the repercussions of persistent and unsustainable fiscal deficits on money supply, inflation and the external balance, macroeconomic stabilization must entail fiscal adjustment (both revenue and expenditure) as a central ingredient. This becomes much harder when a safety net must be provided to avoid social unrest. Perhaps the non-government organizations (NGOs) can play an important role in this regard.

Exchange Rates: Fix or Flex?

It has been shown in the preceding section that when a country follows a fixed exchange rate system, it cannot run an independent monetary policy. In that case money supply responds to changes in net foreign assets due to the balance of payments outcomes (capital flows included). As mentioned earlier, this puts an enormous pressure on the central banks which are trying to sterilize changes in NFA, especially when the capital market is underdeveloped. On the other hand, one main argument in favour of flexible exchange rates is that it gives the monetary authority control over the money supply and hence allows a country to choose its own inflation rate. However there is a body of literature which favours some kind of a fixed or pegged exchange rate system for those developing countries which do not generally have a good inflation record. It is argued that if a country's exchange rate is pegged to the currency of a country with a stable price level history, it acts as a 'nominal anchor' – a bulwark against inflation (Aghevli *et al*, 1991; Corden, 1991; Hossain and Chowdhury, 1996). In the words of Bruno (1993:28–29):

> In a small, open economy the relationship between the general price level and the exchange rate is considerably tighter than between money and prices, primarily because import prices play a large role in the input-output system. Any increase in the cost of imports (say, through a devaluation) quickly feeds into the general price level, which is further enhanced when there is some formal linkage between ... wages ... and the price level. For this reason there is an advantage in anchoring the price level to the exchange rate.

If the exchange rate becomes in effect an anti-inflation tool, how does the exchange rate perform its other role, namely external balance and international competitiveness? The answer lies in the incomes or wages policy. The wages outcomes must be consistent, given the nominal exchange rate, with the required real exchange rates.

Dornbusch and Kuenzler (1993) revisited the debate between fixed and flexible exchange rate systems. They advocate a 'dual rate' approach – one official and the other free market determined – as a pragmatic device in cases of high capital mobility which cannot be controlled effectively. The basic premise of their argument is that exchange rate shifts reflect both changes in economic fundamentals and transient factors such as a sudden surge in capital flows or speculative attacks. When capital flows cannot be controlled effectively, the dual rate can insulate the economy from undue exchange rate volatility arising from transient factors. In such a system, the official rate (fixed) should be used in most trade or current account transactions and the free (flexible) rate for all other transactions. However the caveat is that the dual system must be well managed in order to maintain the premium between the official and free rate within a reasonable range (15–20 per cent). Otherwise it will signal an imminent major realignment of the official rate.

Whatever the merits and demerits of different exchange rate regimes, an appropriate exchange rate policy must follow the simple rule that it must avoid cumulative overvaluation. Both theory and evidence suggest that when exchange rates are distorted and misaligned there can be serious consequences: wasteful allocation of resources, capital flights, rent-seeking, red tape and corruption (Islam and Chowdhury, 1997).

INSTITUTIONAL DEVELOPMENTS

The mechanism through which international transactions were settled prior to the end of World War II was known as the 'gold standard'. The system was based on three principles. First, the price of the domestic currency must be fixed in terms of gold in each participating country. Second, there must be a free import and export of gold. Third, countries should allow their money supply to rise (fall) if they are in surplus (deficit), gaining (losing) gold. The fully-fledged gold standard came into operation in 1880 when most industrial countries joined Great Britain in meeting the conditions of the gold standard. The system survived until the outbreak of World War I in 1914. The system was reintroduced in 1925, but collapsed again in 1931 in the midst of the great depression (see Argy, 1994 for a brief discussion of reasons for the collapse).

The International Monetary Fund and the World Bank[14]

After World War II there emerged the two most important international institutions to regulate international transactions – the International Monetary Fund (IMF) and the World Bank. Little *et al* (1993:9) summarized the objective of the World Bank as 'to intermediate between the private capital markets of the world and capital-short countries, since it was assumed … that private lenders would be loath to lend abroad any time soon'. The IMF was to oversee the rules governing the exchange rate and 'to lend funds to tide countries over temporary imbalances in payments or to ease their adjustment from disequilibrium to a position of payments equilibrium' (Little *et al*, 1993:9). Under Article I, the IMF's purposes are:

1. To promote international monetary co-operation through a permanent institution which provides machinery for consultation and collaboration on international monetary problems.
2. To facilitate the expansion and balanced growth of international trade,

and to contribute thereby to the promotion and maintenance of high levels of employment and real income and to the development of the production resources of all members as primary objectives of economic policy.

3. To promote exchange stability, maintain orderly exchange arrangements among members, and avoid competitive depreciation.
4. To assist in the establishment of a multilateral system of payments in respect of current transactions between members and in the elimination of foreign exchange restrictions which hamper growth of world trade.
5. To give confidence to members by making the general resources of the Fund temporarily available to them under adequate safeguards, thus providing them with an opportunity to correct maladjustments in their balance of payments without resorting to measures destructive of national or international prosperity.
6. To shorten the duration and lessen the degree of disequilibrium in the international balances of payments of members.

According to Article IV of the IMF the exchange rates were fixed, although countries were allowed to vary their exchange rates within a narrow band of 1 per cent. Rates were fixed in terms of the US dollar, which in turn had its value fixed against gold ($35 an ounce). Thus the IMF system, commonly known as the 'Bretton Woods system' can be regarded as a quasi-gold standard. The fixed rates could be adjusted with international agreement to correct a 'fundamental disequilibrium' in the balance of payments. Members were barred from imposing restrictions on transfer of funds on current account transactions without the approval of the IMF (Article VIII). However the system also allowed a wide range of exchange controls, designed to impede international capital flows, which prohibited certain forms of international borrowing and lending (Article XIV). These controls made it easier for central banks to maintain fixed exchange rates by buying (selling/borrowing) foreign currencies (usually the US $) when there was a balance of payments surplus (deficit). Thus, the short-term surpluses would lead to a build up of foreign currency reserves while temporary deficits would cause a decline in reserves or an increase in borrowings from the IMF or other central banks. The intervention of central banks in the foreign exchange market to maintain the par value of currencies meant the loss of control over the money supply. However restrictions on capital flows enabled countries to pursue diverse economic and social policies, in particular to maintain full employment.

Strains started to develop in the Bretton Woods system as world trade grew at an unprecedented rate during the two post-World War II decades. As the system was tied to gold (via the US dollar), the supply of gold could not match the demand which arose from the need to settle rapidly growing international transactions. The deficiency was filled by the US dollar. However as the US itself was experiencing growing deficits in its own balance of payments, the ratio of foreign-held dollars to the US stock of gold grew over time. This made the gold convertibility of the dollar doubtful. Various measures were taken to prevent a run on US gold and the US appealed to allied countries to exercise restraints in converting official dollars into gold (Argy, 1994:19). However, a run on US gold did occur and President Nixon had to suspend the gold convertibility of the US dollar in August 1971 for an indefinite period.[15]

In response to the problem of international liquidity, the member countries agreed to the creation of the Special Drawing Rights (SDR) in 1968. Its short-term aim was to supplement the shortage of reserves while the long-term aim was to make the SDR the principal reserve asset. SDRs are a 'paper' asset with no backing. Its value was fixed at 1/35th of an ounce of gold or one US$. During 1970–72 a total of $9.5 billion SDRs was allocated to member countries. Under the arrangement the deficit countries give up SDRs in return for foreign currencies while surplus countries absorb SDRs. Countries earn (pay) interest only on the excess (deficiency) of holding over the original allocation.

This new arrangement was found to be inadequate as the IMF grossly underestimated the need for SDRs. As a result, after 1 July 1974 the link between the SDR and gold was broken and the SDR was valued in terms of a weighted basket of 16 currencies. In 1978 the rules governing SDRs were made more flexible and the interest rate was linked to the rates in major industrialized countries.

Another reason for the collapse of the Bretton Woods system was its reliance on changes in the fixed exchange rates to correct a fundamental disequilibrium (Little *et al*, 1993:10). Countries were generally reluctant to change their exchange rates and, as they waited to accept that the disequilibrium was fundamental, that disequilibrium became obvious to market speculators. This led to speculative attacks on currencies of deficit countries – buying foreign currencies before devaluation and selling afterwards. These attacks aggravated the reserve crisis of deficit countries, forcing them to devalue more than would have been required according to the fundamentals. Currency speculation became easy and widespread in the 1970s with the revival of the world capital market and made it extremely difficult for the central banks to hold the line on exchange rates (Argy, 1994:22; Little *et al*, 1993:11).

By 1973 most industrialized countries had abandoned the fixed exchange rate system. One of the arguments used at the time was that the flexible exchange rate system would give the countries more freedom to pursue domestic stabilization policies. In particular by not having to intervene in the foreign exchange market, the flexible exchange rate system was thought to give central banks controls over money supply.[16] Later however the European countries moved to some sort of fixed rate arrangement among themselves, known as the European Monetary System (EMS).

These developments led to the amendments to the IMF Articles of Agreement in March 1978, effectively legitimizing the new exchange rate arrangement. Members are now allowed to follow any one of several arrangements. They may float, or maintain the par value with the SDR or some other major currencies, but not gold. The most important of the new provisions is the authority of the IMF to 'exercise firm surveillance over the exchange rate policies of the members'. Under the surveillance provision members are required to provide necessary information to the IMF and the IMF shall adopt specific principles for the guidance of all members with respect to their exchange rate policies.

GATT, WTO, The New International Economic Order and UNCTAD

The basic framework of rules governing trade relations among nations is set by the General Agreement on Tariffs and Trade (GATT). With the exception of the centrally planned (communist) countries, all industrialized and most developing countries were members of GATT.[17] The US, whose Senate blocked the formation of a more ambitious International Trade Organisation (ITO), took the initiative in 1947 to set up GATT as a temporary substitute for ITO. GATT was modelled on the US trade-liberalization agreements of the 1930s. The ITO was supposed to handle problems associated with commodities trade. In its absence, GATT continued as the main forum for settlement of trade disputes and negotiations for multi-lateral trade liberalization until the establishment of the World Trade Organisation (WTO) in 1994, following the successful completion of the Uruguay round of negotiations which lasted for nearly a decade.

GATT's major concerns were with tariffs, quotas, and other more subtle trade barriers such as the placing of government contracts and the setting of safety, environment, human rights and health standards. Its non-discriminatory principle was enshrined in Article I which insists on equal treatment of all trading partners who are members of GATT. If a country extended some trading privileges to another member country then these privileges were to be extended to all other members so that all were accorded 'most favoured nation (MFN) treatment'. Although GATT was regarded as a rich nations' club, the MFN clause brought some benefits to smaller and less developed countries with very little bargaining power.

However developing countries were generally dissatisfied with GATT as its mechanism for tariff reductions was based on reciprocity of concessions and the developing countries felt that they had very little to bargain with. To begin with, most commodities trade, which is the specialization of developing countries, does not attract much tariff in industrialized countries. On the other hand GATT largely failed to remove the quotas and restrictions on imports into industrialized countries of such agricultural products as sugar, beef, grains and vegetable oils from developing countries. Similarly in the areas of manufacturing such as textiles, garments and leather goods in which developing countries enjoy comparative advantage, most imports into industrialized countries from the Third World are controlled and limited by the Multifibres Arrangements and by unilaterally imposed quotas, and GATT did not offer much in removing these restrictions. In addition GATT's charter did not provide for any mechanism to deal with the developing countries' main problem of uncertainty and volatility of commodities trade.

Mirza (1988: 37) notes that:

> The new international economic order (NIEO) is an economic and political concept, variously interpreted, which encapsulates the developing countries' demands for a greater access to the world's economic, financial, and technological resources.

These demands are the result of the realization that existing world trade and financial relations are characterized by 'unequal exchange' between developing and industrial countries which constrains the pace and pattern of development. Recall the Singer-Prebisch thesis of a secular decline of the terms of trade of developing countries whose exports are mainly primary commodities, and the associated problems of fluctuating terms of trade as discussed earlier. In the extreme version NIEO requires not just reform but complete transformation of trade and financial relations between developing and developed nations. In concrete terms the NIEO argues for an 'integrated programme for commodities' which will stabilize the commodity market, extend developing countries' control over processing, distribution and marketing of commodities, and compensate for any shortfall in export earnings resulting from a sudden drop in commodity prices. The call for a NIEO was formally made for the first time by a group of 25 countries at the first Conference of the Non-Aligned Movement held in Belgrade in 1956. The formal negotiations for a NIEO are mostly conducted at the forum of the United Nations Conference on Trade and Development (UNCTAD) which was established following a UN resolution pushed by a group of 77 (G77) developing countries. The G77 now comprises more than 125 countries and there are significant differences in their interests and concerns. For example high income countries such as Singapore and South Korea do reasonably well out of the present order and hence are less radical in their approach. Similarly the wealthy members of OPEC are generally found at odds with most develop-

Table 2.6   A brief chronology of the New International Economic Order

---

1955   The Bandung (Indonesia) conference of 29 newly independent countries calls for stable prices and demand for commodities.

1956   The Non-Aligned Movement is founded by the countries attending the Bandung Conference.

1961   The First Conference of the Non-Aligned Movement calls for a New International Economic Order.

1962   77 developing countries push for a UN resolution for the UNCTAD.

1963   Group of 77 comes into existence.

1964   UNCTAD I convenes in Geneva. Agreement to have a permanent secretariat for UNCTAD in Geneva. Some discussions of an IMF facility to finance shortfalls in commodity earnings and industrialized countries agreed to spend 1% of GNP in aid.

1968   UNCTAD II in New Delhi. The GSP is established and the aid target of 1% of GNP is again agreed. Some attempts at international commodity agreements.

1972   UNCTAD III in Santiago. G77 proposes a comprehensive series of measures on trade, production, multinationals, the IMF voting system and the allocation of new SDRs. However due to internal dissension of G77 and industrial countries' opposition, nothing much is achieved.

1974   UN General Assembly adopts a charter on the Economic Rights and Duties of States. Active push for an NIEO.

1975   The North-South Conference on International Economic Co-operation (CIEC) convenes in Paris.

1976   UNCTAD IV takes place in Nairobi. An Integrated Programme for Commodities for stabilizing prices at a just level is adopted. International Commodity Agreements in cocoa, coffee, rubber, jute, tin and sugar.

1977   CIEC convenes in Paris and industrialized countries agree to discuss all commodities, finance, and trade within the framework of NIEO but no result is achieved. Developing countries regard it as a cynical exercise of industrial countries interested only in the oil price.

1979   UNCTAD in Manila. G77's proposal for changes in the conditionality of IMF fails, but agreement to formulate codes of conduct for multinationals and technology transfer to be monitored by UNCTAD.

1981   A North-South Conference convenes in Cancun following the Brandt Commission Report. Calls for a large scale transfer of resources from rich to poor countries but fails due to US's negative attitude.

1983   UNCTAD VI in Belgrade. Expresses concerns about structural changes in world manufacturing industry, rising protectionism in industrial-

Table 2.6   continued

---

ized countries and debt crisis. Developed and developing countries do not agree on the solution to problems.

1985   The publication of *Global Challenge. From Crisis to Co-operation: Breaking the North-South Stalemate* by the Socialist International. However no action on the part of the industrialized nations.

1987   UNCTAD VII and the Havana declaration by G77. The 1980s is declared 'the lost decade of development' as the developing countries' crises deepen.

1992   UNCTAD VIII heralded *The Spirit of Cartagena*, a partnership for development.

1996   UNCTAD IX at Midrand, South Africa. Frank assessments of UNCTAD's functioning and pledge to build a more effective organization capable of implementing its mandate in a changing world.

Source: Mirza (1988) and The UNCTAD Bulletin (various issues)

ing countries. Nonetheless the G77 has continued to negotiate on a coherent basis.

The call for a NIEO found momentum and achieved a moral dimension following the Independent Commission on International Development Issues (ICIDI), chaired by Germany's ex-Chancellor Willy Brandt. The ICIDI, known as the Brandt Commission, was founded in 1977 at the suggestion of Robert McNamara, then President of the World Bank. Many of the proposals by the G77 on trade, the IMF and multinational corporations were accepted in the Brandt Commission report called 'North-South: A Programme for Survival'. The report proposed a North-South summit which was held in 1981 at Cancun, Mexico. However the summit largely failed to achieve any concrete result, except for a proposal for a second report which provided a blueprint for some proposals at the Sixth UNCTAD. Table 2.6 presents a brief chronology of major events relating to the NIEO.

For the purpose of negotiations, countries are divided into four groups in UNCTAD – A and C (developing countries), B (developed countries) and D (socialist countries). UNCTAD is held every four years. Although many proposals at the UNCTAD are readily agreed on the grounds of justice, there have always been tensions between developing and developed countries. It is worth mentioning that the first conference of UNCTAD, held in 1964, was opposed by industrialized countries. The industrialized countries accuse the developing countries of trying to impose non-market or legally binding solutions too readily and with rigid deadlines. They argue for a voluntary and market-based agreement on the transfer of technology, together with a market solution for the price instability of commodities.

Some of the significant achievements of UNCTAD are the Generalized System of Preference (GSP), the Integrated Programme for Commodities (IPC), the Code of Conduct for Multinationals (CCM) and the International Trade Centre (ITC). Under the GSP industrialized countries are required to lower tariffs against exports of manufactures from developing countries, while retaining tariffs on similar exports from other industrialized countries. The idea was mooted in 1964 and, despite opposition, it was agreed by 1968. Most industrialized countries now have some form of GSP. Although in reality quotas are imposed on labour intensive products such as textiles, footwear, garments and leather and few GSPs have proved as liberal as they initially appeared, many developing countries have gained from GSP. This is especially so, when any foreign investment decision is influenced by the possibility of exports under the GSP from a developing country production base.

The IPC entails international commodity agreements (ICA) to set up a common fund with contributions largely from industrialized and oil exporting countries to finance a buffer stock, with a view to stabilizing primary commodity prices at 'fair and remunerative levels'. The programme was initiated at UNCTAD IV. A common fund of around $6 billion was initially sought but only around $470 million was agreed by the end of UNCTAD VI.

Multinationals are often accused of avoiding taxes through transfer pricing, earning excess profit, corrupting the local officials and interfering in local politics. Thus developing countries sought to have an enforceable code of conduct for multinationals through UNCTAD. However what was eventually achieved is a voluntary code of conduct on transfer of technology.

The International Trade Centre (ITC) was originally set up under GATT in 1964 but became a joint venture between GATT and UNCTAD in 1968. Its main objective is to promote exports from developing countries. ITC generally operates through governments or government bodies in response to requests for advice on trade strategies, analysing export potential and advising on appropriate export markets, export financing, packaging and quality controls. It also provides training for officials from developing countries and trade information for business communities through its publications.

SUMMARY AND CONCLUSION

This chapter has reviewed such important concepts as the balance of payments accounts, exchange rates – nominal and real, purchasing power parity and the terms of trade. It then examined some of the problems and issues faced by developing countries in an interdependent world. It argued that developing countries are potentially vulnerable to various external shocks through terms of trade changes and changes in the economic conditions in industrial country trading partners. Adjustments to these shocks require both expenditure variations and resource reallocation and hence are costly. Adjustment costs usually have a greater adverse effect on the poor, which may make such adjustments politically infeasible. Furthermore adjustments may be blocked by losers in the declining sectors. Whether a country should make costly adjustments depends on the nature of shocks. If the shocks are temporary in nature then the optimal response should be overseas borrowing (or lending in the case of favourable shocks) to smooth out consumption. However there is considerable uncertainty as to the nature of external shocks – it is not easy to predict whether a shock is going to persist or reverse.

This chapter also examined the problems associated with international capital flows. It argued that international capital flows can cause macroeconomic instability. Short-term capital inflows put pressures on domestic money supply if the exchange rate is managed or fixed. The sterilization of these flows imposes quasi-fiscal costs as wealth holders (public and banks) are forced to hold less attractive government bonds. If they are not sterilized, short-term capital inflows can jeopardize the safety of the banking system as the banks expand credit. More importantly these flows are volatile and can reverse very quickly, causing severe liquidity problems.

It has also been demonstrated that there are close links between government budget deficit, money supply and both internal and external imbalance. Thus it is argued that the assignment problem of developing open economies entails the resolution of the government budgetary problem.

The chapter also provided a brief overview of institutional developments such as IMF, GATT, WTO and UNCTAD. IMF and GATT are generally regarded as rich nations' clubs and the benefits of WTO for developing countries are not yet very clear. UNCTAD is an outcome of developing countries' push for greater access to international trade and investment. Although the success of UNCTAD is mixed, it has been an important forum for developing countries.

APPENDIX

The mechanism through which foreign inflation is transmitted to developing countries can be explained by using an input-output framework where production requires a fixed proportion of non-competitive imports.[18] Assuming a two-goods economy, the cost-determined unit price (P_i) of domestic products can be expressed as:

$$P_1 = a_{11}P_1 + a_{21}P_2 + n_1w + m_1P_m \qquad (2.1A)$$
$$P_2 = a_{12}P_1 + a_{22}P_2 + n_2w + m_2P_m$$

where a_{ij} is the per unit input requirement of j from i, n_i is labour-output ratio (inverse of labour productivity), m_i is per unit imported raw material requirement, w is the given wage rate and P_m is an import price index ($=eP_f$).

In matrix form (2.1A) can be expressed as:

$$\mathbf{P}^T = \mathbf{wn}^T(\mathbf{I} - \mathbf{A})^{-1} + P_m\mathbf{m}^T(\mathbf{I} - \mathbf{A})^{-1} \qquad (2.2A)$$

where superscript T denotes transpose and $\mathbf{A}$ is the matrix of input coefficients a_{ij}. Thus we have individual prices as:

$$P_1 = wn_1r_{11} + wn_2r_{21} + P_mm_1r_{11} + P_mm_2r_{21} \qquad (2.3A)$$
$$P_2 = wn_1r_{12} + wn_2r_{22} + P_mm_1r_{12} + P_mm_2r_{22}$$

where r_{ij} are the elements of the inverse matrix $(\mathbf{I} - \mathbf{A})^{-1}$, and capture the direct and indirect input requirements for producing one unit of output.

The equations system (2.3A) shows that the impact of import prices on individual sector prices is amplified due to both direct and indirect import requirements. Consequently any rise in the price of imported raw materials leads to a more than proportionate rise in the unit domestic price.

NOTES

1. The money supply is determined by the financial assets of the central bank, which include foreign exchange reserves and credit to the government (see equation 2.11). Under the fixed exchange rate system, the central bank must be ready to either buy or sell foreign exchange if there is an excess supply or demand at the official rate.
2. This follows from note 1 and equation 2.11. When the central bank buys or sells foreign exchange, it can offset the impact on money supply by selling or buying government bonds through open market operations so that its total financial assets remain unchanged. This action of offsetting the effect of the balance of payments developments on money supply is known as sterilization.
3. This follows Dornbusch (1980).
4. In the absence of trade, BX amount of importables would have required the conversion of BA' amount of exportables. Therefore trade improves the external productivity of a nation.
5. See Bruno and Sachs (1985). The idea can be traced to Klein (1965, 1978).
6. See Gavin (1993) for an analysis of Nigeria's adjustment to terms of trade shocks.
7. See Chapter 7, section 3.
8. See Chapter 7, section 3.
9. See Mundell (1971).
10. One common way of avoiding regulations and effecting the transfer of capital is by over-invoicing imports and under-invoicing exports.
11. This section draws on Islam and Chowdhury (1997).
12. The idea of the 'two-targets two-instruments' approach to internal and external balance

was first coined by Meade (1951); the concept of switching was first introduced by Johnson (1958); the traded and non-traded goods model was developed by Salter (1959).

13. Three very influential approaches to policy making in this general spirit are those of Tinbergen (1952), Theil (1961) and Mundell (1962).

14. This section draws on Little *et al*, (1993) and Argy (1994).

15. In an influential book, Triffin (1960) warned of impending problems in 1960 and Argy (1994) calls the 1960s the 'Triffin awakening'.

16. Friedman (1953) argued in favour of a floating exchange rate system on the grounds that it would insulate economies from external shocks and allow governments to exercise more direct control over their money supplies, which would lead to lower inflation and lower volatility of domestic interest rates.

17. Initially only a few countries joined GATT. However, by 1990, 100 of the 150 members of the IMF and World Bank joined GATT

18. Non-competitive imports means that they have no domestic substitute. This makes them price inelastic.

3.   Open-economy macro models

INTRODUCTION

Open economy macroeconomic models attempt to incorporate the balance of payments, the exchange rate and the terms of trade in a general framework where they interact with income levels (both foreign and domestic), money supply, interest rates (domestic and foreign) and the price level (domestic and foreign). However, '[w]hile there is now a recognizable body of literature on open economy macroeconomics, there is far from universal agreement on the appropriate structure of an analytical model' (Prachowny, 1981:1–2). Thus there is no single standard model that can analyse all the issues. This chapter provides an overview of some of the models designed to analyse issues confronted by open economies and their policy options. Specifically it will review the absorption approach to the balance of payments, the monetary approach to the balance of payments, the Mundell-Fleming (MF) model and the Swan-Salter-Corden (SC) model. The chapter begins with a brief review of the policy dilemma for open developing economies.

POLICY PROBLEMS AND THE TINBERGEN RULE

As mentioned in Chapter 2, the fundamental problems for most open developing economies are current account deficits (external imbalance) and high unemployment/inflation (internal imbalance). However, these economies face a dilemma. Although the general solution to the unemployment problem requires the economy to grow rapidly, the expansionary macroeconomic policies needed for economic growth often cause demand to grow at a faster rate than the supply capacity. This has a number of consequences for the external balance. First, imports rise while the availability of exportables declines, widening the external imbalance directly. Second, the excess demand pressure accelerates the inflation rate, which affects the country's international competitiveness adversely and hence worsens the external balance further. Thus attempts to increase employment worsen the balance of payments on current account.

Section 4 of Chapter 2 highlighted the fact that the conflict between internal and external balance arises from the Tinbergen rule that there must be at least as many effective instruments as there are targets. This is because a policy instrument can have favourable impacts on one target but unfavourable impacts on others. Furthermore not all instruments can be equally effective for every target. Thus what follows is the assignment principle that an instrument be assigned to the objective where it has the maximum effectiveness. This principle is central to the analysis of macroeconomic policy problems of open developing economies.

ABSORPTION AND THE BALANCE OF PAYMENTS

The absorption approach to the balance of payments highlights the policy dilemma of open developing economies. This approach follows from the national income identity:

$$Y = C + I + G + X - M \tag{3.1}$$

where Y is gross domestic product (GDP), C is aggregate consumption, I is aggregate investment, G is government expenditure, and X – M is the trade balance.

Define C + I + G = A as domestic absorption. Then equation (3.1) reduces to:

$$Y - A = X - M \tag{3.1a}$$

Equation (3.1a) shows that the balance of payments on current account is a macroeconomic phenomenon and that it must always be equal to the difference between domestic production and domestic absorption. Therefore the current account deficit arises when domestic absorption grows at a faster rate than the growth of GDP.

One can gain more insight when GDP is classified into its component uses:

$$Y = C + S + T \tag{3.2}$$

where S is domestic private sector savings and T is taxes. A rearrangement of equations (3.1) and (3.2) yields

$$(S - I) + (T - G) = X - M \tag{3.2a}$$

Equation (3.2a) shows that the balance of payments on current account must be equal to the private sector saving-investment gap *plus* the government budget surplus or deficit. According to the 'new Cambridge' school of thought, the private sector saving-investment gap is a stable function of disposable income and hence the current account deficit is caused by the government budget deficit. This is also known as the 'twin deficit' hypothesis.

Historically, developing countries relied heavily on expansionary fiscal policies for economic growth and, according to the twin deficit hypothesis, the chronic balance of payments problem of these countries can be traced to large public sector deficits. Developing countries often attempt to resolve this policy dilemma by introducing import controls. However they cannot succeed, as import controls without absorption reduction merely shift demand to domestic goods and thereby reduce the availability of exportables. This suggests that one of the ways to improve the current account is to reduce domestic absorption which, in this case, means a reduction in government budget deficit. However the difficulty with such a contractionary policy is that it adversely affects employment unless there is either a decline in imports or an increase in exports. This is the theme of the Swan-Salter-Corden model, to be discussed later.

THE MONETARY APPROACH TO THE BALANCE OF PAYMENTS

This approach was developed by economists working at the IMF and it results in the same policy prescription as the absorption approach, namely that the solution to an external imbalance lies in the reduction in domestic absorption, more specifically the government budget deficit. However, unlike the absorption approach which relies mostly on accounting identities, the monetary approach to the balance of payments derives its results from the behaviour of economic agents.

The basis of this model is that if money supply exceeds money demand, people dispose of their excess money holdings by spending on goods and services. The underlying assumption is that money is demanded primarily for transactions purposes, which is not unrealistic for a developing country where the capital market is underdeveloped. That is, the excess supply of money is manifested in excess demand in the commodity market. Therefore as people adjust their actual money holdings to the desired level, the trade balance deteriorates.

As in the absorption approach, the trade account is identically equal to the difference between domestic output and domestic absorption. That is, if domestic absorption exceeds domestic output, there will be a trade deficit as shown by equation (3.1a).

The capital account (KA) is identically equal to net non-official borrowings (lendings) abroad and sale (purchase) of real and financial assets abroad. Therefore:

$$KA = F_f - H_f \tag{3.3}$$

where F_f = sales of financial and real assets abroad and H_f = purchases of financial and real assets abroad.

Equations (3.1a) and (3.3), when combined, will yield the equation for the balance of payments as:

$$BP = (Y - A) + (F_f - H_f) \tag{3.4}$$

Note that the sales of financial and real assets domestically (F_d) must be equal to the purchases of financial and real assets domestically (H_d). Hence equation (3.4) can be written as:

$$BP = (Y - A) + (F - H) \tag{3.5}$$

where $F = F_f + F_d$ and $H = H_f + H_d$

The identity (3.5) shows that a necessary condition for a deficit in the balance of payments is that current purchases by non-central bank domestic residents of goods, services and assets must exceed their total sales of goods, services and assets. This difference can only be financed by domestic residents either running down cash balances (dishoarding) or by selling assets to the central bank. When the central bank purchases assets, it creates domestic credit. Therefore a deficit in the balance of payments necessarily involves either dishoarding (a manifestation of excess supply of money) by domestic residents or an increase in the central bank's creation of domestic credit. If the central bank does not create domestic credit, then a balance of payments deficit can only persist through a continuous dishoarding by domestic residents. In this case the money stock will shrink as the central bank purchases the excess supply of its currency on the foreign exchange market and its foreign exchange reserves decline (under a fixed exchange rate system). The resulting decline in money stock will eventually halt the dishoarding as the domestic residents reach their desired level of money holdings. Therefore a balance of payments deficit cannot persist for a long period of time unless the central bank engages in continuous credit creation. This is the central message of the monetary approach to the balance of payments.

Why then does the central bank indulge in continuous domestic credit creation? The answer lies in the public sector borrowing requirement. Following Easterly and Schmidt-Hebbel (1993), the 'public financing identity' can be written as:

Fiscal/public sector deficit financing (FDF) = Money financing (MF)
+ Domestic debt financing (DDF) + External debt financing (EDF)   (3.6)

To begin with, most developing countries have a low credit rating, and their access to the international capital markets is limited. Moreover the debt crisis of the 1980s is a constant reminder of the danger involved in this route of deficit financing. Given that the domestic capital markets in most developing countries are underdeveloped, their ability to finance public sector deficits by borrowing from the domestic non-bank public is also limited. This leaves them with only one option, namely borrowing from the central bank (MF). Estimates by Little *et al* (1993) show that a typical developing country finances approximately 50 per cent of public deficits through the banking system.

Therefore the key policy message of the above analysis is that assuming monetary control for the external balance must entail assuming control over the government's budgetary position. This is the message the IMF conveys to developing countries.

However neither the absorption nor the monetary approach addresses the problem of simultaneously achieving both internal and external balance. Their predominant concern is external imbalance and, thus, they are partial in focus. The models reviewed below analyse both internal and external balance simultaneously.

THE MUNDELL-FLEMING MODEL

The Mundell-Fleming (MF) model is the best known and most widely used macro model of an open economy. The model is an extension of the standard IS-LM model[1] and is Keynesian in spirit. The basic assumptions of the MF model are:

1. nominal wages (W) and prices (P) are fixed,
2. aggregate demand is positively related to the level of government expenditure (G), exogenous overseas output (Y_f) and the exchange rate (e) and negatively related to the domestic interest rate (r_d),
3. the demand for money is a negative function of the domestic interest rate and a positive function of the domestic income level,
4. the money supply is negatively influenced by the deviation of the exchange rate (e) from some target level (e*),
5. the trade account is determined by the level of domestic output (Y_d) *vis-à-vis* output abroad (Y_f), and
6. the capital account is determined by the home and overseas interest rate differential ($r_d - r_f$).

The assumption of fixed money wages and prices is the key Keynesian feature of the model, implying a perfectly elastic aggregate supply (AS) curve where output is determined by the position of the aggregate demand (AD) curve. The degree of capital mobility determined by the sensitivity to interest rate differential plays a crucial role in the MF model.

Following Argy (1994), the model can be mathematically presented in logarithmic form as follows:

$$\ln Y_d = \alpha_1 \ln e + \alpha_2 \ln G - \alpha_3 r_d + \alpha_4 \ln Y_f \qquad (3.7)$$
$$\ln M_0 - \alpha_5(\ln e - \ln e^*) = \alpha_6 \ln Y_d - \alpha_7 r_d \qquad (3.8)$$
$$B/X_0 = \alpha_8 \ln e - \ln Y_d + \ln Y_f + \alpha_9(r_d - r_f) \qquad (3.9)$$

Equation (3.7) is the commodity market equilibrium condition and hence defines the IS curve. The right hand side of (3.7) summarizes the determinants of the components of AD. For example, the domestic interest rate (r_d) negatively influences investment and consumption, and the exchange rate (e) and foreign income (Y_f) positively influence net exports.

Equation (3.8) gives the money market equilibrium condition and hence defines the LM curve. The right-hand side of the equation describes the demand for money which is negatively influenced by the domestic interest rate and positively by domestic income. The left-hand side states that the money supply has two components – an exogenous component (M_0) determined by the monetary authority and an induced component [$\alpha_5(\ln e - \ln e^*)$] which responds to the difference between the market exchange rate and a target exchange rate (e*). If $\alpha_5 = 0$, money supply is exogenous which is consistent with a flexible exchange rate system or a fixed exchange rate system with full sterilization. If α_5 tends to infinity, it would imply a fixed exchange rate system where monetary policy is used to restore the target exchange rate. For an intermediate regime or managed float, α_5 will lie between zero and infinity.

Equation (3.9) explains the overall balance of payments over initial exports (X_0), where the first three terms determine the trade or current account balance and the last term gives the capital account balance. Thus (3.9) defines the balance of payments (BP) curve along which BP= 0 for various combinations of domestic income and domestic interest rates.

The equations system (3.7) to (3.9) can be solved for three variables, domestic income (Y_d), the domestic interest rate (r_d) and either the exchange rate (e) if the system is flexible ($B/X_0 = 0$) or the balance of payments position for a given e if the exchange rate regime is fixed. In order to show the solution graphically, (3.7) to (3.9) are rearranged as follows:

$$r_d = -1/\alpha_3(\ln Y_d) + \alpha_1/\alpha_3 (\ln e) + \alpha_2/\alpha_3 (\ln G) + \alpha_4/\alpha_3 (\ln Y_f) \qquad (3.7a)$$
$$r_d = \alpha_6/\alpha_7 (\ln Y_d) + \alpha_5/\alpha_7 (\ln e - \ln e^*) - 1/\alpha_7 (\ln M_0) \qquad (3.8a)$$
$$r_d = r_f + 1/\alpha_9 (\ln Y_d - \ln Y_f) - \alpha_8/\alpha_9 (\ln e) \qquad (3.9a)$$

Equation (3.7a) describes a downward sloping IS curve for given values of G, e and Y_f. It is downward sloping because as the interest rate rises, demand for both consumption and investment declines and hence output must decline to maintain equilibrium. Government expenditure (G), the exchange rate (e) and foreign income (Y_f) act as positive shift variables. A depreciation of the exchange rate (a rise in 'e') and a rise in foreign income will induce net exports to rise and hence cause a rightward shift of the IS curve.

Equation (3.8a) is the upward sloping LM curve. It is upward sloping because, as the domestic interest rate rises, demand for money falls and hence income must increase to induce an increase in demand for money so that the money market remains in equilibrium. The money supply variables – both exogenous and induced components – act as shift variables. However if the exchange rate is flexible or fixed (with sterilization), that is $\alpha_5 = 0$, then the LM curve will not shift in response to any balance of payments and exchange rate developments. In that case the only shift variable is the exogenous money supply. When the exchange rate is fixed and capital flows are not sterilized, then a deficit (surplus) in the balance of payments will shift the LM curve upward (downward) to the left (right).

Equation (3.9a) is derived by setting $B/X_0 = 0$. It gives various combinations of domestic income and the interest rate for which the overall balance of payments is in equilibrium. It is upward sloping because as the domestic interest rate rises (for a given foreign rate), capital flows inwards causing a surplus in the capital account, hence income must rise to induce imports so that there is an equivalent deficit in the trade account such that the overall balance of payments will remain in equilibrium. Foreign income and the exchange rate act as shift variables. If, for example, foreign income rises, there will be an increase in exports and the BP curve will shift to the right, implying that for a given domestic interest rate, the trade balance requires a higher level of domestic income so as to induce higher imports to match higher exports. There will be a similar rightward shift of the BP curve if the exchange rate depreciates (a rise in 'e').

The slope of the BP curve shows the degree of capital mobility. If the BP curve is vertical ($\alpha_9 = 0$), there is no capital mobility. On the other hand when the capital mobility is perfect (α_9 tending to infinity), the BP line will be horizontal, implying that a slight deviation between the domestic and foreign interest rate will induce massive capital flows.

Figure 3.1 shows the equilibrium in all three markets – commodity, money and the exchange rate. Point E, where the IS, LM and BP curves intersect, represents both internal and external balance. Points to the right (left) of the IS curve represent an excess supply (demand). This is because for a given interest rate, the supply of output is larger (smaller) than required for an equilibrium in the commodity market. Points to the right (left) of the LM

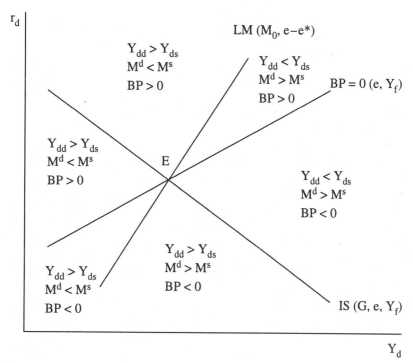

Notes:
Y_{dd} = domestic aggregate demand
Y_{ds} = domestic aggregate supply
M^d = money demand
M^s = money supply

Figure 3.1   Internal and external balance

curve represent an excess demand for (supply of) money. This is because for a given interest rate, the level of income is higher (lower) than is necessary for an equilibrium in the money market. To the right (left) of BP is the balance of payments deficit (surplus). This is because, for a given level of interest rate, capital inflows remain unchanged, but a higher (lower) domestic income level means a larger trade deficit (surplus).

For a fixed exchange rate regime coupled with unsterilized capital flows and a fully flexible exchange rate regime, both internal and external balance require that all three markets are always in equilibrium. For example, if any disturbance shifts the internal balance (the point of IS-LM intersection) to the right of the BP curve causing a deficit in the balance of payments, the LM curve will shift to the left as money supply contracts in response under an unsterilized fixed exchange rate system, until all three schedules intersect at one point. On the other hand if the exchange rate is fully flexible, it will depreciate (a rise in 'e'), causing net exports to rise. As a result, both the IS and BP curves will shift to the right until all three curves intersect at one point again. When the exchange rate regime is fixed and capital flows are sterilized, the IS-LM intersection point may or may not fall on the BP curve, so that the internal balance may co-exist with either a surplus or a deficit in the overall balance of payments.

Relative Effectiveness of Monetary and Fiscal Policies

The relative effectiveness of monetary and fiscal policies in an open economy described by the MF model depends on the degree of capital mobility and the exchange rate regime – with or without sterilization. Despite the substantial opening up of many economies, the recent surge in capital inflows is limited to a small number of countries in the Asia-Pacific region. Most developing countries still do not attract much foreign private capital. This means that the BP curve will be very close to a vertical line, reflecting a limited degree of capital mobility. It is also alleged that the interest rate does not play a major role in the demand for money in most developing countries with a large non-monetized sector. This implies that the LM curve is relatively steep. It is also a fact that most developing countries follow some variants of a fixed exchange rate system. Therefore the case now considered here is where the exchange rate is fixed (or managed) and capital mobility is limited, as depicted in Figure 3.2. The two graphs show the situation where the LM curve is flatter/steeper than the BP curve respectively.

Point E_0 is the initial equilibrium where all three schedules intersect. An expansionary monetary policy shifts the LM curve to LM_1 and the internal balance (the IS-LM intersection) moves to E_1, which is to the right of the BP curve. Thus at E_1, the balance of payments will be in deficit as a lower interest rate induces capital outflows and a higher income level induces more imports for a given level of exports. If the country is following a fixed exchange rate system, the central bank will have to intervene and supply foreign exchange at the official rate to protect the target rate. This will reduce the central bank's reserves of foreign currencies and hence its assets, unless sterilized by acquiring other financial assets (buying government bonds). As a result, the money supply will decline and the LM curve will return to the original position (LM_0). Thus there will be no impact of either an expansionary or contractionary monetary policy on output and employment under the fixed exchange rate system (unsterilized). As can be seen from the two graphs, this result holds regardless of the degree of capital mobility.

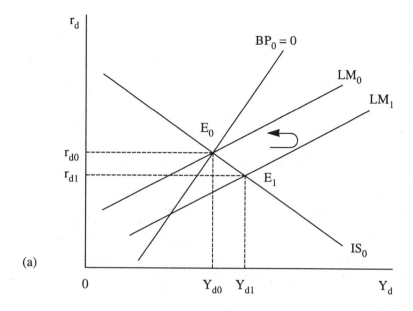

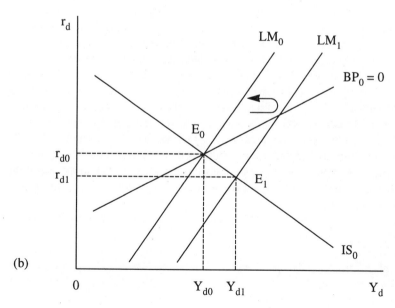

Figure 3.2   Effectiveness of monetary policy under the fixed exchange rate system

Figure 3.3 shows the comparative statics for fiscal policy. An expansionary fiscal policy shifts the IS curve to IS_1. In the first graph where the BP curve is steeper than the LM curve, the new internal balance causes a balance of payments deficit. As the central bank intervenes in the foreign exchange market, the LM curve shifts leftward reducing the effectiveness of the expansionary fiscal policy. On the other hand, when the BP curve is flatter than the LM curve (graph (b)), the new internal balance (point E_1) produces a balance of payments surplus. In response, the money supply increases (if the capital inflows are not sterilized) and the LM curve shifts to the right enhancing the effectiveness of an expansionary fiscal policy. Thus, under the fixed exchange rate system, the effectiveness of fiscal policy is enhanced with the increase in capital mobility.

Figure 3.4 depicts a situation where a country follows a flexible exchange rate system. In this case, the deficit in the balance of payments due to an expansionary monetary policy will be adjusted through an exchange rate depreciation. The depreciation will improve the country's international competitiveness and, as a result, both the BP and IS curves will shift to the right and intersect the new LM curve (LM_1) at E_2, making monetary policy very effective.

Figure 3.5 illustrates the effectiveness of an expansionary fiscal policy in a flexible exchange rate regime. When the BP curve is steeper than the LM curve (graph (a)), an expansionary fiscal policy will cause a balance of payments deficit. As the exchange rate depreciates, both the IS curve and the BP curve will move further to the right. The new equilibrium point is E_2, where the effectiveness of an expansionary fiscal policy is greatly enhanced. However when the BP curve is flatter than the LM curve (graph (b)), an expansionary fiscal policy will cause a surplus in the balance of payments due to a rise in the interest rate. In response the exchange rate will appreciate, reducing the country's competitiveness. As a result both the IS and BP curves will shift to the left, establishing both internal and external balance at E_2. Thus, the degree of capital mobility affects the effectiveness of fiscal policy if the exchange rate is flexible. In contrast to the fixed exchange rate case, the higher the sensitivity of capital mobility to interest rate changes, the less is the effectiveness of fiscal policy.

Effectiveness of Devaluation

Devaluation is applied as an exogenous policy instrument when a country follows a fixed exchange rate system. Devaluation makes exports cheaper in foreign currency and imports dearer in domestic currency. If, as a result, export demand increases in a greater proportion than the decline in foreign currency price of exports and, similarly, import demand declines in a greater

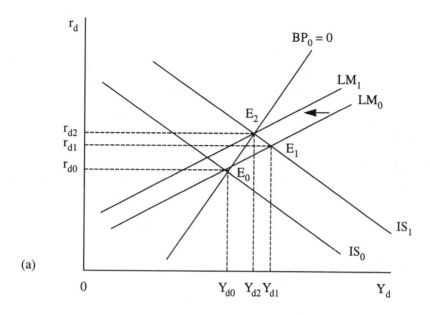

(a)

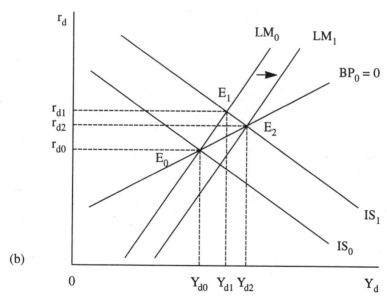

(b)

Figure 3.3 Effectiveness of fiscal policy under the fixed exchange rate system

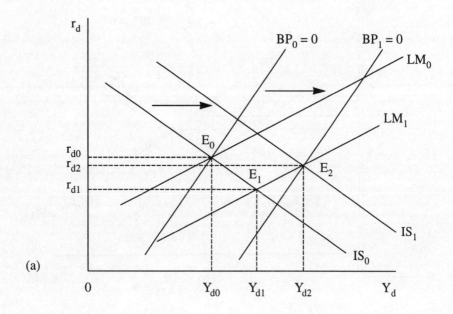

(a)

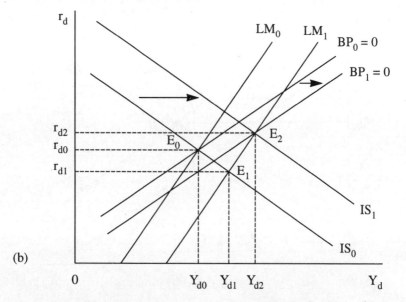

(b)

*Figure 3.4   Effectiveness of monetary policy under the flexible exchange
rate system*

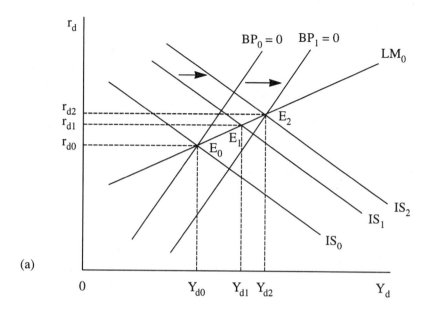

(a)

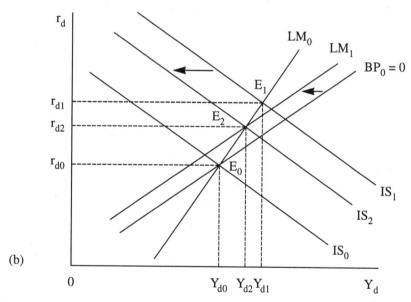

(b)

Figure 3.5   Effectiveness of fiscal policy under the flexible exchange rate system

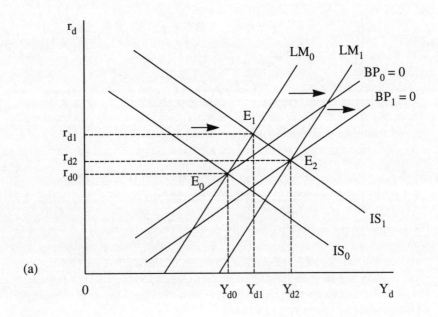

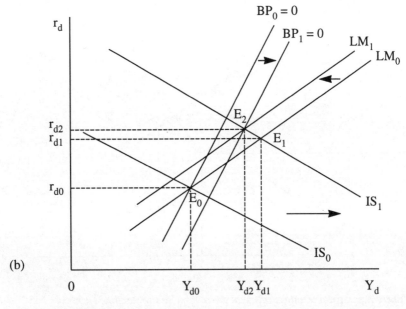

Figure 3.6   Effectiveness of a devaluation

proportion than the rise in domestic currency price of imports then the balance of payments on current account will improve. In other words, the price elasticity of both exports and imports must exceed unity for devaluation to have a favourable impact on the current account. Strictly speaking this condition, known as the Marshall-Lerner condition, requires that the sum of export and import price elasticities must exceed unity.

Therefore if the Marshall-Lerner condition holds, a devaluation will shift both the BP and IS curves to the right. Figure 3.6 shows two cases of a devaluation. In graph (a) where the LM curve is steeper than the BP curve, the new internal balance (E_1) causes a balance of payments surplus. If unsterilized this will result in the expansion of the money supply, shifting the LM curve to the right. The new internal and external balance will be at E_2. In graph (b) where the LM curve is flatter than the BP curve, two scenarios are possible. First, the IS curve can shift more than the BP curve, intersecting the LM curve to the right of the new BP curve (BP_1). In that case the balance of payments will be in deficit, pushing the LM curve leftward, and thereby will reduce the impact of a devaluation. Second, if the shift in the BP curve is larger than the shift in the IS curve, the new internal balance will cause a surplus in the balance of payments. This will shift the LM curve to the right and enhance the impact of a devaluation.

THE MUNDELL-FLEMING MODEL WITH WAGES AND PRICE ADJUSTMENT

In this section, one fundamental assumption of the MF model is relaxed by allowing wages and prices to vary. This is achieved by adding the labour market to the model. In this extended model, the aggregate supply (AS) curve is not perfectly elastic but, under reasonable assumptions about wage-price flexibility, is upward sloping:

The labour market:
$$\ln Y_{ds} = -\beta_1(\ln W - \ln P_d) \tag{3.10}$$
$$\ln W = \beta_2 \ln P \tag{3.11}$$
$$\ln P = \beta_3 \ln P_d + (1 - \beta_3)\ln e \tag{3.12}$$

The commodity market:
$$\ln Y_{dd} = \alpha_1(\ln e - \ln P_d) + \alpha_2 \ln G - \alpha_3 r_d + \alpha_4 \ln Y_f \tag{3.13}$$
$$\ln Y_{dd} = \ln Y_{ds} \tag{3.14}$$

The money market equilibrium:
$$(\ln M_0 - \ln P_d) - \alpha_5(\ln e - \ln e^*) = \ln P_d + \alpha_6 \ln Y_d - \alpha_7 r_d \tag{3.15}$$

The foreign exchange market:

$$B/X_0 = \alpha_8(\ln e - \ln P_d) - \ln Y_d + \ln Y_f + \alpha_9(r_d - r_f) \qquad (3.16)$$

where P_d is the domestic price level and W is the nominal wage rate. All other variables are as defined earlier.

Equation (3.13) is the aggregate domestic demand (AD). It is no longer equal to aggregate supply at all levels of output as in the fixed price model, except at equilibrium. The commodity market equilibrium is given by equation (3.14). In contrast to equation (3.7) of the simple MF model, AD in the extended model is a function of real exchange rate ($\ln e - \ln P_d$). The real exchange rate also enters the overall balance of payments equation (3.16). The change in the money market relations is that the domestic price P_d enters into the equation to determine the real money supply.

The aggregate supply is determined by the conditions in the labour market. Equation (3.10) states that AS (Y_{ds}) is a negative function of the real wage rate ($\ln W - \ln P_d$). Equation (3.11) defines a rule of wage-indexation. If $\beta_2 = 1$, then there is full indexation, and when $\beta_2 = 0$, there is no indexation. Equation (3.12) defines the consumer price index as a weighted average of the price of home goods and the price of imported goods, reflected in exchange rate movements (as the foreign price level is assumed given and unchanged).

Substitution of equations (3.11) and (3.12) in equation (3.10) and rearrangements yield the equation for the AS curve as:

$$\ln Y_{ds} = \beta_1(1 - \beta_2\beta_3)\ln P_d - \beta_1\beta_2(1 - \beta_3)\ln e \qquad (3.10a)$$

When there is full wage indexation ($\beta_2 = 1$), the AS curve becomes:

$$\ln Y_{ds} = -\beta_1(1 - \beta_3)(\ln e - \ln P_d) \qquad (3.10b)$$

Equation (3.10b) states that when wage indexation is perfect, real wage becomes fixed and output is determined solely by the real exchange rate. According to this relationship, output must fall (rise) when there is a real devaluation – a rise in the real exchange rate (a real appreciation – a fall in the real exchange rate). In other words, output cannot change if the real exchange rate remains unchanged. However for the real exchange rate to fall (rise), the real wage rate must also fall (rise). This can be shown by equating equations (3.10) and (3.10b), which gives:

$$\ln W - \ln P_d = (1 - \beta_3)(\ln e - \ln P_d) \qquad (3.10c)$$

The relationship between real wages, the real exchange rate and output supply can be illustrated by using the following example. Assume that domestic and import prices rise by 6 and 2 per cent respectively, causing a real appreciation. According to equation (3.12), the consumer price index will rise by something between 6 and 2 per cent depending on the weights. Therefore under full-indexation wages will rise by less than 6 per cent, causing a fall in real wage. As real wage falls, employment and output will rise. Hence this gives a positive relationship between real appreciation and output supply as depicted in equation (3.10b).

The above extension of the MF model captures

1. the degree of exchange rate flexibility (represented by money supply coefficient α_5),
2. the degree of capital mobility (the balance of payments coefficient α_9) and
3. the degree of wage indexation (coefficient β_2).

In order to examine the relative effectiveness of fiscal, monetary and exchange rate policies within this model, the IS, LM and BP curves have to be derived as before. The IS curve is derived from equation (3.13) by setting $\ln Y_{dd} = \ln Y_d$. Simple algebraic manipulations yield:

$$r_d = -1/\alpha_3(\ln Y_d) + \alpha_1/\alpha_3 (\ln e - \ln P_d) + \alpha_2/\alpha_3 (\ln G) + \alpha_4/\alpha_3 (\ln Y_f) \quad (3.17)$$

The negative slope is $-1/\alpha_3$, and the real exchange rate, government expenditure (G) and foreign income (Y_f) act as shift variables.

From the money market equilibrium condition, the LM curve is obtained:

$$r_d = \alpha_6/\alpha_7 (\ln Y_d) + \alpha_5/\alpha_7 (\ln e - \ln e^*) - 1/\alpha_7 (\ln M_0 - \ln P_d) \quad (3.18)$$

The positive slope is given by α_6/α_7. Balance of payments developments (depending on sterilization and the exchange rate regime) and real money balances are shift variables.

The overall balance of payments curve BP is:

$$r_d = r_f + 1/\alpha_9 (\ln Y_d - \ln Y_f) - \alpha_8/\alpha_9 (\ln e - \ln P_d) \quad (3.19)$$

The positive slope is given by $1/\alpha_9$ and the real exchange rate acts as a shift variable. For simplicity, ignore the foreign interest rate and income as they are exogenously given.

The extended IS-LM-BP model is depicted in Figure 3.7. It can be used to derive the AD curve for the economy described by this model. Consider a fall in domestic price (P_d). This will increase the growth of real money supply ($\ln M_0 - \ln P_d$) and shift the LM curve to the right. There will also be a rise in

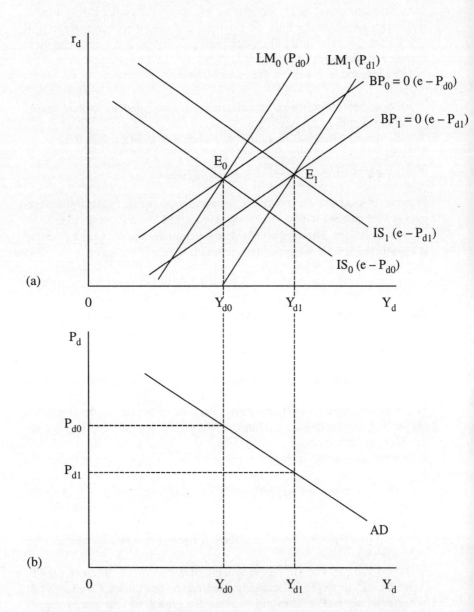

(a)

(b)

Figure 3.7   The extended IS-LM-BP model and the aggregate demand curve

the real exchange rate $(e - P_d)$, causing a rightward shift of both the IS and BP curves as net exports increase in response to a real depreciation. Thus a new IS-LM-BP equilibrium is attained at E_1, giving a higher level of Y_d. In other words Y_d increases when P_d falls. This gives a downward sloping AD curve.

Figure 3.8 shows the AD-AS equilibrium for the extended MF model. The AS curve is given by equation (3.4b) and is drawn for a given money wage rate. (The effect of foreign price and the exchange rate is captured by the wage rate through indexation.) The horizontal AS curve depicts the simple MF model (with fixed wages and prices).

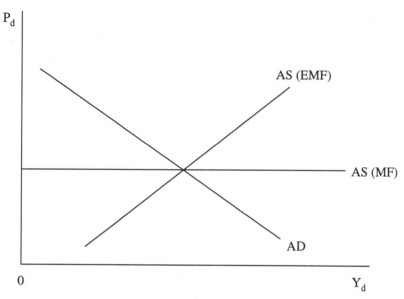

Figure 3.8   Equilibrium in the extended MF model

Relative Effectiveness of Monetary and Fiscal Policies

The AD-AS representation (as in Figure 3.8) of the extended MF model can be used to examine the relative effectiveness of monetary and fiscal policies and a devaluation. First consider the case of a fixed exchange rate regime where the monetary authority does not sterilize the balance of payments developments. In this case monetary policy will be totally ineffective as in the simple MF model, as the money supply adjusts downward to a balance of payments deficit despite the fact that wages and prices are allowed to vary. Any open market operation will be offset by an opposite movement in the international reserves.

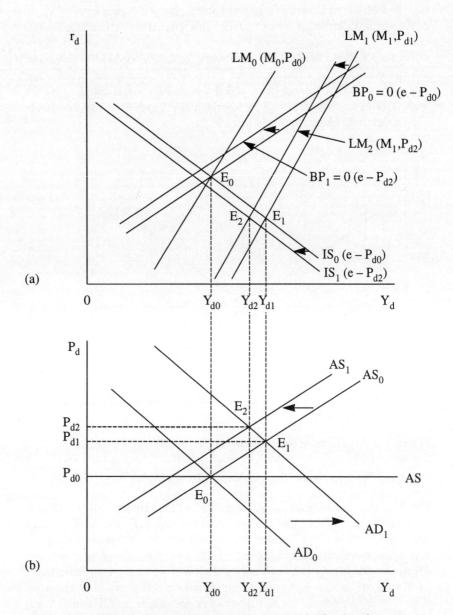

Figure 3.9   Effectiveness of monetary policy under the fixed exchange rate system (sterilized)

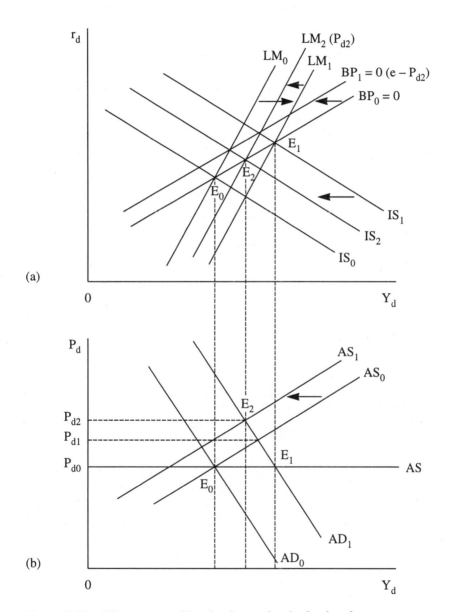

Figure 3.10 Effectiveness of fiscal policy under the fixed exchange rate system (unsterilized)

If the balance of payments developments are sterilized, the internal balance will co-exist with a balance of payments deficit (E_1 in Figure 3.9a). In terms of the AD-AS model, the AD curve will shift to the right (Figure 3.9b). The domestic price level will rise, real money supply will decline, the interest rate will rise and hence domestic demand will fall. The rise in P_d will also reduce international competitiveness and net exports will fall. Both together will cause a movement upward along AD_1. As the nominal wage rate adjusts upward in response to a higher P_d, the AS curve will shift to the left and the final equilibrium will be at E_2.

An expansionary fiscal policy shifts the IS curve to the right and (with the BP curve flatter than the LM curve) there will be a balance of payments surplus. When the exchange rate is fixed and the balance of payments surplus is not sterilized, the money supply will increase and the LM curve will shift to the right (Figure 3.10a). Recall that in the simple MF model the effectiveness of fiscal policy is enhanced. This is shown by the rightward shift of the AD curve which establishes a new equilibrium (with a horizontal AS curve) at point E_1 (Figure 3.10b). In the extended model, when the AS curve is upward sloping there will be an increase in the domestic price level (P_d). The rise in P_d will reduce the real money supply, causing the interest rate to rise. Furthermore international competitiveness will decline, causing leftward shifts of both the IS and BP curves. Thus aggregate demand will fall along the new AD_1. The higher domestic price level will also trigger an upward wage adjustment and the AS curve will shift to the left. The final equilibrium is at E_2. Thus fiscal policy is less effective than it is in the case of both the MF model and the extended model (without wage indexation).

The qualitative result remains the same when the balance of payments developments are sterilized. However in the latter case the LM curve will not shift and hence the AD curve will shift less. This essentially reduces the overall effectiveness of fiscal policy compared with non-sterilization.

Consider now the case of flexible exchange rates. Recall the simple MF result that the effectiveness of an expansionary monetary policy is enhanced (Figure 3.4). This means that the AD curve shifts to the right considerably and, as a result, the domestic price level will rise more. When wages adjust fully the AS curve will shift to the left. Once again, when wages and prices are allowed to vary, the effectiveness of monetary policy is reduced compared with the simple MF model.

An expansionary fiscal policy with a flexible exchange rate in the simple MF model is less effective (Figure 3.5). This means that the AD curve will shift less (compared with an expansionary monetary policy). The rise in P_d and the shift in the AS curve will therefore be less. As a result, the effectiveness of fiscal policy (which is less to begin with) will be reduced less.

Recall that the effectiveness of fiscal policy depends on capital mobility. In the simple MF model, the effectiveness of fiscal policy (under a flexible exchange rate system) declines with the degree of capital mobility. In the extended model however the result is reversed. To illustrate this, consider the extreme case of zero capital mobility. It is known from the labour market equilibrium condition that output increases if there is a real appreciation (equation 3.10b). However due to both increase in output and real appreciation, there will be a trade deficit unmatched by capital inflows (zero capital mobility). The result will be a balance of payments deficit and disequilibrium in the foreign exchange market. To have equilibrium in all three markets, the interest rate and domestic prices must rise and currency must devalue in proportion. The rise in the domestic price level reduces the real money supply. The equilibrium in the money market results in a high enough interest rate which fully neutralizes the effect of any fiscal expansion (complete crowding out), and the goods market returns to the original equilibrium. The proportionate devaluation leaves the real exchange rate unchanged and hence the labour market stays at the initial equilibrium. With all markets returning to their original equilibrium situation, there will be no effect of a fiscal expansion on output and employment.

On the other hand, with capital mobility there will be a real appreciation and output will rise. The resultant trade deficit will be matched by capital inflows in response to a higher interest rate. When the capital flow is perfect, fiscal policy is fully effective.

In total, the effectiveness of monetary and fiscal policies is reduced in the extended MF model when wages and prices are allowed to adjust in response to an expansion in aggregate demand. In extreme cases, when nominal wage adjusts fully to domestic price rises (perfect wage indexation) and the original real wage is restored (vertical AS curve), demand management policies will be totally ineffective. In other words, money becomes neutral and cannot affect real variables.

Effectiveness of Devaluation

The simple MF analysis has shown that a devaluation increases aggregate demand (the shift of the AD curve will depend on capital mobility). In the extended model the following will happen:

1. The home price will rise proportionately as wages adjust to higher import prices leaving the real exchange rate unchanged.
2. The level of output will remain unchanged as the real exchange rate remains unaltered.
3. With a rise in the domestic price level, the real money supply will fall.

This will neutralize the initial impact on money supply of the balance of payments surplus immediately following a devaluation.
4.   There will be no effect on the current account balance.

When the balance of payments outcomes are sterilized, the nominal money supply remains fixed. With the rise in domestic price however, the real money supply declines and hence the interest rate rises. This exerts a deflationary pressure on the economy and output falls. The deflationary pressure also means that home prices do not rise as much and there will be a real devaluation. Both the fall in output and a real devaluation will improve the current account balance.

Two points are worth emphasizing when money wages and prices are allowed to vary. First, if the balance of payments developments are not sterilized, a devaluation is completely impotent in improving the current account position. The rise in wages and prices will neutralize the effect of a nominal devaluation leaving the real exchange rate unchanged. Second, when the balance of payments developments are sterilized, a devaluation works to attain the external balance through a deflationary pressure and hence at the cost of internal balance. As the current account improves, unemployment increases. These important messages are carried to the Swan-Salter-Corden model.

TRADABLE AND NON-TRADABLE SECTOR MODEL

The tradable non-tradable sector model of internal and external balance, originally developed by Salter (1959) and later extended by Corden (1981), has been found extremely useful in analysing the problems faced by open developing economies. In fact this model provides the basic theoretical underpinning of the IMF adjustment programme for developing countries with a serious balance of payments problem. It explicitly shows the conflict between the internal and external balance and the usefulness of the policy rule that there must be at least as many effective policy instruments as there are targets.

The distinguishing feature of the model is that it divides the gross domestic product into tradables and non-tradables. Non-tradables are those goods ' ... which do not enter into world trade; their prices are determined solely by internal costs and demand' (Salter, 1959:226). Tradable is a composite product of exportables and importables. Exportables consist of actual exports together with products which could have been exported but are sold domestically. Importables are likewise actual imports and import substitutes which are produced and sold domestically. Traditionally agriculture, mining and manufacturing are regarded as tradables, and services and construction sectors as non-tradables.[2] It is possible to lump both exportables and importables into one tradable product if the relative price of exports and imports (the terms of trade) remains fixed. This assumption is consistent with the small country assumption that it cannot affect export or import prices.[3]

The model is based on the following assumptions:

1. Gross domestic product (GDP) is decomposed into tradables and non-tradables.
2. The country is small and cannot affect export or import prices. The prices are determined in the world market.[4]
3. The domestic excess supply of exportables is actual exports, and domestic excess demand is actual imports.
4. The prices of non-tradables are determined by domestic demand and supply.
5. Non-tradable prices are rigid downward.
6. There is initial equilibrium in the market for non-tradables.
7. There is no capital mobility and the country follows a fixed exchange rate system.

Assumption 3 implies that the balance of payments is in equilibrium if domestic excess demand for tradables is zero. Assumption 6 is the condition for an internal balance. Thus, if the non-tradable sector is in equilibrium (assumption 6) and there is a domestic excess demand for tradables, then it will create a situation of internal balance but an external imbalance.

Policy Implications

The domestic excess demand means that domestic absorption (consumption, investment and government expenditure) exceeds income. Therefore it requires contractionary fiscal and/or monetary policy. A contractionary policy may help to improve the external balance in two ways. First, it will reduce the demand for exportables and thereby release more to be exported. Second, it will reduce the demand for imports.

However the problem is that although the external balance improves with the reduction in domestic absorption, it may worsen the internal balance. This occurs because when the demand for non-tradables falls, producers respond by cutting production rather than price (prices are assumed rigid downward – assumption 5). Furthermore, with the prices of tradables being fixed (in the world market), the relative price between tradables and non-tradables remains unchanged so that the fall in demand will be uniform across both sectors. This means that a fall in domestic demand for exportables may not be matched by an increase in demand for non-tradables.

Once again this conflict highlights the simple policy rule that an absorption reduction policy must be supplemented with a switching policy. Devaluation as a switching policy raises the relative price of tradables (in domestic currency). This induces a shift of domestic demand away from tradables to non-tradables and resources (labour and capital) from non-tradables to tradables. Expenditure and resource switching ensures that the overall domestic demand does not fall and thus the internal balance is maintained. Both the switching of domestic demand away from tradables and the reduction in domestic demand for tradables help improve the external balance. This means that the cut in domestic demand for the improvement of the current account need not be as large if it is coupled with a switching policy.[5]

Just as absorption policy alone cannot achieve two targets, the switching policy by itself will not be sufficient. A devaluation will initially improve the external balance through both resource and expenditure switching. However at constant absolute prices for non-tradables there will be an excess demand for non-tradables, as demand switches towards them and resources switch away from non-tradable production. The prices of non-tradables will rise which will eventually negate the initial switching. Resources switch back to the non-tradable sector and expenditure away from it, until the relative price returns to the original level. This means that the original balance of payments problem reappears.

The policy outcomes of the tradable non-tradable model can be illustrated with the help of Figure 3.11. TT' is the full employment transformation curve between tradables and non-tradables. The initial relative price GG' determines the initial production at B where it is tangential to TT'. GDP and initial expenditure in terms of non-tradables are OG and OH, respectively. Therefore expenditure exceeds income by GH. The initial absorption point is D, where the internal price ratio HH' (parallel to GG') is tangential to the community indifference curve. The community indifference curve represents a constant level of real absorption. The line OZ through D is a sort of Engel curve. As D is directly above B (the production point), demand for non-tradables is equal to their supply (internal balance). However the demand for tradables exceeds their supply by BD, which is the initial external imbalance.

If the price ratio is kept unchanged but demand is reduced, the absorption point will move down OZ towards O. When expenditure is reduced to OG (that is, HH' coinciding with GG') the consumption point will be at C, where income will be equal to expenditure, but there will be an excess supply of non-tradables and a residual balance of payments deficit. Further cuts in expenditure (such as point E) can remove the balance of payments deficit but there will be a substantial excess supply of non-tradables (EB). This will induce cuts in production (a rise in unemployment) of non-tradables until production and consumption coincide at E.

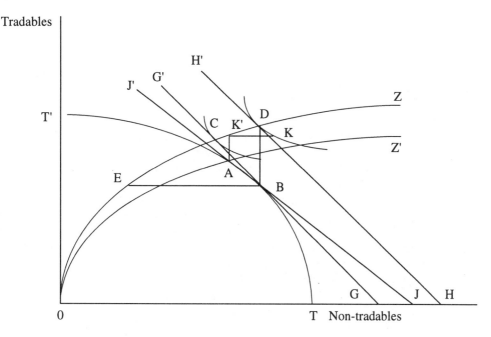

Figure 3.11   Absorption and switching policies in the Salter-Corden model

Now consider a devaluation which raises the domestic price of tradables. The price ratio is represented by JJ' which is tangential to both the indifference curve and the transformation curve (TT') at A. That is, it achieves both internal and external balance. The switching policy essentially brings the absorption pattern to some point on a new Engel curve OZ', while the absorption reduction policy brings the absorption level to A. The resource-switching effect of a devaluation moves the production point to A, which represents a higher level of tradables and a reduction in non-tradables production. Thus both production and consumption points coincide. A devaluation unaccompanied by an appropriate absorption policy will move the absorption point to K on the same indifference curve as D (that is, the real absorption remains unchanged), leaving the production point at A. At K, there will be an excess demand for non-tradables (KK'). This will raise the price of non-tradables and hence negate the impact of a devaluation on the relative price.

Contrary to the assumption of initial internal balance (assumption 6), a typical developing country faces both internal and external imbalance. Yet the analytical component of this model applies to a developing country without much modification. The internal imbalance is manifested in both unemployment and inflation.

Thus, the short-run macroeconomic policy targets for a developing country can be listed as

1. unemployment,
2. inflation, and
3. a current account deficit unmatched by capital inflows.

Three targets require three policy instruments – absorption policy (monetary and fiscal), switching policy (devaluation) and wages (incomes) policy. The policy rule with regard to assignment of instruments requires that an instrument be assigned to a target where it has the maximum potential. For example while a devaluation can also improve the external account, it is best in maintaining the internal balance. Therefore devaluation should be assigned to prevent unemployment from rising while the wages policy maintains international competitiveness (Corden, 1984, 1987). Likewise monetary and fiscal policies are best in achieving the external balance. This follows from the monetary approach to the balance of payments.

A typical developing country situation is depicted in Figure 3.12. TT' is the transformation curve, CC' is the consumption expansion path and QQ' is the production expansion path. The initial production and consumption points are A and B respectively. Point A, being below the transformation curve (TT'), represents unemployment. The consumption point B, being above the production point, implies a trade deficit (=AB). If fiscal and/or monetary policies shift the production point from A to D to achieve full employment (with unchanged relative price P_1P_1), the consumption point will move to E, creating a larger trade deficit (=DE). If however due to a devaluation, the relative price changes to PP_2 (in favour of tradables), CC' and QQ' will come closer and the production and consumption points will be at F where PP_2 is tangential to the transformation and community indifference curves. (In this figure there is no community indifference curve).

There is one more complication, which arises if workers demand higher wages to compensate for higher prices following a devaluation. This phenomenon is known as 'real wage resistance'. The higher wages, if accommodated through monetary expansion, will lead to higher domestic price level. This will erode the competitiveness that was achieved through a devaluation in the first place and may even reduce output. This type of outcome is a prediction of structuralists, such as Taylor (1983). Structuralists argue that developing countries are plagued with rigidities so that their supply elasticities of exports are very low. At the same time, as their imports are mostly essentials, the demand elasticity of imports is also low. These effectively negate the Marshall-Lerner condition. Structuralists also argue that as real wages in developing are already too low, workers are likely to resist any cut in their real wages.

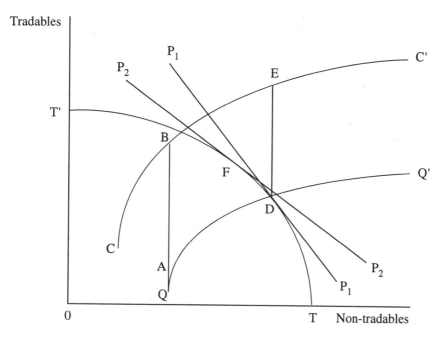

Figure 3.12   The internal and external balance problem in a developing economy

Furthermore, any rise in costs of imported raw materials may exacerbate the cost-push induced stagflation. Although structuralist views appear plausible, there is little evidence that supply elasticities in developing economies are low.

Moreover it does not necessarily imply that the switching and absorption reduction policies will adversely affect all workers (Corden, 1981). The income distribution effect of a devaluation will depend on factor mobility between the tradable and non-tradable sectors and their factor intensity. For example, if capital is immobile (sector specific) but labour is mobile between the two sectors and there is a constant money wage, the real profit in the tradable sector will rise and that in the non-tradable sector will fall as tradable prices rise relative to non-tradable prices due to a devaluation. However as tradable prices rise and non-tradable prices fall, the average price level may rise or fall (or remain unchanged) depending on the magnitude of these price changes in opposite directions. Therefore real wages may rise, fall or remain constant. On the other hand, if both capital and labour are mobile between the sectors (neo-classical trade model) and the tradable sector is more labour-intensive, then the change in relative price in favour of the tradable sector will raise the real income of labour. This shows the importance of following a labour-intensive export oriented industrialization strategy.

The analysis also shows that there is no reason for labour to be worse off in general. There will be some gainers and some losers. The losers will obviously attempt to block any structural adjustment measures or seek to maintain their real wages. The problem is to find some institutional mechanism whereby gainers are required to compensate the losers. Perhaps the non-government organizations (NGOs) can play a significant role here.

It should be noted that a devaluation only prevents the internal imbalance from further deterioration due to a reduction in absorption. In order to have a real impact on unemployment in developing countries with rapid population growth, it is essential that the economy grows at a faster rate. This means that the above macro policies must be supplemented by growth promoting policies, such as policies that enhance saving and investment rates. It is argued that macroeconomic stability itself provides an environment that encourages savings and investment. Furthermore it is essential that the tradable sector grows at a faster rate so that the current account problem does not re-emerge as the economy grows. In terms of Figure 3.12, the transformation curve (TT') shifts out (growth of GDP) but the shift in the tradable sector is larger than the non-tradable sector (structural change) so that it becomes steeper. As a result the required change in relative prices to be brought about by a devaluation would be less. Here lies the importance of microeconomic reform.

In summary, the four long-term macroeconomic goals for an open developing country are:

1. growth and employment,
2. price stability,
3. external balance and
4. structural change.

In terms of the above analysis the assignment rule should be absorption policy to external balance, switching policy to structural change, wages policy to price stability for international competitiveness and microeconomic reform to growth and employment. This policy rule does not imply that only the specified objectives will be achieved for each policy. For example microeconomic reform will also impact on structural change and thereby will minimize the need for a deeper devaluation. The assignment rule is based on the maximum impact of a policy instrument on a target. It is also worth emphasizing that under a fixed exchange rate system, there cannot be any independent monetary policy. This is also the case given the linkage between fiscal deficits, external imbalance and money supply.

SUMMARY AND CONCLUSION

This chapter has provided an overview of some of the open economy macro models used to analyse macroeconomic issues and policies. Although there is no universally applicable model for all the possible macro policy issues of an open economy, the Mundell-Fleming model is regarded as the bench-mark model. This model is particularly useful in analysing the effectiveness of fiscal and monetary policies but has one flaw, which is a lack of the supply-side. The extended model, discussed here, includes aggregate supply considerations and allows the exchange rate to influence the domestic price level.

The two-sector open economy model, based on the distinction between tradable and non-tradable sectors, is found to be useful when examining the policy dilemmas of internal and external balance. When taken together with the monetary approach to the balance of payments, it provides the basic theoretical framework for the IMF structural adjustment programme for developing countries. It shows that for the attainment of both internal and external balance, countries need both absorption and switching policies. The success of devaluation as a switching policy depends on wage restraint. This places developing countries in a difficult situation where the real wage is already low and any further reduction in real wage may not be feasible.

This chapter also highlighted the close linkage between the fiscal deficit, external imbalance and money supply. A consistent theme that emerged is that the resolution of the assignment problem boils down in essence to the resolution of the fiscal problem.

NOTES

1. See any standard intermediate macroeconomics textbook, such as Taslim and Chowdhury (1995) or Dornbusch and Fischer (1994), for a review of the standard IS-LM model.
2. For an open economy, trade related services and international tourism are included in the tradable sector.
3. If one wants to allow for terms of trade changes then there must be at least three sectors, exportables, importables and non-tradables. See Corden (1981) for the introduction of the terms of trade effects.
4. The price-taker role in international goods markets comes from Swan, who coined the term 'dependent economy' to describe 'a small country which trades in world markets that are competitive in the sense that the prices it receives for exports and pays for imports are independent of its domestic conditions of demand and supply' (Swan, 1960:53).
5. As a matter of fact, devaluation also affects absorption. If, for example, fiscal and monetary policies keep the money expenditure constant, then devaluation will mean a fall in real expenditure as it raises the domestic price level. It is more evident in the monetary approach to the balance of payments.

4. Foreign capital and economic growth

INTRODUCTION

Why do some economies grow rapidly while others exhibit periods of stagnation? This is an important question in modern growth theory, for economic growth determines the wealth of nations. The production function approach provides four major explanations of economic growth – the growth of the labour force, the accumulation of physical capital, technological progress and the behaviour of economic agents (Burda and Wyplosz, 1993).

Accumulation of capital is the fundamental determinant of economic growth, at least during the early stages of economic growth and development. This is the point which has been repeatedly emphasized by leading economists. For example Heinz Arndt (1987) points out that the cornerstone of economic development in its first phase is physical capital accumulation. Ragner Nurkse (1953) considered it 'a necessary condition of progress'. Arthur Lewis (1955) shared such a view and pointed to the low investment rate as the key difference between a developed and an underdeveloped economy. This theme was indeed common in the writings of classical economists from Adam Smith to Karl Marx and took a central position in the growth theory of Roy Harrod and Evsey Domar (Rostow, 1990). Thus it is not surprising that Meier and Baldwin (1957) have characterized poor countries as being 'capital hungry'. Amartya Sen (1983:751) is equally forceful in his acknowledgment of the role of capital accumulation in economic growth:

> Altogether, so far as growth is concerned, it is not easy to deny the importance of capital accumulation or of industrialisation in a poor pre-industrial country.

Such an acknowledgment of physical capital as a key factor of economic growth is one thing; how to accumulate productive capital[1] in low-saving developing economies is another. By definition, net investment should be positive in order to increase the volume of capital.

What is the constraint on investment? Classical economists were of the view that prior savings are the determinant of investment. This is the basis of the traditional policy recommendation that in order to increase the pace of economic growth, savings need to be increased to spur capital formation.[2] An acceptance of the classical view would mean that savings determine investment and economic policies which increase savings are growth-promoting. Within this paradigm, the role of government is to pursue policies that promote savings (both public and private).

This chapter reviews economic policies and issues related to the accumulation of capital in developing countries from foreign sources – both official development assistance and private capital flows. The major theme that emerges from this review is that, as many poor countries are unable to generate adequate investable funds from domestic sources for both economic and political reasons, capital accumulation from foreign sources remains an important source of economic growth. For a better understanding of this contention, the link between saving and economic growth is formalized here and is extended to consider the role of foreign capital in economic growth.

Saving and Economic Growth

Modern growth theory starts with the Harrod-Domar model (Domar 1946,1947; Harrod, 1939). It shows that the rate of economic growth[3] (g_y) in the steady state equals the productivity of capital (σ) multiplied by the rate of saving or investment (s), such that :

$$g_y = \sigma s \qquad (4.1)$$

If, for simplicity, the productivity of capital is considered fixed, economic growth is found to be directly linked with the rate of saving. To go a step further, this may be postulated as a causal relationship between the rate of saving (or investment) and economic growth. This causal relationship could be uni-directional running from saving to economic growth or bi-directional as is commonly observed during the phase of rapid economic growth.[4]

Raising the rate of saving thus remains the key to economic growth. How to do it in a poor economy however is unclear, if not mysterious. For example Arthur Lewis (1955:208, 225, 226, 236) emphasizes the key role that capital plays in economic growth and suggests that underdevelopment of capitalist sectors is one explanation for the low rates of saving and investment in poor countries:

> All the countries which are now relatively developed have at some time in the past gone through a period of rapid acceleration, in the course of which their rate of annual net investment has moved from 5 per cent [of national income] or less to 12 per cent or more. This is what we mean by an Industrial Revolution... The central problem in the theory of economic growth is to understand the process by which a community is converted from being a 5 per cent to a 12 per cent saver – with all the changes in attitudes, in institutions and in techniques which accompany this conversion... If the process of converting an economy from a 5 to a 12

per cent saver is essentially dependent upon the rise of profits relatively to national income, it follows that the correct explanation of why poor countries save so little is not because they are poor, but because their capitalistic sectors are so small. No nation is so poor that it could not save 12 per cent of its national income if it wanted to; poverty has never prevented nations from launching upon wars, or from wasting their substance in other ways. Least of all can those nations plead poverty as an excuse for not saving, in which 40 per cent or so of the national income is squandered by the top 10 per cent of income receivers, living luxuriously on rents. In such countries productive investment is not small because there is no surplus; it is small because the surplus is used to maintain unproductive hordes of retainers, and to build pyramids, temples and other durable consumer goods, instead of to create productive capital.

Foreign Capital-led Economic Growth

As indicated earlier, the rates of saving and investment are low in many poor countries. This is often explained in terms of what is popularly known as the 'vicious circle of poverty' (Meier and Baldwin, 1957; Nurkse, 1953). The basic idea is that poor countries with low rates of saving and investment grow slowly, which in turn keeps the rates of saving and investment low.[5] This portrays a pessimistic picture of poor countries. However the reality is not so gloomy as it sometimes appears.

Assuming that there is a saving/investment constraint to economic growth for poor countries, it may not be binding for two reasons. First, as the neoclassical theory shows, in a relatively poor economy with an initial low capital-labour ratio, the marginal productivity of capital will be high and this can trigger greater savings and investment at the early stages of development (Naqvi, 1996). Second, even if the rate of saving does not increase in response to a high rate of return, the rate of investment may remain high in an economy which allows the inflow of foreign capital. This is the basis of the view that, in an open economy with perfect capital mobility, economic growth may not be constrained by a low rate of domestic saving. That is, any shortage of domestic saving can be supplemented by foreign capital and thereby high rates of investment and economic growth can be maintained. In the spirit of this logic, the basic Harrod-Domar model can be extended for an open economy.

Let foreign capital inflows as a proportion of aggregate output be denoted by k^f. The Harrod-Domar model can then be written as

$$g_y = \sigma (k^f + s) \qquad (4.2)$$

Such an open-economy extension of the Harrod-Domar model formalizes the role of foreign capital in economic growth. In addition, this provides a developmental role for the government as 'all three of the variables on the right side are highly subject to government influence, directly and indirectly, positively and negatively' (Riedel, 1994:30). For example, government policies are a crucial determinant of foreign capital inflows (k^f).

The Two-gap Approach: an Early Economic Rationale for Foreign Development Assistance

In the 19th and early 20th centuries, foreign private capital played a key role in economic growth in European settled countries such as Argentina, Australia, Canada, New Zealand and the USA. During this period some foreign private capital also flowed to European colonies in both Asia and Africa, but their contribution to economic growth was limited.

After World War I, private capital flows to developing countries dried up. The prevailing view was that foreign private capital was not much suited to poor countries because of their 'specific economic conditions', implying the lack of developed markets and other institutions. The Great Depression of the 1930s and World War II further diminished the revival of any private capital flows to non-European poor countries. After World War II, many former European colonies in Asia and Africa gained political independence. As mentioned in Chapter 1, for the next two to three decades these newly independent countries opted for an inward-looking strategy for development and discouraged foreign private investment. However they have relied heavily on official aid from both developed countries and multilateral financial institutions. In 1985 the World Bank's World Development Report provided a rationale for official assistance to poor countries along the lines of the arguments made in favour of public goods. The Report offered five reasons for underprovision of private funds to poor countries. Eaton (1989:1308) has summarised them as:

1. sovereign risk;
2. capital market regulations in developed countries;
3. investment opportunities in poor countries that 'yield social returns, but may yield benefits that are not readily capturable or in the short run earn little or no foreign exchange with which to service foreign commercial loans';
4. private lenders' lack of information about investment opportunities and the repayment capacity of poor countries; and
5. commercial banks' aversion to long-term lending.

The role of official assistance in economic growth in poor countries was rationalized and formalized by leading development economists in the 1950s and 1960s. The two-gap approach is one model which provided a strong economic justification for foreign capital and the role it plays in the economic growth of poor countries.[6]

The basic model

The two-gap model is based on three interrelated assumptions. First, imported capital goods are essential for domestic production in poor countries. Second, the availability of foreign exchange to import capital goods, rather than the availability of domestic savings, constrains the growth of the economy. Third, external demand, rather than domestic supply of exportable goods, is the constraint on the ability of poor countries to earn foreign exchange through export. When these assumptions are valid, foreign capital can raise the rate of economic growth, not by raising resources available for investment but by increasing the availability of foreign exchange to import capital goods (Eaton, 1989). Following Findlay (1984), this basic idea of the two-gap model is explained here with the aid of Figure 4.1.

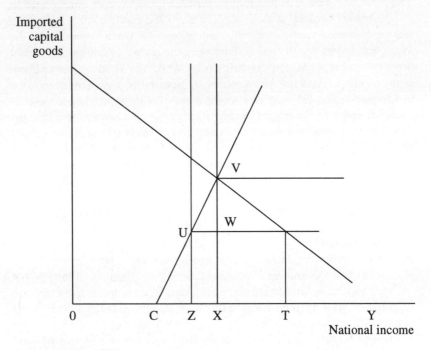

Source: Findlay (1984)

Figure 4.1   Economic growth under a foreign exchange constraint

Assume that domestic output (or income) (Y), measured by the distance OY, depends on a given capital stock. This output can be exchanged at a fixed rate for imports of capital equipment. Consumption is assumed to be a fraction of domestic output and is equal to OC. The propensity to save is given by

CY/OY. Assume that domestic investment requires both imported capital equipment and domestically produced goods but in fixed proportions. The levels of investment are represented by L-shaped isoquants with C as the origin. For an investment level at the point V, VX is the imported capital equipment acquired by exporting XY amount of domestic goods and CX is the domestic component of investment. The growth rate of output is determined by the rate of investment, corresponding to the isoquant at V, divided by the capital stock (assuming that the marginal and average capital-output ratios are equal). This shows that the output growth rate is constrained by the saving rate.

Assume now that exports are constrained by foreign demand and not by domestic supply. If the country exports TY of domestic goods (given foreign demand), UZ will be the maximum level of imports obtainable and this will restrict investment to the isoquant at U. This shows that, as exports of TY are adequate to finance UZ of imports, ZT of domestic exportable output will remain redundant in the sense that they cannot be used for investment, either directly or through exports. A foreign exchange gap of VW is thus created. The output growth rate, corresponding to the isoquant at U, is lower than that at V and this is precisely due to the lack of imported capital equipment. Under these circumstances foreign aid can fill the foreign exchange gap and raise economic growth by increasing investment through increased imports of capital equipment.[7]

FOREIGN AID FLOWS

The Size of Foreign Development Assistance

Table 4.1 lists the top 20 aid recipients and the top 15 aid donors in 1990. It shows that there are a few countries which receive the bulk of foreign aid. The size of official development assistance from developed to poor countries was US$5 billion in 1960 and US$54 billion in 1990. This increase in the nominal value of foreign assistance hides the fact that the real value of it has been declining since the early 1970s. Moreover in terms of the percentage of developed country GNP allocated to official development assistance, there has been a decline from 0.51 per cent in 1960 to 0.35 per cent in 1990. This figure is significantly lower than the internationally agreed United Nations target of 0.7 per cent. The allocation of aid by region or country is also rather arbitrary on economic criteria. Most independent observers believe that the bulk of foreign aid is given based on military and political considerations.[8]

Table 4.1   Major aid recipients and aid donors, 1990

Recipient countries	Development assistance		Donor countries	Development assistance	
	(US$ million)	(% of GNP)		(US$ million)	(% of GNP)
Egypt	5 584	17.2	Norway	1 207	1.17
Bangladesh	2 081	10.5	Finland	846	0.64
China	2 064	0.5	Denmark	1 171	0.93
Indonesia	1 717	2.0	Netherlands	2 580	0.93
India	1 550	0.5	Sweden	2 007	0.90
Philippines	1 266	3.0	Switzerland	750	0.31
Turkey	1 259	1.7	Canada	2 470	0.44
Tanzania	1 155	37.5	Italy	3 395	0.32
Pakistan	1 108	2.8	United Kingdom	2 639	0.27
Kenya	989	11.3	France	6 277	0.52
Morocco	965	4.4	Austria	389	0.25
Mozambique	923	77.4	United States	10 166	0.19
Jordan	884	16.7	Germany	6 320	0.42
Ethiopia	871	14.6	Japan	9 054	0.31
Zaire	816	9.2	Australia	955	0.34
Thailand	787	1.2			
Sudan	768	9.5			
Senegal	724	15.4			
Côte d'Ivoire	674	7.2			
Sri Lanka	659	9.1			

Source: UNDP (1992)

Macroeconomic Effects of Foreign Aid

Besides relieving the foreign exchange constraint and thereby enhancing growth through capital augmentation as captured in the two-gap model, there are at least four other channels through which foreign aid can influence a country's growth and development.

First, when capital assistance goes to specific projects to particular sectors, donors can use those projects to improve practices in those areas and initiate a self-sustaining growth. One prominent example of this is foreign assistance in spreading the high-yielding variety technology in South Asian agriculture. With the application of this technology South Asian countries have become almost self-sufficient in food. Second, through technical assistance donors can help to develop the administrative, managerial, scientific and educational standards of poor countries. Third, donors, through conditionality, can influence economic policies of the poor countries. Although most poor countries try to maintain their policy autonomy, there is overwhelming evidence that the structural adjustment measures that many developing countries have undertaken since the early 1980s have been largely under pressure from aid donors, including the World Bank and the IMF. Fourth, the international aid establishment directly and indirectly supports a large group of university scholars, professional consultants, aid administrators and others, from both the industrial and developing countries, who conceive and eventually popularize the new ways of thinking about development issues. This diverse group has, over time, influenced the way developing country scholars and policy-makers think about issues such as economic reform, trade strategy, fiscal policy and rural development. Once policy-makers are influenced in this way, foreign aid may become far more effective in serving development strategies because its basic premises are shared by recipients and donors (Cassen, 1986; Cassen *et al*, 1987).

However despite such plausible channels through which foreign aid can influence economic growth, there has long been an intense debate on the effectiveness of foreign aid in economic growth and development. This debate has been conducted against the background that although foreign aid has played an important role in economic development in some middle-income countries such as Taiwan, South Korea, Colombia and Israel, there has been no discernible impact of foreign aid on the macroeconomic performance of most of the developing countries. The contemporary debate on foreign aid has multiple themes – aid effectiveness, aid fatigue and the volume of aid (Burki and Ayres, 1986).

Critique of Foreign Aid

The question which is repeatedly asked is whether foreign aid can encourage economic growth in poor countries. Although there is no shortage of arguments in favour of foreign aid, the reality is that unless the volume of foreign aid is substantial, the impact of it on major macroeconomic variables cannot be easily detected and quantified. Early studies, such as Friedman (1958), Bauer and Yamey (1992) and Griffin (1978), argued that foreign aid retards rather than promotes economic growth through various channels, including disincentive effects on saving and the lowering of efforts toward economic self-sufficiency. Some radical economists even consider that foreign aid is an instrument for keeping poor countries poor and dependent on industrialized countries.

In general empirical economists have examined the impact of foreign aid on a number of macroeconomic indicators, such as domestic saving, investment and government tax effort, to assess the overall contribution of aid to economic growth. Some of the widely cited studies are by Griffin and Enos (1970), Rahman (1968), Chenery and Eckstein (1970), Weisskopf (1972) and Areskoug (1973). These suggested that foreign aid might not raise productive resources because it lowers domestic saving in both the private and public sectors. Papanek (1972) has criticized the studies which showed a negative impact of foreign aid on domestic saving on statistical grounds; for example, these studies were not corrected for simultaneity between domestic saving and foreign aid. However Chenery and Syrquin (1975), in a broad cross-country study, confirmed the earlier finding that foreign aid has a depressing effect on domestic saving. Recent studies also confirm that foreign aid can have an adverse effect on domestic saving. For example Hadjimichael and Others (1995) show that foreign aid has a negative effect on domestic saving, although it increases overall saving. Studies by Levy (1988) and the World Bank (1994) show that, on average, about 40 per cent of foreign aid goes into consumption. The major impact of foreign aid is on the government's saving efforts. Although savings and investment are the major channels through which foreign aid affects economic growth, there are studies which investigate the direct effect of foreign aid on economic growth. For example Mosley, Hudson and Horrell (1987), in a cross-country study, found no evidence to support the view that aid promotes economic growth.

While the findings of these studies raise considerable doubt about the general usefulness of foreign aid in economic growth, there are critics in both aid donor and recipient countries who simply want the discontinuation of foreign aid programmes, albeit for different ideological reasons. As indicated earlier the radical critics in aid-recipient countries argue that foreign aid programmes stifle the growth of self-sufficiency in poor countries and/or make them dependent on aid donors. In their view, as aid serves the economic and non-economic interests of aid donors, it is not surprising that it has little impact on economic growth. Hogendorn (1992:169) captures this sentiment:

> The proceeds may go not for additional capital formation but to finance further consumption; they may also substitute for domestic saving. The programs may largely benefit politicians, the educated élite, the civil service, the military, and, more generally, urban areas as opposed to rural. When aid givers prefer monuments to their own generosity to projects with a high rate of economic return, the effect on growth will be smaller yet.

Critics in donor countries are no less hostile. In foreign aid programmes they see a transfer of resources from the poor taxpayers of developed countries to the rich of poor countries. Such a view has some credence as stories of economic mismanagement and endemic corruption among political and economic élites in poor countries find sympathetic ears in rich countries. In fact, on the basis of anecdotal evidence and popular examples, some leading economists have reached the conclusion that foreign aid prolongs the agony of poor countries as they become complacent and pursue repressive economic policies which retard economic growth and exacerbate poverty. For example Bauer and Yamey (1992:306) put it rather bluntly:

> There are... untoward implications and repercussions of foreign aid which are far from trivial. Aid enables governments to pursue policies which patently retard growth and exacerbate poverty, and there is a long list of such policies. These include ... restraints on the activities of traders and even the destruction of the trading system; restriction on the inflow of foreign capital, enterprise and skills; voluntary or compulsory purchase of foreign enterprises... Aid also impairs the international competitiveness of economic activities in the recipient countries by helping to create or maintain overvalued exchange rates or to increase the domestic money supply... Foreign aid also makes it easier for governments to pursue imprudent financial policies. Unless aid is increasingly forthcoming, these policies lead to disruptive domestic inflation and to balance of payments difficulties, which in turn are apt to engender a crisis atmosphere and a flight of capital.

In response to such extreme criticisms, there has been some rethinking about the design and scope of aid programmes in fostering economic growth in poor countries. An emerging view is that although most studies do not find a positive impact of foreign aid on economic growth, there are examples that show that foreign aid can play a positive role. Some developing countries which received substantial foreign assistance for political reasons, such as South Korea, Taiwan and Israel, indeed benefited from aid. The World Bank-IMF Task Force 1982 investigated the subject of aid effectiveness in poor countries by carrying out a systematic review of four central aspects of concessional aid:

1. the contribution made to economic growth of recipient countries,
2. poverty alleviation in the poorest countries,
3. improved policies and institutions through policy dialogue and enhanced market forces, and
4. development of the private sector.

The major conclusion it reached was that aid is productive and helpful to economic development. Therefore, despite limitations, Cassen (1986:14) defends foreign aid programmes in poor countries:

> While donors and recipients have no cause for complacency, they need not be too defensive about the record of aid. There is much that can be criticized – particularly where error is repeated – but there is much more that is laudable: from aid's many contributions to raising food production in South Asia to experimental rural education in Africa; from infrastructure investment to self-help rural development

schemes; from widespread support for strengthening developing country institutions to population programs in a great variety of countries; and, not least, the new initiatives to promote policy reform, that, one may hope, will enhance the effectiveness of all aid and accelerate development itself.

FOREIGN PRIVATE CAPITAL FLOWS

Forms and Types of Foreign Private Capital Flows

Foreign private capital flows to developing countries fall into three forms: bond finance, bank loans and foreign investment.

Bond finance
To raise capital for investment at home, developing countries can issue bonds to foreign investors. Such bonds can be denominated in the domestic or foreign currency. Each type of bond carries a particular risk to foreign investors. When bonds are issued in the domestic currency, they are subject to inflation risk and a higher than expected inflation in the issuing country lowers the real redemption value of bond. When bonds are issued in the foreign currency, they are subject to default risk in the sense that a poor country may not be able to redeem the bond.

Commercial bank loans
When developing countries cannot raise capital through selling bonds, they may decide to borrow from foreign commercial banks. Such bank loans, short-term or long-term, may be made at fixed or flexible rates of interest by a single bank or a syndicate of banks.

Foreign investment
Foreign investment is another form of capital flow to developing countries: a multinational company may acquire equity in a domestically owned business, it may expand an existing subsidiary and/or set up a completely new enterprise. Direct investment is a popular form of multinational investment in developing countries. Such investments give multinationals ownership and control over businesses they set up and acquire.

The above forms of foreign capital flows to developing countries can be classified as either debt finance or equity finance, depending on the terms of repayment obligations. Debt finance, which includes bonds and bank loans, requires the debtor country to repay the principal with interest, irrespective of its economic condition. This contrasts with equity finance whereby foreign investors own shares or have direct control of companies. Repayments are then in the form of profits, dividends and changes in the capital values of companies and hence are linked with the performance of those companies.

Private capital flows to developing countries in historical perspective[9]

Private capital flows from developed to developing countries are not a recent phenomenon; historically they were a part of European colonialism. In the 19th century London was the financial centre of Europe. However Germany and France became important rival centres of finance in the later part of the 19th century.[10] Table 4.2 reports the major creditor and debtor countries in 1914 and shows that the United Kingdom, Germany and France were the main creditors.

Table 4.2   Gross creditor and gross debtor positions: 1914

Gross creditors	Percentage of total	Gross debtors	Percentage of total
United Kingdom	40.9	Europe	27.3
France	20.4	Latin America	19.3
Germany	13.2	United States	15.5
Benelux	12.5	Canada	8.4
United States	8.0	Asia	13.6
Others	5.0	Africa	10.7
		Oceania	5.2

Source: Cardoso and Dornbusch (1989:1390)

Table 4.3 shows the distribution of foreign investments of the United Kingdom, Germany and France in 1913. As can be seen, both German and French investments were concentrated in Europe while the United Kingdom's investments were located throughout its global empire.

The newly settled regions, such as Australia, Argentina, Canada and the USA, lacked both labour and capital. Alongside the large immigration of people from Europe, these countries raised capital from European capital markets, mainly for infrastructural development. This is the basis of the view that European labour and capital built the infrastructure of the New World and played a key role in its development. As Table 4.3 shows, a portion of Europe's capital flowed to heavily populated countries in Asia, Africa and Latin America. This capital was for direct investment, mainly in plantations and mining. Thus the contribution of foreign capital to economic development was somewhat different in the newly settled countries from that in Asia, Africa and Latin America. In the newly settled countries European capital

Table 4.3   Approximate distribution of foreign investments of the United Kingdom, Germany and France in 1913

	United Kingdom (% of total)	Germany (% of total)	France (% of total)
United States and Canada	33.7	15.7	4.4
Europe	5.8	53.2	59.5
Russia	2.9	7.7	25.1
Austria-Hungary	0.2	12.8	4.9
Spain and Portugal	na	7.2	8.7
Turkey	0.6	na	7.3
Latin America	20.1	16.2	13.3
Africa	na	8.5	16.2[a]
South Africa	9.8	na	na
Asia	na	4.3	4.9
India and Ceylon	10.0	na	na
Australia and New Zealand	11.1	na	na
Others	9.5	2.1	1.7

Notes:
(1)   na = absence of detailed statistics.
(2)   [a] = French colonies plus Egypt, Suez and South Africa.

Source: Cardoso and Dornbusch (1989:1390)

generated employment for immigrants and created the infrastructural base for future development. In contrast direct investments in plantations and mining in Asian and African countries did not contribute much to their overall development because such investments created dualistic economies with limited linkage between the relatively modern and traditional sectors. Moreover profits from investments in plantations and mining were repatriated to Europe rather than invested in the colonies.

Private capital flows to developing countries in the 19th century were not without problems. While European private capital played a role in economic development in newly settled countries, there were instances of debt crises, such as Argentina's inability to meet debt service payments in 1890, and of gun-boat diplomacy for the recovery of debts. Cardoso and Dornbusch (1989:1389) aptly describe these two representations of capital flows in the 19th century:

> The nineteenth-century experience with international capital flows has given rise to two broad representations of the facts. One is of states with persistently poor

public finance defaulting on one loan after another and of gun boat diplomacy employed for the recovery of debts. The second one is an image of dramatic economic progress in the new world resulting from international lending, together with migration. Both are correct.

Although the United States was a net debtor in the 19th century, it became a net exporter of capital during the aftermath of World War I. By the 1920s the United States started international lending on a massive scale. The centre of international lending shifted from European cities to New York. Lending went to Canada, Europe, Latin America and South East Europe and continued until the outbreak of the great crisis in world trade and capital markets in 1929. This was the beginning of the Great Depression that affected both developed and developing countries. Between 1929 and 1933 commodity prices fell sharply in the world market and the decline in world trade reduced the attractiveness of foreign loans. Latin America was hard hit when exports from this region fell sharply and the US bankers abruptly halted foreign lending to Europe and Latin America. Without new loans and with reduced export earnings and deflation, many debtors could not service their debts except at the cost of deep recession. Latin American debtors opted for moratoria and default of debt servicing to avoid creating deep recession. This created a debt crisis. The immediate effect of the crisis was a sharp decline in bond prices for all debtors, especially those in Latin America (Cardoso and Dornbusch, 1989). The effects can be seen in Table 4.4.

Table 4.4 Latin American gold bond prices in the 1930s

Country (interest rate, maturity)	1930		1939	
	High	Low	High	Low
Bolivia (8%, 1947)	100.0	35.0	5.0	2.5
Brazil (6.5%, 1957)	88.2	47.5	23.0	9.5
Chile (7%, 1942)	103.3	87.0	18.4	12.0
Colombia (6%, 1961)	83.0	55.0	34.6	19.8
Costa Rica (7%, 1951)	91.0	65.0	30.8	16.5
Guatemala (8%, 1948)	97.0	85.0	39.0	24.0
Mexico (4%, 1934)	17.4	8.0	1.4	0.8
Peru (7%, 1959)	100.0	52.5	13.5	7.5
El Salvador (8%,1948)	110.2	98.0	21.5	13.5

Source: Cardoso and Dornbusch (1989:1395)

Unlike Latin American debtors, Canada, Australia and New Zealand continued to service their debts despite a sharp decline in prices of their export commodities. An explanation for this is that, unlike Latin America, trade remained open for them under imperial preferences. The Royal Institute of International Affairs (1937:2) provided another explanation:

> Maintenance of debt service upon the foreign capital invested in a country is affected by a number of factors. In the first place, creditors' receipts will be dependent not merely upon the ability but also the willingness of debtors to pay. Many countries have discontinued service payments on their debts even when their financial position was sufficiently sound to enable such payments to be made. Usually, defaults have taken place when the possibility of obtaining fresh supplies of capital seemed remote, and when appearances suggested that there were little to be gained – except in prestige – from the fulfillment of obligations.

Following the recovery of commodity prices in the late 1930s and increased trade opportunities during World War II, the trade position of Latin American debtors improved. This led them to resume debt servicing and to buy back their bonds at the low prices at which they were trading. However, the cleaning-up of Latin American debt default was not completely over until 1960 (Cardoso and Dornbusch, 1989).

The Latin American debt crisis changed the patterns of international lending to developing countries after World War II. Private lending to developing countries dried up. The 1950s saw the beginning of a phase of direct investment and/or subsidized official loans to developing countries.

The New Wave of Foreign Private Capital Flows

Table 4.5 reports capital flows to developing countries during the period 1956 to 1984. It shows that the total flows of capital to developing countries during this period were relatively small. In the distribution of foreign capital, direct investment was dominant during the 1950s and 1960s but declined sharply after the early 1970s. A major change occurred during the period 1975 to 1979 when the share of bank financing and bond issues was about 42 per cent of capital flows to developing countries. This was possible as the banks in the industrialized countries received large deposits from the OPEC following the oil price rise in 1973. The composition of direct investment also changed sharply. For instance, whereas in the interwar period and earlier US direct investment in Latin America was concentrated on mining and petroleum, in the 1980s it shifted to manufacturing (Cardoso and Dornbusch, 1989).

One of the consequences of the rise in bank and bond financing of Latin American countries' fiscal and trade deficits was the debt crises of the 1980s. In general the OPEC oil price shock of 1973 caused non-oil developing

Table 4.5   Capital flows to developing countries, 1956–84

	Total average annual flow (US$bn)	Portfolio and direct investment (% of total)	Direct investment (% of total)	Export credits (% of total)
1956–59	7 082	44.2	31.1	5.2
1960–64	9 904	34.1	18.8	7.3
1965–69	11 865	42.9	21.4	11.0
1970–74	20 805	45.9	24.3	9.6
1975–79	55 384	60.5	19.0	13.4
1980–84	80 923	56.8	13.2	9.6

Source: Cardoso and Dornbusch (1989:1400)

countries to borrow more to finance the increased imports cost of oil, without cutting back their development programmes. The Latin American countries in particular regarded the oil shocks as a temporary phenomenon and did not adjust their absorption. They opted for large-scale borrowings from international commercial banks. Some oil exporting countries, such as Nigeria and Mexico, regarded their windfalls as if they were permanent rather than transitory. By the early 1980s high interest rates on borrowed funds and the recession in industrialized countries after the oil shocks initiated the debt crisis in Mexico, Brazil and Argentina. Facing the debt crises, most developing countries undertook the World Bank-IMF adjustment programmes lasting over a decade or so. Such adjustment programmes were not painless and for Latin America and Africa the 1980s were a lost decade of economic growth and development. Until the late 1980s, even though the debt crisis was not in the front page news, the future of large debtor countries appeared bleak as they were cut off from international capital markets.

The 1990s have begun with new developments in international finance. Most observers have been surprised to see an unprecedented surge of private capital flows to developing countries since the early 1990s. This is a startling development against the backdrop of Latin American debt crisis that caused a drying up of foreign private capital for most developing countries. Even high performing East Asian countries were unable to attract money from foreign commercial banks or to sell bonds or equities internationally (Dean, 1996; IMF, 1995a,b).

By the early 1990s the major countries of the Western Hemisphere had experienced a repatriation of capital and developed links with international capital markets. This has created an optimism for increased investment and growth in developing countries. However not all developing countries have been successful in attracting foreign capital. Most capital flows have been concentrated on East Asia and Latin America. The countries of Africa and South Asia received little and are still dependent on subsidized capital from official sources.

Table 4.6 reports data for capital flows to developing countries since the mid-1970s. It shows that in the 1980s annual average capital flows to developing countries were roughly US$9 billion. In contrast, since the early 1990s such capital flows have jumped to more than US$100 billion. There has also been a marked regional difference in the composition of the capital flows.

Table 4.6   Capital flows to developing countries[a], 1977–94

Annual averages, US$bn	1977–82	1983–89	1990–94
All developing countries[b]			
Total net capital flows	30.5	8.8	104.9
Net foreign direct investment	11.2	13.3	39.1
Net portfolio investment	−10.5	6.5	43.6
Others[c]	28.8	−11.0	22.2
Asia			
Total net capital flows	15.8	16.7	52.1
Net foreign direct investment	2.7	5.2	23.4
Net portfolio investment	0.6	1.4	12.4
Others[c]	12.5	10.1	16.3
Western Hemisphere			
Total net capital flows	26.3	−16.6	40.1
Net foreign direct investment	5.3	4.4	11.9
Net portfolio investment	1.6	−1.2	26.6
Others[c]	19.4	−19.8	1.6
Other developing countries[b]			
Total net capital flows	−11.6	8.7	12.7
Net foreign direct investment	3.2	3.7	3.8
Net portfolio investment	−12.7	6.3	4.6
Others[c]	−2.1	−1.3	4.3

Notes:
[a]   flows exclude exceptional financing
[b]   excludes capital exporting countries, such as Kuwait and Saudi Arabia
[c]   includes bank lending

Source: IMF (1995b)

About 40 per cent of capital flows to developing countries since 1990 has been in the form of portfolio investment in tradable bonds and equity shares and 37 per cent has been foreign direct investment. Portfolio investment in Asia represented about 24 per cent of capital flows while 45 per cent was foreign direct investment. In the Western Hemisphere capital flows were concentrated in yield-sensitive and liquid portfolio flows, which accounted for 66 per cent of gross capital flows. Foreign direct investment was about 30 per cent of capital flows in this region.

Reasons for the surge in private capital flows to developing countries

The recent surge in capital flows to developing countries was initially attributed to the domestic developments, such as sound macroeconomic policies, of some developing countries. Later it became clear that the phenomenon was widespread, affecting countries with diverse characteristics. Reisen (1996) shows that Asia (in particular East Asia) and Latin America, which received the bulk of foreign capital, differed markedly with respect to macroeconomic prerequisites for capital inflows (Table 4.7).

Calvo *et al* (1996) suggest that several domestic and international factors interacted in the early 1990s to make the developing countries of Latin America and Asia fertile territory for the renewal of foreign lending. In general there are both domestic and international factors behind capital flows to developing economies. First, in terms of policies and future prospects there have been positive developments in both Latin America and East Asia. Having been cut off from international capital markets for a decade or so, Latin American countries re-entered these markets in the 1990s. Their entry has been facilitated by restructuring of commercial debts, combined with the implementation of restrictive macroeconomic policies and wide-ranging structural reforms, including financial reforms. East Asian economies have performed superbly since the mid-1980s, even in the midst of structural adjustment measures. High and sustained economic growth in East Asia and their maintenance of macroeconomic stability have attracted foreign investment. To some extent creditworthiness of the recipient country has played a role in determining the geographic destination of capital flows. Capital flows to one or two large countries have generated some externalities for smaller neighbouring countries – the contagion effect.

Second, while the above developments acted as a pull factor, there was a push factor in industrialized countries. Low interest rates in those countries caused an outflow of capital into the emerging market economies of Asia and Latin America. Investors were attracted to these economies because of their high investment yields and improving economic prospects. Note that, given the high external debt burden of many of these countries, low world interest rates have improved their creditworthiness.

Table 4.7 Prerequisites for the 1990s episode of capital flows to Asia and Latin America

Country	Average seigniorage, 1970–88 (% of GDP)	Budget deficit/ surplus, 1988–93 (% of GDP)	Public debt 1994 (% of GDP)	Average black market premium[a]	Average annual export growth, 1980–92 (%)
Asia:					
China (P.R.)	na	−2.6	n.a.	88.0	11.9
India	1.5	−7.4	45	23.8	5.9
Indonesia	1.4	−0.6	39	8.9	5.6
Korea, Rep.	1.6	0.5	22	3.0	11.9
Malaysia	1.3	−3.7	58	0.0	11.3
Philippines	1.0	−3.3	96	4.6	3.7
Thailand	1.0	3.3	16	1.2	14.7
Latin America:					
Argentina	4.2	−5.9	22	21.1	2.2
Brazil	2.3	−46.9	40	51.7	5.0
Chile	3.7	2.0	18	16.1	5.5
Colombia	2.1	−0.4	22	12.9	12.9
Mexico	3.1	−3.2	32	10.3	1.6
Peru	3.6	−4.0	42	11.5	2.5

Notes:
[a] Post-trade reform up to 1992.
na not available

Source: Reisen (1996:80)

Table 4.8   Behaviour of financial indicators in response to capital inflows caused by the pull and push factors

Indicator	Upward shift of money demand curve	Increase in productivity of domestic capital (sustained inflows)	External factors, such as falling international interest rates (temporary inflows)
Asset prices			
Interest rates	Increase	Increase	Decrease
Yield curve	Flattens	?	Becomes steeper
Exchange rate	Appreciates	Appreciates	Appreciates
Equity prices	Decrease	Increase	Increase
Real estate prices	Decrease	Increase	Increase
Inflation	Decreases	Increases	Increases
Monetary and credit aggregates			
Real money balances	Increase	Likely to decrease	Increase
Base money	Increases	Increases	Increases
International reserves	Increase	Increase	Increase
Bank credit	Likely to increase	Increases	Likely to increase
Foreign currency deposits	Decrease	?	May decrease
Balance of payments			
Foreign direct investment	?	Increases	?
Portfolio investment	Increases, especially in short-term flows	Increases, in both short- and long-term flows	Increases, especially in short-term flows

Note: ? indicates that the effect is uncertain.

Source: Haque, Mathieson and Sharma (1997:4)

Third, there has been a trend towards international diversification of investments in major financial centres and growing integration of world capital markets (Gooptu, 1993). Increasing amounts of funds managed by life insurance companies and mutual funds have entered emerging markets. Regulatory changes in the United States and Europe have also made it easier for foreign firms to place their equity and bonds and make them attractive to investors. The ongoing international diversification of rapidly expanding institutional portfolios (mutual funds, insurance companies, pension funds, proprietary trading of banks and securities houses) has contributed to the inflows of capital into emerging markets (IMF, 1995b).

Haque, Mathieson and Sharma (1997) have developed an analytical framework to identify the causes of capital flows to developing countries. These fall into three major categories:

1. autonomous increases in the domestic money demand,
2. increases in the domestic productivity of capital and
3. external factors, such as falling international interest rates.

The first two of these are referred to as pull factors, the third as push factors. Table 4.8 shows how various financial indicators are likely to behave in response to capital inflows caused by the pull and push factors.

From an analytical viewpoint this classification is useful. However one shortcoming of it is that although the movement of each of the financial indicators may provide some information on the likely causes of capital flows to developing countries, disentangling the factors affecting various indicators can be complex. In order to make any sensible judgement on the likely causes of capital flows to developing countries and the need, if any, for a policy response, additional information from other sources is required.

PROBLEMS WITH, AND MANAGEMENT OF LARGE CAPITAL FLOWS

Using the Mundell-Fleming model, Chapter 3 analysed the relative effectiveness of fiscal and monetary policy in achieving both internal and external balance under fixed and flexible exchange rate systems. It was shown that the relative effectiveness of fiscal and monetary policy is dependent upon both the choice of exchange rate regime and the degree of capital mobility. In fact one of the crucial parameters determining the effectiveness of both fiscal and monetary policy in an open economy is the degree of financial integration of that economy with the rest of the world, as reflected by the mobility of capital internationally (Pilbeam, 1992). With perfect capital mobility, monetary policy is more effective under a floating exchange rate regime while fiscal policy is more effective under a fixed exchange rate regime. However Tobin (1978:154) argues that the highly integrated world capital markets leave little room for national authorities to pursue independent monetary and fiscal policies:

> National economies and national governments are not capable of adjusting to massive movements of funds across the foreign exchanges, without real hardship and without significant sacrifice of the objectives of national economic policy with respect to employment, output and inflation. Specifically, the mobility of financial capital limits viable differences among national interest rates and this severely restricts the ability of central banks and governments to pursue monetary and fiscal policies appropriate to their national economies.

Why is 'Too Much Capital' a Matter of Concern to Policy-Makers?

Foreign capital flows to developing countries since the debt crisis have generally been considered to be a positive development. Such capital flows have relaxed financial constraints to investment in debtor countries and helped the financial systems of those countries to integrate with the global economy. Investors of developed countries have benefited from investment opportunities to developing countries through diversification of their investment portfolios. Foreign private capital has been particularly welcome as it has been directed at the private sector and is predominantly in the form of equity capital rather than debt financing.

Despite these benefits from capital inflows, there has been concern that too much foreign capital may have undesirable consequences. The dramatic reversal of portfolio capital flows to Mexico in December 1994 caused a sharp depreciation of Mexican currency (peso). This incident encapsulated concerns about the sustainability of capital inflows in their portfolio forms and allied to this, concerns about the sustainability of exchange rates (Dean, 1996). Since this incident a large body of literature has grown on the actual or potential problems associated with large flows of capital to developing countries and Corbo and Hernandez (1996) summarised the problems as below.

Appreciation of the real exchange rate
Large capital inflows can cause an appreciation of the real exchange rate, defined as the price of tradables to the price of non-tradables. The appreciation of the real exchange rate may be a matter of concern for those countries which have recently introduced trade reform policies to increase their integration into the world economy. As the appreciated real exchange rate may delay the supply response of export-oriented sectors and increase competition for import-competing sectors, large capital inflows can work at cross purposes with the liberalization of trade and may undermine the credibility of

trade reforms and retard improvement in long-run external competitiveness by eroding the profitability of the traded-goods sector. Many developing countries which intend to adopt a flexible exchange rate system to have more control over their monetary policy may find it difficult to do so in the presence of 'hot money' entering into their underdeveloped financial systems and then creating excessive volatility in both the nominal and real exchange rates. The evidence on the behaviour of the real exchange rate presents a mixed picture. In most Latin American countries capital inflows have been associated with a marked real exchange rate appreciation. In Asia such an appreciation is only evident in the Philippines; for the remaining Asian countries, the real exchange rate remained stable through the inflow period.

Accumulation of foreign exchange reserves

A substantial portion of the surge in capital inflows is often channelled to accumulation of foreign exchange reserves. From 1990 to 1994 the share going to reserves was 59 per cent in Asia and 35 per cent in Latin America. Although the pace of reserve accumulation has shown signs of slowing in recent years, an increasing portion of capital inflows is taking the form of larger current account deficits. This happens because an increase in capital inflows causes an appreciation of the real exchange rate which, along with interest payments for debt servicing, increases the current account deficit.

Current account deficits

Developing countries may like to maintain a sustainable current account deficit (as a percentage of GDP) in the long run. When there is a sudden increase in current account deficit due to capital inflows (particularly when such capital inflows are found to be linked with a consumption boom), the risk premium of the country may increase and the future access of the country to international capital markets may be restricted as a result. Many observers note that capital flows to Asia and Latin America have been associated with widening current account deficits and this should be a matter of concern. The widening of the current account usually involved both an increase in national investment and a fall in national saving, implying a rise in private consumption spending.

Monetization of capital inflows

For high inflationary developing countries which have been pursuing stabilization programmes with a fixed or pre-announced nominal exchange rate as an anchor for domestic prices or with price stability as an objective, large capital inflows could be a matter of concern because of the monetization effect of capital inflows on inflation. Note that besides increasing the money supply, large capital inflows may increase the demand for money by lowering interest rates and increasing economic activity. Therefore the net effect of capital inflows on inflation would depend on the relative effect of capital inflows on money supply and money demand.

Banking crisis

Large capital flows to developing countries with weak banks (that is banks with low or negative net worth and a low ratio of capital to risk-adjusted assets) and poor banking supervision may exacerbate moral hazard problems associated with deposit insurance. When large funds are intermediated through weak banks, those banks may lend money for riskier projects resulting in a financial bubble and, eventually, a financial crisis (Haque, Mathieson and Sharma, 1997). The experience of Asian developing countries during 1997–98 shows that this is a real possibility. McKinnon and Pill (1996) have elaborated the channels through which large capital flows may increase the risk structure of a newly liberalized banking system. They identify the following risks:

1. *Credit risk* – exposure to the failure of a borrower to repay a loan – will increase as bank lending rises. A sudden increase in the availability of loanable funds through capital inflows may encourage greater investment in risky projects, such as lending to real estate or securities market participants.

2. *Foreign exchange exposure* can increase dramatically if the inflows are foreign currency denominated while the banks enjoy a comparative advantage (information or otherwise) in domestic lending in local currency. Lack of experience and absence of derivatives markets may make managing such risks more problematic in developing countries than in developed nations.

3. *Real exchange rate risk* rises because the profitability of traded goods industries is lowered as more capital flows in.

4. *Settlement risk* rises if the payments system is incapable of dealing with the magnitude or direction of cross-border settlements.

5. *Liquidity risk* may rise if the size of the capital inflows is large relative to that of domestic securities markets. If banks attempt to invest the inflows in domestic markets (say, real estate) they may simply bid up the prices of housing, helping to create bubbles in real estate and equity prices and inducing destabilizing herding behaviour among market participants. The surge in portfolio flows to the Asian and Latin American countries has been accompanied by a sharp increase in stock and real estate prices.

6. *Risks arising from the supervisory and regulatory framework* – regulators face larger and different challenges in assessing the risks borne by the supervisory institutions when capital inflows are considerable and the risks described above multiply.

7. *Greater systematic risk* – all these risks can lead to a greater systematic risk. That is, there is an increased risk of contagion between different banks as credit, liquidity and settlement risks rise.

Real adjustment costs

If capital inflows are volatile or temporary, any reversal of such capital may cause real adjustment costs originating from resource re-allocation, bankruptcy hysteresis (that is the asymmetrical problems resulting from the fact that it is easier to exit a business than to enter it) and other market imperfections.[11]

Private Sector Overborrowing

The above discussion suggests that developing countries should remain cautious about the possibility of overborrowing by the private sector following any financial liberalization. Given its importance, this issue is elaborated here.

It is generally believed that any premature opening of the capital account in the balance of payments during economic reforms may generate macroeconomic instability and destabilizing capital flows. McKinnon (1973, 1982) and Dornbusch (1983, 1984) suggest that any early opening of the capital account may result in large destabilizing capital outflows when the domestic capital market is repressed and interest rates are fixed at low levels. However, Edwards (1984) has developed a partial adjustment model to demonstrate that after restrictions on capital inflows are lifted, there may be rapid inflows of capital because of the accumulated large gap between the desired level of external debt and actual debt (Figure 4.2). His capital flow equation is given by:

$$\Delta K = [\min (\gamma(D^* - D_{-1}), \Delta K_o] \tag{4.3}$$

where ΔK is capital inflows, D^* is desired external debt, D_{-1} is actual external debt in the previous period, γ is the partial adjustment coefficient, and ΔK_o is the maximum amount of net capital inflows allowed by the authority in every period. Over time the amount of capital flows will decline to the equilibrium level ΔK^*.

As financial reform includes opening of the capital account in the balance of payments, it may create an external debt problem when the private sector

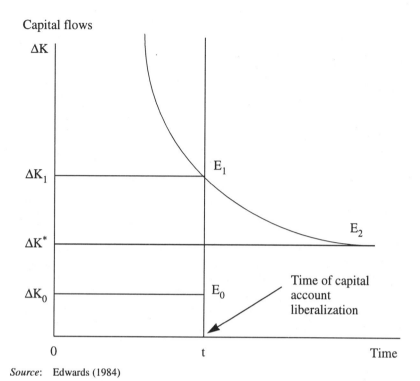

Capital flows

Source: Edwards (1984)

Figure 4.2 Behaviour of capital flows following a capital account liberalization

takes the opportunity to borrow excessively from overseas at interest rates which are often lower than domestic interest rates. It has been observed in many developing countries that, following financial reforms, the private sector borrowed heavily when foreign financial institutions were eager to lend without properly evaluating the credit risk and without charging interest rates which included a risk premium. Hanson and de Melo (1985) found that financial liberalization and the opening of the capital account contributed to increased indebtedness in Uruguay which, after generating two asset bubbles, led to widespread default when the loan rates rose. Following the opening of the capital account and the removal of controls over private borrowing, Chile also encountered an external debt problem. Foreign banks were eager to lend to Chilean banks when the latter encountered an excess, or false, demand for credit. In the early stage of financial reforms the official view in Chile was that the private sector debt should not be a matter of concern because any debt servicing difficulty would be solved through bankruptcy procedures.

However any distinction between private and public debt became artificial when the Chilean government finally had to nationalize a large proportion of non-guaranteed private debt (Edwards and Edwards, 1987).

Following McKinnon (1991), the tendency to private overborrowing after financial reform can be explained by a simple model (Figure 4.3). When the government of a borrowing country explicitly or implicitly guarantees foreign loans by the private sector, an individual borrower in the foreign capital market faces a horizontal supply curve for finance (S_F) rather than an upward-sloping curve (ACF). An upward-sloping supply curve captures the increase in riskiness of any private borrower as it increases its exposure. As Figure 4.3 shows, the horizontal supply curve for finance, given the demand curve for finance (D_f), allows the private borrower to borrow more than is optimal in the absence of any guarantee by the government. It has also been pointed out by Edwards and Edwards (1987:17) that '[t]o the extent that the private sector knows that it will be bailed out by the government, moral hazard type behavior becomes highly likely'. An implication is that to avoid any external debt problem there should be an indirect form of control over private foreign borrowing by phasing out implicit or explicit official guarantees of private loans. Any government policy or declaration in this regard must be time consistent, otherwise it will not be credible and effective.

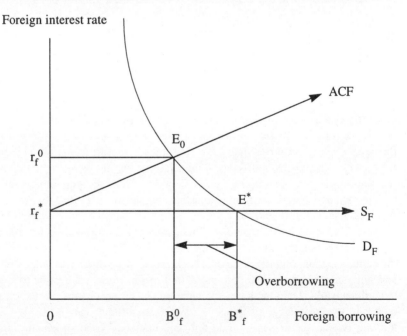

Figure 4.3   Private sector overborrowing

Symptoms of overborrowing

Following McKinnon and Pill (1996) the main distinguishing features of an overborrowing episode include:

1. *Rapid growth of domestic credit* largely financed out of capital inflows intermediated through the domestic banking system, leading to higher levels of domestic consumption.
2. *Widening of any current account deficit* on the balance of payments, as greater availability of financing from abroad eases the external constraint.
3. *Weaker domestic monetary control* and rising or sustained high domestic price inflation, typically associated with problems in attempting to sterilize the capital inflows.
4. *Appreciation of the real exchange rate*, appropriately defined, with higher inflation concentrated in the nontradable goods sector; prices of domestic assets, especially real estate or house prices, typically increase.
5. *Overseas deposits placed with the domestic banking system* forming a large proportion of the capital inflow, increasing pressure on the government to broaden the base of insured deposits.
6. *Greater vulnerability* to adverse shocks and increased likelihood that the stabilization programme will be derailed and thrown into reverse.
7. *Culmination in a financial crisis, capital flight and recession*, often forcing an uncontrolled, deep devaluation of the currency with a resurgence of inflation.

Policy responses to overborrowing

How should policy-makers respond to the possibility of overborrowing in the course of an otherwise successful liberalization programme? Improved banking regulation with higher capital and reserve requirements could help. However such measures are unlikely to prove fully effective given the banking industry's inherently asymmetric information structure. The authorities may wish to impose other financial controls to limit the potential for damage should overborrowing arise and controls on cross-border movements of financial capital are one appropriate tool. The various policy options are

1. *Restrain short-term capital flows*, particularly those intermediated through the domestic banking system. The preferred policy instrument is probably reserve requirements rather than direct administrative controls. These do not discriminate between domestic and foreign sources of funds and are harder to evade. Marginal reserve requirements could be increased if capital controls become unduly large.
2. *Be more liberal with direct investment*, perhaps in the form of joint ventures with domestic partners. Direct investment brings new technol-

ogy into the economy and bypasses the banking system, thus avoiding market failure problems.
3. *Limit organized consumer borrowing* – say on bank credit cards – and restrict access to mortgage finance. Such measures should help to prevent the runaway excess demand for consumer durables and non-traded services that may reignite domestic price inflation.
4. *Consolidate compulsory social security contributions into a Singapore-style provident fund.* A fully funded compulsory saving programme – geared to preventing the dramatic falls in private saving seen during overborrowing episodes – should be considered earlier rather than later in the liberalization process.

Managing the Risks of Volatile Capital Inflows

The above discussion highlights the fact that too many foreign capital flows, particularly portfolio investment which is volatile or temporary in nature, carry with them certain risks. Such capital inflows need to be managed properly so that they do not diminish the economic advantages of greater integration into global capital markets. As explained earlier, among many consequences the main risks of a surge in capital inflows are that they may cause an appreciation of the real exchange rate, an inflationary expansion of domestic money and credit, an unsustainable current account deficit and a more vulnerable banking system. Some of the policy problems associated with capital inflows are akin to the Dutch Disease policy problem of preventing the erosion of the tradable goods sector in the event of a natural resource discovery. In general the menu of policy responses to capital flows to developing countries includes intervention in foreign exchange markets (with or without sterilization of the monetary impact of such intervention), fiscal consolidation and capital controls. Table 4.9 reports the summary measures that a selection of developing countries of Asia and Latin America have used to minimize the costs of large capital inflows.

Sterilization
Sterilization has been widely used by those developing countries which experienced large capital inflows. Through this policy intervention capital-receiving countries under a floating or managed floating exchange rate system have tried to prevent nominal appreciation of their currencies and avoid monetary expansion associated with an accumulation of foreign reserves.

There are a number of ways through which sterilization is conducted. Open market operations are the most common and straightforward method. In the absence of well-developed capital markets, the increase in reserve requirements is the only available method for sterilizing the monetary expan-

Table 4.9 Policy responses to capital inflows, 1988–94

Country[a]	Fiscal restraint	Revaluation	Increased exchange rate variability	Sterilized intervention	Controls on capital inflows	Liberalization of capital outflows	Trade liberalization accelerated
Argentina (1991)	no	no	no	no	no	no	no
Chile (1990)	yes	yes	yes	yes	yes	yes	no
Colombia (1991)	no	yes	yes	yes	yes	yes	yes
Indonesia (1990)	no	no	no	yes	yes	no	no
Malaysia (1989)	yes	no	yes	yes	yes	yes	yes
Mexico (1990)	no	no	no	yes	no	yes	yes
Philippines (1992)	no	no	yes	yes	no	yes	no
Sri Lanka (1991)	no	no	no	yes	no	no	yes
Thailand (1988)	yes	no	no	yes	no	yes	yes

Note: [a] The year next to the country name denotes the first year of the surge in inflows.

Source: IMF (1995b)

sion associated with foreign exchange market interventions. However this presupposes the existence of a well-developed secondary market for government securities.

The difficulty with sterilization is that sterilized intervention is neither fully effective nor free from negative side effects. Sterilization through open market sales of government securities or central bank bills prevents the interest rate differential from narrowing. It is also possible that open market sales of government securities increase the domestic-international interest rate spread sufficiently so as to attract more short-term capital. Instead of stopping, sterilization may thus prolong capital inflows. In addition sterilization has significant quasi-fiscal costs which arise from the difference between the yield on foreign exchange acquired by the central bank and the higher interest rate paid on government or central bank securities.

Concern with both the costs and ineffectiveness of sterilization via open market operations induced several Asia-Pacific countries to increase commercial bank reserve requirements, with the intention of lowering the value of the money multiplier and the money supply from an increased level of monetary base. While this technique solved the problem of quasi-fiscal costs, it created a wider spread between bank loan and deposit rates.

Several Asia-Pacific countries, including Indonesia, Malaysia, Singapore, Taiwan and Thailand, have sterilized capital inflows by shifting public sector deposits or pension funds from commercial banks to the central bank. This has the effect of reducing the banks' deposits (reserves) at the central bank and therefore their ability to create money. The advantages of this type of sterilization are that first, it avoids or reduces the central bank quasi-fiscal costs associated with open market operations; second, it does not seem to increase interest rates as much as sales of sterilization bonds; and third, it does not tax bank intermediation as does a reserve requirement increase.

Fiscal policy

Fiscal consolidation is another possible response to capital inflows. The intended effect is that the deflationary impulse of fiscal consolidation may offset the expansionary impact of unsterilized portions of foreign exchange intervention. The result may be a downward pressure on interest rates, particularly if the government borrowing requirement is perceived to be declining.

Tighter fiscal policy in response to capital inflows can be accomplished either by reducing government spending or by raising taxes. The mechanism is to reduce both aggregate demand (and therefore the inflationary impact of the inflows) and upward pressure on the real exchange rate. Reducing government spending may be more effective than raising taxes if government spending is more heavily weighted toward non traded goods than is private spending. Moreover the impact of increased taxes on disposable income and spending may be frustrated if consumer credits are easily obtainable – as is typically the case under heavy capital inflows – and if the tax is thought to be temporary.

Capital controls

Many developing countries have employed various direct measures that discourage capital inflows. These measures included imposing or tightening prudential limits on banks' offshore borrowing and foreign exchange transactions, taxing some types of capital inflows, and quantitative restrictions. Note that Tobin (1978) argues that much of the disruptive exchange rate movements under a floating exchange rate system have been caused by short-term capital flows. He suggests that a tax be imposed on all foreign exchange transactions 'to throw some sand in the wheels of our excessively efficient money markets' (p.154). Such a tax is expected to reduce speculators' incentives to suddenly flood money into and out of a currency in response to small interest rate changes. There have been numerous criticisms of the Tobin proposal, the prominent one being that, unless it is implemented internationally, the tax is most likely to be evaded by shifting the transaction to a tax-free zone (Argy, 1994; Kearney, 1996). Another criticism is that not all short-term capital movements are undesirable and the tax may prevent some stabilizing capital movements. Note that some countries, such as Hong Kong and Singapore, have managed large capital inflows without recourse to capital controls or taxes. For developing countries which do not have monetary-fiscal discipline, it is precisely the threat of sudden exchange rate movements owing to a withdrawal of capital that imposes a degree of discipline on national authorities' conduct of economic policies (Pilbeam, 1992).

The above discussion suggests that the policy response to large and volatile capital inflows may require multiple instruments, including measures that seek to discourage capital inflows or change their character, and co-ordination of policies, monetary, fiscal and exchange rate, to ensure that recipient countries can derive benefits without incurring much of the costs. As a guide Haque, Mathieson and Sharma (1997) have developed a matrix (Table 4.10) showing the appropriate use of policy instruments for managing capital inflows caused by the pull and push factors. According to them, the appropriate policy response to capital inflows should be determined not only by the causes of capital inflows but also by the degree of flexibility allowed by the domestic institutional structure and the existing policy stance. Countries that pursue relatively balanced macroeconomic policies may find it easier to deal with disruptions caused by capital inflows than countries which have unbalanced policies.

The matrix shows the appropriate use of each instrument for countries with balanced macroeconomic policies. It shows that when capital inflows are

Table 4.10 Instruments for managing capital inflows for countries with balanced macroeconomic policies

	Upward shift of domestic money demand curve	Increase in productivity of domestic capital (sustained inflows)	External factors, such as falling international interest rates (temporary inflows)
Sterilization	May be needed to smooth fluctuations.	May be needed to smooth fluctuations.	Is appropriate.
Exchange rate appreciation	Equilibrium real effective exchange rate does not change.	The warranted appreciation of the equilibrium real effective exchange rate can be achieved partly through nominal appreciation and partly through increases in the prices of nontraded goods.	Equilibrium real exchange rate need not change. Temporary nominal appreciation of the exchange rate may be warranted if there are constraints on sterilization.
Fiscal policy	No policy response is required.	Fiscal policy tightening is generally required, especially if the absorptive capacity of the economy is limited relative to the size of the inflows.	If the constraints on sterilization are too severe and the external competitive position is weak, some fiscal tightening may have to be considered.

Source: Haque, Mathieson and Sharma (1997:5)

associated with an upward shift in the money demand function, no policy action is required because the expansion of the monetary base caused by capital inflows may not cause inflation or threaten external stability. However, it may be necessary for the central bank to invervene in the relatively thin money and foreign exchange markets to smooth fluctuations in the exchange rate and interest rates.

Policy responses should also depend on whether capital inflows are sustained or temporary. If capital inflows are sustained due to, say, an increase in the productivity of domestic capital, policymakers must decide how best to achieve the required appreciation of the equilibrium real exchange rate. For economies with flexible exchange rate arrangements, the required appreciation of the real exchange rate may be achieved through an appreciation of the nominal exchange rate rather than a rise in the prices of non-traded goods. If capital inflows are temporary in nature – for example, one resulting from a fall in the international interest rate, sterilization may be the appropriate response.

As in countries with unbalanced financial policies, short-term capital inflows are largely determined by domestic interest rates and expected exchange rate movements, the appropriate policy response should be adjustment of fiscal and monetary policies to bring policy discipline.

Sustaining Foreign Private Capital Flows to Developing Countries

Although the recent surge in capital flows to developing countries presents significant problems for macroeconomic policies, it must not be forgotten that such capital flows carry the potential for an increase in investment and economic growth. Although it is true that some portfolio capital flows to developing countries are temporary in nature and have the danger associated with a sudden reversal, the thrust of the policy response should be on creating conditions for the use of foreign capital productively. To reap the maximum benefits, inflows of foreign capital should be sustained. Fernandez-Arias and Montiel (1996:57) are perceptive about the various issues involved:

> ... the possibility that capital inflows may be welfare reducing does not mean that they are invariably harmful... the stimulus to aggregate demand provided by the arrival of inflows may be welcome in economies with excess productive capacity. Moreover, if the inflow of capital is sustained, it need not be associated with increased macroeconomic instability. The upshot is that the nature of the policy problem posed by the receipt of capital inflows depends on a complex array of factors, such as the allocative efficiency of the domestic economy, the causes of the inflow, the domestic macroeconomic context, and factors that determine the sustainability of inflows.

In order to sustain foreign capital inflows, developing countries may undertake the following policy measures (Dean, 1996; Calvo *et al*, 1996; IMF, 1995b):

1. A favourable macroeconomic and regulatory climate for investors is essential to sustain portfolio investment. To create macroeconomic stability, the government should pursue sound financial policies and correct structural problems, such as excessive government intervention, labour market distortions and inefficient tax and trade policies. The government should also design and implement appropriate policies to mitigate the appreciation of the real exchange rate that may result from large capital inflows.
2. After bringing macroeconomic discipline and ensuring that the country's macroeconomic fundamentals are right, the next task should aim at increasing foreign investment and its benefits. This would depend on whether the country's microeconomic fundamentals are also right (that is, few regulatory barriers, proper taxation, and ease of entry and exit by foreign investors).
3. The government may need to introduce some sectoral policies or develop institutions to channel increased capital flows. The banking system should be developed and the central bank must take its prudential and supervisory functions seriously. The choice of intermediary for capital flows – the banking system or stock market or, more likely, some combination of the two – could be pivotal because the intermediary affects the final uses of the funds and the possible negative effects on the economy when funds are withdrawn. In general a country can benefit more from portfolio inflows if it has a healthy and properly regulated banking system.
4. Provided that the above measures are taken, developing countries should encourage portfolio investment by lowering implicit or explicit barriers, including legal hurdles, lack of credit ratings of companies, limits on the size of emerging stock markets, the absence of a solid regulatory and accounting framework and investor protection, inadequate clearing and settlement procedures, lack of modern communications and too few internationally listed securities.

SUMMARY AND CONCLUSION

This chapter has reviewed various issues and policies associated with foreign capital flows to developing countries. Given that economic growth is responsible for a general rise in standards of living, the importance of capital accumulation in developing countries cannot be exaggerated. For various reasons the rates of saving and investment in most developing countries are low, which constrains economic growth. In some developing countries, despite high rates of investment, the rates of economic growth are low because of low efficiency of investment.

The role of foreign capital in economic development can be examined from two perspectives. First, foreign capital may supplement domestic saving/investment and raise economic growth. Second, foreign capital may increase the average productivity of investment and promote economic growth. Historically foreign capital has played an important role in economic growth in newly settled countries as well as in those countries which, although lacking capital, had already developed economic, social and political institutions. However foreign capital (or aid) has not been successful in raising economic growth in most developing countries. Some developing countries which have been successful in attracting foreign private capital have had mixed results.

The 1950s and 1960s witnessed the proliferation of foreign aid programmes in the newly independent countries of Asia and Africa to promote economic growth and development. By the 1970s all aid programmes came under criticism, largely for their apparent failure to promote economic growth and partly due to disenchantment with foreign aid as most developed countries experienced serious macroeconomic problems, such as unemployment, inflation and current account deficits. Along with the so-called aid-fatigue, the 1980s debt crisis was a major shock to the international financial system and caused a sea of change in international finance. For most of the 1980s developing countries were virtually cut off from international capital markets. However one good thing appears to have come out from this trauma: most developing countries willingly or unwillingly have undertaken structural adjustment measures since the mid-1980s and maintained macroeconomic stability. Despite the shadow of the debt crisis a substantial amount of private capital has flown to many developing countries, in part because of improvements in those countries' economic policies and prospects. Reform measures and policy changes have also contributed to developing countries' integration with international capital markets. Although the developing countries as a whole have become more integrated internationally over the last decade or so, the level and pace of integration have varied widely between countries. For example only a dozen of the East Asian and Latin American countries received the bulk of private foreign capital. For most low-income countries, official aid remains dominant.

Rapid integration with international capital markets has major implications for developing countries where new opportunities are created as well as challenges. The new opportunities come from wider markets for trade, an expanding array of tradables, larger private capital flows and increased access to latest technology. By opening up their economies and adopting outward-oriented development policies, developing countries have indeed improved their economic prospects.

The new opportunities have been accompanied by new challenges of economic management. Integration with international capital markets requires the adoption and maintenance of a liberal trade and investment regime. In trade, competition is increasingly stiff and the rapidly changing possibilities for trade favour the more agile. In finance, international capital market integration and the potential volatility of capital flows that comes with it are making macroeconomic management more complex. Policy-makers have the difficult task of maintaining the confidence of markets, both domestic and international. In this setting sound economic policies command a rising premium: the pay-offs are larger, but so are the penalties for policy errors. What is more, globalization increases competition between policy regimes; with greater capital mobility, investors are increasingly exploring opportunities worldwide and assessing a country's policies not only in the absolute but also relative to those in other countries (IMF, 1995a,b).

NOTES

1. In many poor countries, savings/investment often take such forms which are not so productive. For example savings/investment in the forms of gold and palatial houses do not generally raise the productive capacity of the economy, although they are good hedges against inflation and taxes.
2. Economists of the Keynesian persuasion do not think so. According to them, investment can be increased by the government without prior savings and financed through inflation. This is known as the 'forced savings approach to development', where investment precedes savings. (For details see Chapter 1).
3. Harrod (1939) called it the warranted rate of growth.
4. The positive effect of saving on economic growth is straightforward: a high rate of saving raises economic growth by increasing capital accumulation. For such an interpretation of the data, see Mankiw, Romer and Weil (1992). Economic growth can also raise the rate of saving. For example the high-saving, high-growth countries of East Asia experienced high growth before their saving rates rose. An implication is that an acceleration of growth in developing countries is possible in the absence of an initial jump of saving (IMF, 1995a). The Granger causality tests conducted by Carroll and Weil (1994) confirm the link from growth to saving. One consensus view emerging is that there is 'a virtuous circle between growth and saving'. Increases in growth raise the saving rate, which in turn feeds back to increase growth.
5. Bauer and Yamey (1992) have strongly criticized the vicious circle of poverty hypothesis. They point out that if the circle was so vicious, there would be no developed countries because all developed countries were once underdeveloped. There would also have been none of the progress that has been made by many underdeveloped countries.
6. For a detailed discussion on two-gap models and their formalization, see Chenery and Bruno (1962), Chenery and Strout (1966), McKinnon (1964), and Findlay (1973).
7. Findlay (1984) has described a situation where foreign aid is more growth-promoting when given to a poor country whose economic growth is constrained by the shortage of foreign exchange rather than by domestic savings. Although the idea of foreign exchange-

constrained growth was widely accepted in the 1950s and 1960s, its validity has come under challenge since the 1980s. For example Lal (1992) is critical of the two-gap model and the implied foreign exchange constraint to economic growth. He argues that most poor countries are constrained in their growth by current savings. The apparent foreign exchange difficulties of poor countries are not signs that they are in a structural foreign exchange bottleneck, as postulated by the proponents of the two-gap model, but rather they result from the maintenance of an overvalued real exchange rate. This argument against the theory of the foreign exchange bottleneck counters one of the conclusions of two-gap models that the productivity of foreign capital is higher in countries faced by a foreign exchange constraint than in those faced by a savings constraint.

8.   As Todaro (1994:539–540) aptly puts it:

> ODA is allocated in some strange and arbitrary ways. In terms of regional distribution, South Asia, where nearly 50% of the world's poorest people live, receives $5 per person in aid. The Middle East, with three times South Asia's per capita income, receives 11 times the per capita aid, $55... If we now look at the country distribution and calculate aid as a proportion of GNP, the results vary dramatically and inexplicably – 0.5% for India, for example, 17% for Egypt, 38% for Tanzania, and 77% for Mozambique... If we next look at the relationship between aid allocation and poverty, we find even stranger results. For example, only 27% of aid goes to the 10 LDCs with 72% of the world's poorest people... Moreover, the richest 40% of the Third World's people receives more than twice as much per capita aid as the poorest 40%. And this ratio has risen substantially since 1970. Finally, if we compare ODA allocation to LDCs with large and small military expenditures, we find that countries that spend more on their military (greater than 4% of GNP) receive twice as much aid per capita as countries that spend much less.

9.   This section draws materials from both Krugman and Obstfeld (1989) and Cardoso and Dornbusch (1989).

10. Most capital flows from Europe to the New World before World War I came from private sources. Investments were concentrated in the form of bonds issued by private railroads and utilities companies. However government bond issues were prevalent in the interwar period (1918–1939) (Eaton, 1989).

11. Reisen (1996:73) draws attention to such imperfections:

> ... global capital markets suffer from three major distortions: the problem of asymmetric information causes herd behavior among investors and, in good times, congestion problems; the fact that some market participants are too big to fail causes excessive risk taking; and the global financial markets feature multiple equilibria, unrelated to 'fundamentals'.

5.   Debt crisis and capital flight

INTRODUCTION

Chapter 4 examined the macroeconomic issues relating to capital flows to developing countries. It was found that capital flows from developed to developing countries were not an uninterrupted phenomenon. There was a major debt crisis in Latin America and Europe in the 1930s, which caused an interruption of private capital flows to developing countries for a considerable period of time. A similar debt crisis happened in Latin America in the 1980s, which virtually cut off all developing countries from international finance for about a decade. Capital flight from developing countries was another phenomenon closely related to the debt crisis.

Although the debt crisis was concentrated on Latin America and is no longer front page news, it had far reaching economic, social and political consequences. In general it cast a shadow over the economic horizon of developing countries and the latter had no other realistic alternative but to undertake structural adjustment programmes of various forms under the pressure of aid donors, including the IMF and the World Bank. Many analysts refer to the 1980s as a lost decade of socio-economic development for many developing countries, especially within Latin America. This chapter examines the causes and consequences of the debt crisis in, and capital flight from, developing countries in greater detail.

THE 1980S DEBT CRISIS

Origins and Consequences of the Debt Crisis

Although a large body of literature exists on the Latin American debt crisis, there is a lack of consensus on factors which might have caused it. An emerging view is that both internal and external factors played a role in the crisis. Sachs and Larrain (1993:692) aptly put it as follows:

> Explaining why the debt crisis occurred is no simple task. As it normally happens with complicated phenomena, there is no single factor that can explain the debt crisis. The extent of the crisis provides a crucial clue, however. The fact that

dozens of countries succumbed *simultaneously* suggests international factors (such as higher world interest rates) played a key role in the onset of the crisis. On the other hand, the fact that some countries were hard hit while others were not suggests that domestic factors, that is factors internal to the debtor countries, also played a role. How else can we explain the fact that Latin America fell into a deep crisis while East Asia did not?

Cardoso and Dornbusch (1989:1401) are more explicit about the reasons for the debt crisis:

Economic management in debtor countries had been exceptionally poor. Budget deficits had increased vastly; exchange rates were overvalued; capital flight and excessive consumer imports were the rule. All this was financed by external debt accumulation without much regard for the future cost in terms of debt. Lenders did not pay much attention to reasons for borrowing and hence made the excessive accumulation of debt possible. But an essential ingredient in the outbreak of the debt crisis was the sharp deterioration in the world economic environment, just as in the 1930s. The US shift to tight money in 1980–1981, together with tighter money in other OECD countries, raised interest rates and thus led to a recession in the world economy. As a result debt burdens increased and export revenues of debtors fell.... Debtors could not pay and creditors would not lend: the 1982 debt crisis was ready.

The OPEC oil shocks

For an elaboration of the above analysis one must start with an historical evolution of the debt crisis, beginning at least since the 1973 OPEC oil shock. This oil shock caused non-oil developing countries to borrow more to finance the increased cost of imported oil without cutting back their development programmes and/or consumption. As mentioned in Chapter 2 some oil exporters, such as Mexico and Nigeria, borrowed heavily as they expected that earnings from oil exports would continue for a long period. Such an increase in demand for funds for import financing was matched by an increase in availability of loanable funds in the Western commercial banks. The latter received huge deposits from the OPEC countries, which had large current account surpluses from oil exports. The Western banking system was thus able to develop a recycling scheme in which OPEC surplus funds were loaned out to non-oil developing countries on comparatively easy and favourable terms. This recycling scheme gave a breathing space to non-oil developing countries and allowed them to delay necessary economic adjustments. However, they experienced difficulties in servicing their variable interest short-term commercial loans after the second oil shock in 1979, when their export earnings fell sharply because of recession in the industrialized economies.

The debt crisis started in August 1982 when Mexico was unable to pay scheduled debt payments, declared a moratorium and began negotiations for rescheduling its debt. This shocked the large Western banks, who were exposed to huge risky loans to countries such as Brazil, Mexico and Argentina; all of them were close to default. Perhaps as an overreaction, Western banks scrambled to reduce their risks by refusing to extend new loans or renew old ones. This caused the debt crisis to spread to other countries. By the end of 1986 more than 40 countries in Latin America, Africa and elsewhere encountered severe external financing problems. However the countries in East Asia (except the Philippines) maintained debt servicing throughout the recession and avoided the need to reschedule their debts (Krugman and Obstfeld, 1989).

There is no doubt that if all the Latin American countries had defaulted on their debts, the large Western banks could have gone bankrupt and triggered an international banking collapse. To avoid such a nightmare, rescue operations were called for. The US government, large banks and the IMF engaged in intense negotiations with debtor countries and were able to design policies and programs that allowed the debtor countries to reschedule loans and receive new credits. In return the debtors agreed to adopt adjustment policies to correct macroeconomic imbalances. It should be noted that despite stringent conditions of debt rescheduling, the debtors were reluctant to repudiate debts because that could have led to reprisals from the Western governments. While the face-saving measures were able to bring some form of normality to the international financial system, the IMF became the villain in the eyes of most debtors as the austerity measures that were implemented in debtor countries had the IMF seal of approval (Ethier, 1995). Austerity measures indeed lowered investment[1] and halted economic growth. The poor suffered the most as social expenditures were severely cut (Sachs and Larrain, 1993).

The contribution of government to the debt crisis

Since the debt crisis there has been a lot of discussion centred on whether the governments in debtor countries contributed to the debt crisis. The structure of developing country debt (Table 5.1) in 1982 indicates that in both Latin America and Africa, the bulk of the debt was owed by governments. Latin American governments borrowed heavily from commercial banks, whereas African governments borrowed from other governments as well as international financial institutions. This indicates that the Latin American debt crisis was a crisis of governments that owed too much to private commercial banks, while the African debt crisis was a crisis of governments that owed too much to other governments and to international financial institutions, such as the World Bank.

Sachs and Larrain (1993) emphasize the part played by domestic factors in the debt crisis which, they suggest, was the mirror image of a fiscal crisis. Unsustainable large budget deficits were financed by borrowing from interna-

Table 5.1   Structure of developing country debt, 1982

By creditor	(%)	By debtor	(%)
All developing countries	100.0	All developing countries	100.0
Official	29.9	Public and publicly guaranteed	81.8
Commercial banks	51.2	Private nonguaranteed	18.2
Other private	18.9		
Africa	100.0	Africa and the Middle East	100.0
Official	48.0	Public and publicly guaranteed	95.8
Commercial banks	32.4	Private nonguaranteed	4.2
Other private	19.6		
Latin America and		Latin America & the Caribbean	100.0
the Caribbean	100.0	Public and publicly guaranteed	73.9
Official	12.2	Private nonguaranteed	26.1
Commercial banks	67.8		
Other private	20.0		

Source: Sachs and Larrain (1993)

tional commercial banks. The eagerness of commercial banks to finance deficits merely reprieved the national authorities from required adjustments in public sector spending and taxes. In general although the oil shocks were the proximate causes of external borrowing by non-oil developing countries, most Latin American and African countries adopted populist policies and also distorted trade policies in favour of capital-intensive import-substituting industrialization. Such policies contributed to the debt crisis by misusing resources and by creating a trade regime that lowered exports. The link between populist macroeconomic policies and macroeconomic crises is explored in Chapter 9.

Comparison Between the 1930s and 1980s Debt Crises

Cardoso and Dornbusch (1989) have made the following broad comparisons between the 1930s and 1980s debt crises.

1. The 1980s, like the 1930s, presented a situation of simultaneous, widespread debt service difficulties. The world recession and the retrenching of capital flows were the proximate explanations. The preceding wave of lending provided the essential vulnerability.

2. By comparison with the 1930s the decline in world trade and prices in the 1980s was small. For example between 1929 and 1932 Latin American exports declined by 75 per cent, whereas between 1979 and 1982 they increased by 76 per cent. The sharp decline in Latin American terms of trade and a fall in their export quantum were largely due to protectionist measures of both West European and North American countries (Diaz Alejandro, 1983). In the 1980s however, foreign trade remained relatively open. It appears that the sharp rise in interest rates created severe interest burdens on debtors.
3. As Table 5.2 shows, except for Chile, the debt service ratios in the 1980s were of the same order as those in the 1930s.
4. The 1980s debt crisis was concentrated largely on Latin America, unlike the 1930s when many European countries, including Germany, defaulted.
5. Bonds were the primary form of debt in the interwar period. In contrast, commercial bank loans and official credits were the main forms of debt in the 1980s crisis.
6. Unlike the 1980s crisis, in the interwar crisis investment income accounted for a large share of investment income payments.
7. In the 1930s, following the abandonment of gun-boat diplomacy, negotiations for debt rescheduling on behalf of bondholders were conducted by less powerful and resourceful protective councils. They recommended settlements after a lengthy period of suspension of debt service. In con-

Table 5.2   Ratios of debt service to exports in selected Latin American countries

Year	Argentina	Bolivia	Brazil	Chile	Colombia	Mexico	Peru
1926–29	9.3	7.4	14.7	8.2	6.8	na	4.8
1930	18.2	13.5	23.5	18.0	14.0	na	9.5
1931	22.5	24.5	28.4	32.9	15.6	na	16.3
1932	27.6	50.0	41.0	102.6	21.8	na	21.4
1933	30.2	38.5	45.1	81.9	29.6	na	21.7
1980	30	30	56	38	10	38	37
1981	34	30	57	57	17	35	52
1982	38	34	72	62	22	44	44

Notes:
+   The data for the interwar period refer to public debt service, those for the 1980s to total debt service.
++   na = not available.

Source: Cardoso and Dornbusch (1989)

trast, in the 1980s governments and international institutions were at the centre of the rescheduling process from the beginning. Debt negotiations were facilitated by the existence of stand-by credits and the framework of IMF programmes. The involvement of governments and international institutions was made possible as debt problems of developing countries were seen as a threat to the banking system and to the stability of international finance.

CAPITAL FLIGHT

The 1980s debt crisis was accompanied by a large scale capital flight from developing countries, especially from Latin America. Whether the debt crisis caused capital flight or capital flight caused the debt crisis remains a debatable issue. There is, however, no doubt that while the debtor governments of Latin America were borrowing from Western commercial banks, the private citizens of those countries were engaged in transferring funds to acquire foreign assets. In some Latin American countries, capital flight took a pervasive form in the sense that the size of capital flight was greater than the size of external debt (Sachs and Larrain, 1993).

What is Capital Flight?

There is no commonly accepted definition of capital flight; what constitutes capital flight remains a matter of judgement. Capital flight is a concept in international finance which can be explained from an historical perspective. That is, capital flight has been found to be linked with political and economic upheavals in capital-losing countries. Cardoso and Dornbusch (1989:1421) put it as follows:

> [Capital flight] occurred in the great political upheavals of Europe in the nineteenth century, it abounded in the 1920s and 1930s from Europe, and it has come to the surface once again in the 1970s and 1980s from Latin America.

This is a clear indication that capital flight is a symptom of economic and political upheavals in capital-losing countries. Having said this, it is possible to narrow down the conceptual meaning of capital flight in a general context.

In the recent literature, capital flight has two conceptually different meanings, stemming from different perceptions about the causes and consequences of capital flight. Some economists look at the issue of capital flight from developing countries from a normative viewpoint. As developing countries are capital poor, when capital leaves these countries it reduces investable resources and potential growth. From this viewpoint, all private capital outflows from developing countries, be they short-term or long-term, portfolio or equity investment, can be termed capital flight. This definition of capital flight has been suggested by Erbe (1985) and Rodriguez (1987) and takes an extreme position. In an open economy where private wealthholders are expected to maximize their return on investment and minimize the risk of their portfolio, capital outflows from developing countries could be seen in the same way as capital inflows and both could occur in the course of normal portfolio diversification. This has led Dooley (1986), Lessard and Williamson (1987) and Deepler and Williamson (1987), among others, to argue that capital flight should be distinguished by its motivations rather than by its consequences for national welfare. From this perspective there has been less ambiguity about specific motivations for capital flight from either Europe or Latin America. They were fear of capital loss from risks of expropriation, debt repudiation or the introduction of market distortions, such as capital controls, taxation and financial repression (Cardoso and Dornbusch, 1989). Although in the 1920s and 1930s political instability in Europe was the prime cause of capital flight, since the debt crisis of the 1980s the usage of the term capital flight has been generalized to include any situation in which domestic residents in the debtor countries hold their wealth offshore (Sachs and Larrain, 1993). In essence some judgement is necessary to distinguish capital that is fleeing from capital outflows in the course of normal portfolio diversification.

How Does Capital Flight Occur?

Capital flight can occur in both legal and illegal ways. In countries where there are no foreign exchange or capital controls, domestic residents can transfer funds abroad at the prevailing exchange rates. In countries where capital controls are cumbersome and/or not effective, the authorities authorize, in one form or the other, transfers of funds at the official exchange rates. When domestic residents can transfer funds easily through the official channels, there can be a massive capital flight in response to an expected devaluation of the domestic currency unless the authorities introduce measures for capital control which are effective. One main reason why there was a large scale capital flight from Argentina, Mexico and Venezuela was that these countries had free payments systems and large foreign exchange reserves. The authorities either did not try or failed to impose controls over capital outflows which were effective.

In general capital controls in one form or the other are prevalent in most developing countries. When capital cannot be transferred through official channels, the implicit cost of transferring funds abroad increases. However those controls also create various illegal channels through which capital can be transferred to acquire foreign assets. Mis-invoicing of trade transactions is often used for capital flight. Although both underinvoicing of exports and overinvoicing of imports can be used for capital flight, underinvoicing of exports is more effective for the transfer of funds as it can be used to avoid the payment of import taxes. Other methods of capital flight include outright smuggling of foreign currencies bought in black markets and/or of valuable commodities and assets (such as gold and rare stamps). It is no mystery that in developing countries where there are controls over foreign exchange and capital flows, there are also black markets for foreign currencies. Such markets are sometimes located offshore and therefore remain out of the jurisdiction and control of domestic authorities. For example there is a well-developed and extensive *Hundi* market in the Middle East in which are traded the currencies of a number of Asian countries which have exchange controls. Although in such markets most expatriate workers of Asian countries exchange their foreign earnings for home currencies at competitive rates, residents of those countries also purchase foreign currencies in those markets by paying in local currencies. Other methods of transferring capital overseas include commissions and agents' fees paid by foreign contractors directly into foreign bank accounts of domestic residents, and the payment of fictitious medical bills and/or children's educational expenses (Agenor and Montiel, 1996; Cardoso and Dornbusch, 1989; Khan and Haque, 1987).

The Reasons for Capital Flight

There are both domestic and external factors that can cause capital flight. Cardoso and Dornbusch (1989) see it as an issue for portfolio holders whose concerns can be identified as firstly inflation/exchange rate risk, which leads investors to shift from domestic currency to foreign currency assets; secondly political risk, which leads investors to shift assets to a safe haven; and thirdly tax reasons, which involve taking assets underground or to foreign tax shelters.

Expected depreciation of the exchange rate
The basic portfolio problem in terms of a choice between domestic and foreign currency (by denomination and location) involves the comparison of rates of return on capital.

Let r be the expected after-tax return on a domestic asset, r^* the after-tax return abroad and x the expected rate of depreciation of the home (that is developing country) currency. Foreign assets will be more attractive than home assets if the expected return from tax evasion and expected depreciation exceeds the home rate of after-tax return:

$$(1 + r^*)(1 + x) > (1 + r).$$ (5.1)

Alternatively, looking at real rates of return:

$$(1 + rr^*)(1 + \delta) > (1 + rr)$$ (5.2)

where δ is the expected rate of change of the real exchange rate. The above criterion shows that with an anticipated real depreciation, capital would move abroad unless home real interest rates exceed those abroad. There is an emerging consensus that one principal cause of capital flight from developing countries is the likelihood of a sharp devaluation of currency. This happened in both Argentina and Mexico (Cardoso and Dornbusch, 1989; Sachs and Larrain, 1993).

Financial repression
Expected devaluation of currency is not the only factor that may cause capital flight. Underdeveloped financial systems or financial repression could be another major cause. In general controls over interest rates and the lack of financial assets with high yields encourage wealthholders to transfer funds abroad. Until recently most developing countries had extensive controls over interest rates, which created negative real interest rates because of high rates of inflation. The result was that there was an incentive for wealthholders to transfer funds abroad. The lack of both institutional safeguards, such as credible deposit insurance, and opportunities for investing in domestic securities also make domestic investments riskier than foreign assets.

Fiscal and monetary indiscipline
Most developing countries lack macroeconomic stability. In the absence of disciplined policy-making there remain uncertainties about key macroeconomic variables such as inflation, exchange rates and interest rates. Most economists believe that fiscal and monetary indiscipline in Latin America, which created inflation and balance of payments problems in the 1970s and 1980s, was the root cause of capital flight. Capital flight caused by macroeconomic indiscipline is essentially a defensive mechanism for domestic residents who try to avoid paying inflation and other taxes associated with unsustainable budget deficits.

Perceived risk factor
There is a relatively high risk (actual or perceived) associated with investments in developing countries as compared with that in developed countries. Developed countries have well established political systems with constitu-

tional arrangements that provide for an institutional infrastructure that is conducive to saving and investment (Khan and Haque, 1987).

Other factors

Although most discussions on capital flight from developing countries point to disincentives to hold funds at home, there are also in-built incentives for wealthholders in developing countries to transfer funds elsewhere. Some developed countries are practically tax havens for the non-residents of developing countries. As many rich and powerful people in developing countries acquire wealth through illegal means, they find it an attractive proposition to transfer funds to developed countries to avoid detection of such wealth from domestic authorities, in case their political fortune turns against them. The case of Marcos of the Philippines is an example.

The Costs of Capital Flight

Capital flight has both short-run and long-run effects on the economy. These fall into three broad categories: macroeconomic destabilization, the undermining of tax morality, and lowering of economic growth.

Macroeconomic management

Capital flight can have destabilizing effects on interest rates, exchange rates and foreign exchange reserves. A sudden outflow of capital can raise the interest rate by creating a shortage of liquidity, depreciate the exchange rate under a floating exchange rate system, and reduce foreign exchange reserves under a fixed exchange rate system. When a capital-losing country experiences a sharp depletion of foreign exchange reserves, it cannot defend the exchange rate for long. Krugman (1979) has developed a model which shows how unsustainable budget deficits can lead to a full blown balance-of-payments crisis when domestic residents scramble to transfer their capital to acquire foreign assets. Chapter 6 discusses this model and its policy implications.

Tax morality

Capital flight undermines tax morality and in developing countries tax morality is already low. For both administrative and economic reasons, there is only a small proportion of people who pay direct taxes. In addition to the fact that the scope for tax evasion is enormous in developing countries, rich people can avoid paying taxes when their assets are outside the jurisdiction of the national authorities. Cardoso and Dornbusch (1989:1428) explain why capital flight further undermines tax morality:

[Tax morality is undermined] in several ways. In moving assets abroad, over- or underinvoicing is often an immediate byproduct. Underinvoicing of exports invariably filters down into the tax transactions of exporting firms and is also reflected in reduced tax payments. Once assets are abroad it would be altogether exceptional if taxes were paid on the earnings. Hence tax revenue is reduced at this level also. Finally, once external assets have become part of the culture, they become convenient vehicles for the payment of fraud and bribes.

Economic growth

When capital flight is permanent in nature it can retard economic growth. The major channel through which economic growth is affected is the decline in both private and public investment. Public investment may decline because of the government's loss of tax revenues due to capital flight. When the government borrows from overseas to maintain its investment, it creates debt servicing obligations that may lower investment in the future. Khan and Haque (1987:5) have identified three channels through which capital flight retards economic growth.

First, there is a reduction in available resources to finance domestic investment, leading to a decline in the rate of capital formation and adversely affecting the country's growth rate. Second, capital flight reduces the government's ability to tax all the income of its residents, because governments have difficulty in taxing both the wealth held abroad and the income that is generated from that wealth. Capital flight thus reduces government revenues and the ability to service external public debt. Third, as government revenues fall with the erosion of the tax base, there is an increased need to borrow from abroad, thereby increasing the foreign debt burden.

Currency substitution

Currency substitution is linked with capital flight. Currency substitution describes a situation where domestic economic agents use foreign currencies as a medium of exchange, unit of account and store of value. Often referred to as dollarization, this is predominantly a Latin American phenomenon. It is, to a lesser extent, also found in some Asian and other developing countries.

One major problem with currency substitution is that as people hold foreign currencies in increasing amounts, the domestic government loses substantial amounts of seigniorage to the governments of countries whose currencies substitute the domestic currency. It is also claimed that currency substitution raises inflation to a higher level than would otherwise be the case. However it presupposes that the causality between currency substitution and inflation runs from the former to the latter and ignores the possibility of a reverse causation.

From the monetary policy point of view, the important aspect of currency substitution is that it introduces instability in the demand for domestic money function (McKinnon, 1981, 1982). Edwards (1993a:1) has summarized the problem of currency substitution for macroeconomic management:

How is macromanagement affected with the existence of currency substitution? Two things are involved here: (a) money-demand instability. It is clear that the demand for money is much more unstable once we have currency substitution, in particular the one that allows domestic banks to issue foreign-currency denominated deposits, and (b) the effectiveness of exchange-rate policy under currency substitution – in particular the issue of devaluation.

Furthermore when wealthholders respond to changes in the relative opportunity costs of holding foreign money balances, foreign monetary disturbances have the potential to destabilize the domestic economy through changes in the demand for domestic money. In other words currency substitution makes the insulation property of the flexible exchange rate system weaker. To illustrate, if the monetary authority of country A increases its domestic supply, the inflation rate in A will rise and money holders will expect A's currency to depreciate. With a flexible exchange rate system, A's monetary authority does not intervene in the foreign exchange market. The expected depreciation of A's currency will then increase the opportunity cost of holding it relative to country B's currency. This will result in a decline in the demand for A's currency and an increase in the demand for B's currency in both countries. If B follows the policy of maintaining a targeted monetary growth, it will mean a higher interest rate in B than would otherwise have been the case without currency substitution. On the other hand if B follows the policy of pegging the domestic interest rate, it will have to increase the money supply. Thus, if there is currency substitution the policy action taken by country A leads to a similar action by country B, even in a world of flexible exchange rates. In other words the monetary authority cannot have an independent monetary policy which the flexible exchange rate system is supposed to provide.

Policy Options

High, real interest rates, undervalued exchange rates, capital controls, and taxes on expatriate asset holdings are some of the policy options that are often suggested for reducing capital flight. However all these policies have undesirable consequences. For example high, real interest rates lower investment, and an undervalued exchange rate may have an inflationary impact and hence lower the standards of living of wage earners (Cardoso and Dornbusch, 1989). Capital controls are often ineffective and, instead of imposing taxes on expatriate asset holdings, most industrialized countries have built-in incentives for capital flight. Therefore Khan and Haque (1987) suggest that a stable financial and macroeconomic environment is a major requirement for arresting capital flight. The experiences of debtor countries showed that capital flight was pronounced in countries which had high and variable inflation, large fiscal deficits, and overvalued currencies. By removing controls over interest rates, bank credits and capital movements, and by creating a menu of financial assets with competitive yields, developing countries can develop their financial systems to stop capital flight. Low rates of taxes, insurance for domestic investment and other institutional development may help to reduce capital flight.

SUMMARY AND CONCLUSION

This chapter has examined the key issues related to the 1980s debt crisis in, and capital flight from, developing countries. An emerging view is that both internal and external factors played a role in the debt crisis of the 1980s. This debt crisis had far reaching economic and political consequences for developing countries. Most debtor countries have learnt a lesson about the costs of indisciplined economic policies. Facing multidimensional problems, these countries have undertaken various structural reforms since the mid-1980s. This has changed international perception about the riskiness of investment and loans in developing countries, including heavily indebted countries, and is reflected in the recent upsurge in capital flows to developing countries.

NOTE

1. Foreign debt affects investment in two ways – debt overhang and credit rationing. Debt overhang occurs where countries are unable to service their debt in full and actual payments are determined by negotiations between the debtor country and its creditors. In these circumstances the amount of debt payments becomes linked to economic performance of the debtor country, rather than by any contractual terms of the debt. In such a situation, if economic performance of the debtor country improves, a part of its gains will be absorbed by higher debt repayments. Hence at least part of the return on investment will be accrued to creditors as bigger debt service payments. The past accumulated debt then acts as a foreign tax on current and future production, weakening incentives to invest and encouraging capital flight even if finance is available. The disincentive effect of debt overhang is also likely to discourage government efforts to undertake adjustment policies and might also adversely affect private sector incentives to hold domestic assets.
    The credit rationing effect arises in a situation where a non-performing debtor is unable to obtain any new foreign loans. To achieve an equilibrium of savings and investment, its domestic interest rates may then have to be kept higher than the rates in international financial markets, thus adversely affecting its ability to invest (Borensztein, 1989).

6. Budget deficits, inflation and balance of payments

INTRODUCTION

Chapters 4 and 5 analysed the economics of foreign capital flows to and from developing countries. In general foreign capital was found to be beneficial to developing economies as it supplements domestic saving and raises investment and economic growth.[1] Foreign investment in particular raises the productivity of capital through the introduction of modern technology and management and by raising the skill base of the labour force. The experiences of East Asia and Latin America show that foreign capital flows to developing countries and their beneficial effects are dependent on the economic policies and prospects of capital-receiving countries. Sound economic policies and bright economic prospects are key factors that encourage foreign capital flows, while the Latin American experience shows that macroeconomic indiscipline and mismanagement are the root cause of capital flight. The contribution of foreign capital to domestic economic performance is indeed greater when a country has a high level of both competition and openness. From this perspective the main objective of a developing country should be to create an open, stable and competitive economy.

Fiscal policy is a dominant policy instrument of governments in developing countries. Although the fiscal balance is a useful indicator of macroeconomic health, developing countries in general run persistent budget deficits as a matter of policy. As indicated in Chapters 2 and 3, this is a matter of concern insofar as it lies at the root of macroeconomic instability. In fact the common perception is that large budget deficits are the root of most macroeconomic problems, such as high inflation, large current account deficits, overindebtedness and low economic growth.[2] This chapter reviews the major macroeconomic consequences of persistent budget deficits in developing countries.

THE MACROECONOMIC CONSEQUENCES OF BUDGET DEFICITS

Contrary to popular perception, recent empirical studies show that, as in developed countries, the relationship between budget deficits and any indicator of macroeconomic imbalance is not straightforward but depends on how budget deficits are financed and for how long. In general, as noted in Chapter 3, budget deficits can be financed from at least three sources: by selling bonds to the public, by overseas borrowings, by printing money or by some mixture of these three. Over reliance on any of these sources of finance is likely to create macroeconomic imbalances. Over reliance on domestic borrowing, if practicable, may cause a rise in the real interest rate which may lower private investment. Over reliance on foreign borrowing can cause appreciating real exchange rates, widening current account deficits, unsustainable external indebtedness and dwindling foreign exchange reserves. Over reliance on money creation may cause high inflation. This is known as inflationary finance of budget deficits.

While these are the standard consequences of persistent budget deficits, they themselves do not automatically imply macroeconomic problems. If public investment is sufficiently productive, it can generate future income flows to cover the servicing costs of debts incurred. For long-term macroeconomic management, budget deficits can be justified as being one practical way of spreading the costs of a sharp rise in large scale spending owing to temporary factors. The absorptive capacity of the economy is another factor of consideration. In general persistent deficits are somewhat easily absorbed by countries with high rates of private saving and well-developed capital markets. However in a low-saving, highly segmented economy with distorted relative prices, even small deficits could be destabilizing. Given that most developing economies have a low rate of saving, are highly segmented and have distorted relative prices, a consensus view is that developing countries should try to pursue a prudent fiscal policy. Such a fiscal policy would maintain the public deficit at a level that is consistent with other macroeconomic objectives: controlling inflation, promoting private investment and maintaining external creditworthiness (World Bank, 1988).

Budget Deficits and Macroeconomic Performance – Some Recent Findings

Before discussing the consequences of budget deficits in detail, the major findings of a recent study by Easterly *et al* (1994) on budget deficits in selected developing countries are summarised here:

1. Budget deficits are unambiguously bad for growth. Reliance on taxation of financial assets to finance deficits – through surges of monetary financing or issuing of domestic debt at controlled nominal interest rates – is bad for private investment and for growth. Reduction of budget deficits through conventional tax increases is no more contractionary of

short-run demand than taxing financial assets, and is far preferable for long-run growth.

2. Large budget deficits are mostly explained by conscious policy choices and not by external shocks or by feedback from domestic economic conditions.

3. Although large temporary accelerations of monetary financing of budget deficits do not consistently result in higher inflation, the long-run association between monetary financing of budget deficits and inflation is indisputable.

4. There is evidence against the conventional view that public investment is good for private investment. In fact public investment, other than infrastructure, has a negative impact on private investment, indicating that public investment replaces rather than complements private investment.

5. Budget deficits lead to current account deficits and overvalued currencies. This may lower economic growth. Conversely fiscal stabilization is a prerequisite for external adjustment and real depreciation of the currency.

6. Increasing public saving (reducing budget deficits) is an effective policy measure in raising national saving.

Although these findings are broadly consistent with conventional views on the consequences of persistent budget deficits, they vary significantly from country to country and from time to time. This is an important message of the Easterly *et al* (1994:2) study:

> From country to country, deficits may lead to high and variable inflation, to debt crises, or to low inflation with crowding-out of investment and growth, while in some countries moderately high deficits seem not to generate macroeconomic imbalances at all.

The Government Budget Constraint[3]

The effects of budget deficits on macroeconomic variables are commonly analysed within an analytical framework which is centred around the government budget constraint. This concept is outlined here.

When revenues fall short of recurrent and capital outlays, the government incurs a deficit which requires financing from monetary and/or non-monetary sources. The government budget constraint is one way of showing the linkage between budget deficits and alternative sources of deficit financing. This is an essential tool in understanding both the linkage between monetary and fiscal policies and the macroeconomic consequences of budget deficits.

The government budget deficit can be defined and linked with changes in government net debt as follows:

$$D_g - D_{g-1} = (G + I_g - T) + r\, D_{g-1} \tag{6.1}$$

where $(D_g - D_{g-1})$ is the change in government net debt between the current and previous period; G is government consumption spending; I_g is government investment; T is taxes net of transfers; and r is the nominal interest rate. The right-hand side of equation (6.1) measures the budget deficit and the equation shows that the change in government net debt is equal to the budget deficit.

When the government's budget is in deficit, the Treasury needs to finance this deficit by raising funds through issuing bonds. The buyers of bonds can be classified into four categories: foreigners (public or private), domestic households and firms, the domestic banking system and the country's central bank. In developing countries the central bank often buys the bulk of Treasury bonds issued to finance deficits because there is limited demand for Treasury bonds from other buyers. The government may also be unwilling to sell large Treasury bonds to the public because that would require paying interest in the future. Considering the fact that the central bank is often a key organ of the government, it may not have a choice but to buy Treasury bonds or monetize the deficit.[4]

Except in such an extreme situation, Treasury bonds are held by both the public and the central bank. Thus a change in debt held by the central bank $(D_{gc} - D_{gc-1})$ equals the overall change in debt $(D_g - D_{g-1})$ less the change in debt held by the public $(D_{gp} - D_{gp-1})$:

$$D_{gc} - D_{gc-1} = (D_g - D_{g-1}) - (D_{gp} - D_{gp-1}) \tag{6.2}$$

The effect of a budget deficit on the money supply can be shown from the following equation for changes in the monetary base (MB):

$$MB - MB_{-1} = (D_{gc} - D_{gc-1}) + e\,(R_c - R_{c-1}) + (L_{cb} - L_{cb-1}) \tag{6.3}$$

where R_c is foreign reserves at the central bank; e is the nominal exchange rate measured in terms of domestic currency per unit of foreign currency; and L_{cb} is the stock of loans made to commercial banks through the discount window. If the discount window component of changes in the monetary base is ignored, equation (6.3) can be written as:

$$MB - MB_{-1} = (D_{gc} - D_{gc-1}) + e\,(R_c - R_{c-1}) \tag{6.3a}$$

Substituting the expression for $(D_{gc} - D_{gc-1})$ from equation (6.2) into equation (6.3a) and rearranging the resulting expression yields:

$$(D_g - D_{g-1}) = (MB - MB_{-1}) + (D_{gp} - D_{gp-1}) - e\,(R_c - R_{c-1}) \qquad (6.4)$$

This equation, which is another form of equation (3.6), can be called the fundamental equation for financing the budget deficit. It shows that there are three ways to finance the deficit, which is equal to the change in the government's net debt $(D_g - D_{g-1})$:

1. by an increase in the monetary base, $MB - MB_{-1}$;
2. by an increase in the public's holdings of Treasury bonds, $D_{gp} - D_{gp-1}$; or
3. by a loss of foreign reserves at the central bank, $e\,(R_c - R_{c-1})$.

In short, to finance the budget deficit the government will have to print money, borrow from the public, or run down foreign exchange reserves. As Easterly *et al* (1994:17) put it, each of these sources of deficit financing can cause a particular kind of macroeconomic problem:

> The consequences of deficits depend on how they are financed. As a first approximation each major type of financing, if used excessively, brings about a macroeconomic imbalance. Money creation to finance the deficit often leads to inflation. Domestic borrowing leads to a credit squeeze – through higher interest rates or, when interest rates are fixed, through credit allocation and ever more stringent financial repression – and the crowding-out of private investment and consumption. External borrowing leads to a current account deficit and real exchange rate appreciation and sometimes to a balance of payments crisis (if foreign reserves are run down) or an external debt crisis (if debt is too high).

Budget Deficits and Inflation

As indicated earlier, budget deficits are considered the root cause of inflation in developing countries. Consider the following statements by Fischer and Easterly (1990) and the World Bank (1988), which suggest that high inflation is essentially a fiscal phenomenon:

> Milton Friedman's famous statement that inflation is always and everywhere a monetary phenomenon is correct. However, governments do not print money at a rapid rate out of a clear blue sky. They generally print money to cover their budget deficit. Rapid money growth is conceivable without an underlying fiscal imbalance, but it is unlikely. Thus rapid inflation is almost always a fiscal phenomenon. (Fischer and Easterly, 1990:138)

> Inflation ... is often a fiscal phenomenon: it is caused by governments with no alternative source of deficit finance resorting to money creation at a higher rate than the growth in money demand. Any hope of controlling inflation without reducing government deficits is then in vain. Excessive reliance on money creation is particularly risky if inflation worsens the deficits, because expendi-

tures keep pace with rising prices while revenues do not. This means that still
more money creation becomes necessary – further worsening the inflationary
spiral. (World Bank 1988:57)

This suggests a transmission mechanism of deficit-induced inflation: budget
deficits caused by both economic and non-economic factors lead to money
creation, which causes high inflation. If this reasoning is valid, there should
be a link between budget deficits and money creation, and between budget
deficits/money growth and inflation.

The Dornbusch-Reynoso model

Given the key role of budget deficit in high inflation, attempts have been
made by several leading economists to develop a budget deficit-induced
inflation model for developing countries. For instance Dornbusch and Reynoso
(1993) show that inflation in developing economies represents an interaction
of four factors:

1. deficit finance, which governs the growth of the money supply;
2. financial institutions, which determine the demand for money;
3. shocks to the government budget; and
4. ability to react to these shocks by corrective fiscal measures.

High inflation possesses two characteristics. First, a large portion of budget
deficit is financed by money creation. Second, there are indexation arrangements, which link current inflation to past inflation.

In the model, in the tradition of Mundell (1971), the budget deficit is a
fraction (α) of real income, and the demand for high-powered money is a
linear and increasing function of inflation. A fraction (β) of the deficit is
financed by creating money. Making such assumptions, as shown in Chapter
2 Dornbusch and Reynoso develop the following relationship between the
growth rate of high-powered money (μ) and the budget deficit:

$$\mu = \alpha\beta(\rho + \gamma\pi) \qquad (6.5)$$

where ρ and γ are parameters of a velocity function. In the steady-state, with
a growth rate of real output (g_y) and a unitary income elasticity of money
demand, the inflation rate (π) is shown equal to:

$$\pi = (\beta\rho\alpha - g_y)/(1 - \beta\Delta\alpha) \qquad (6.6)$$

This model makes three basic points. First, the link between inflation and the
budget deficit financed by money creation is non-linear. A minor increase in

the deficit when the deficit is already high, significantly raises the inflation rate required to finance the budget.

Second, the financial structure affects the inflationary impact of money-financed deficits. The more sophisticated the financial structure, the higher the coefficients ρ and γ are and, accordingly, the higher the inflation associated with a given deficit.

Third, economic growth dampens the inflationary impact of deficit finance. A percentage point decline in the growth of income raises inflation by a multiple that is higher when the deficit is higher and velocity is more responsive to inflation. A major downward shift in real income growth can therefore be an important contributing factor to inflation.

Empirical evidence

Budget deficits and money growth   How strong is the link between budget deficits and money supply growth? This is an empirical issue. Table 6.1 presents some estimates of budget deficits (as a percentage of GDP) and the proportion of central bank's credit to the government, as well as the average annual growth rates of narrow money in selected developing countries for two sample periods. It shows that a significant proportion of the central bank's credit went to the government, implying that there was an association between the proportion of credit to the government and the growth of the money supply.

Budget deficits and inflation   Although the data reported in Table 6.1 support the general hypothesis that there is some link between budget deficits and the growth of money supply, such a link does not often produce a direct link between budget deficits and inflation, at least in the short-run.[5] In fact the relationship between budget deficits and inflation is often found to be zero or negative in the short run. Figure 6.1 shows this weak relationship between budget deficits and inflation in selected developing countries.

Agenor and Montiel (1996) suggest a number of reasons why there is such a weak link between budget deficits and inflation in developing countries:

First, budget deficits can be financed by issuing bonds rather than money; although such a policy is not sustainable over a long period of time because of the government's solvency constraint, it may imply a weak link between budget deficits and inflation in the short run.

Second, a change in the composition of the sources of deficit financing over time (in particular, a substitution of foreign financing for domestic financing) may imply a low inflation without any reduction of budget deficit.

Third, the correlation between budget deficits and inflation may be low if the money demand function is unstable, if expectations are slow to adjust, or

Table 6.1   *Budget deficits and money supply in selected developing countries*

	1963–1973			1973–1988		
	GBD	CBC	GM1	GBD	CBC	GM1
Ecuador	2.7	48.2	16.5	1.2	38.4	27.9
Honduras	1.3	24.2	10.4	8.0	38.5	10.7
Mexico	2.0	42.9	12.9	9.1	56.9	69.8
Nicaragua	1.2	22.8	12.0	22.9	74.3	214.4
Uruguay	2.3	44.2	16.5	3.0	46.1	27.9
Ghana	4.8	51.4	12.7	1.2	50.9	47.4
Kenya	3.8	10.8	14.8	4.2	62.4	12.0
Nigeria	2.1	41.2	13.7	4.7	77.6	11.4
Tanzania	4.6	25.4	13.4	5.9	93.3	21.9
Uganda	6.5	47.7	26.0	3.9	86.5	105.5
India	4.3	82.3	11.1	7.9	74.6	15.2
South Korea	0.8	33.4	29.1	0.6	15.1	13.3
Malaysia	5.4	5.6	13.0	8.2	17.6	9.1
Singapore	0.3	na	13.1	−2.4	na	7.2
Sri Lanka	6.6	84.5	5.9	9.2	67.8	15.2

Notes:
(1) GBD = government budget deficit as a percentage of GDP
(2) CBC = proportion of central bank's credit to the government
(3) GM1 = average annual growth rate (per cent) of the narrow money (M1).
(4) na = not available

Sources: Edwards and Tabellini (1991: Tables 7A and 8); and IMF, International Financial Statistics, various issues.

if inertial forces prevent the economy from adjusting rapidly to changes in inflationary pressures.

The fourth argument relies on the existence of strong expectational effects linked to perceptions about future government policy. Private agents in an economy with large budget deficits may at different times form different expectations about how the deficit would eventually be closed. For instance, if the public believes at a given moment that the government will attempt to reduce its deficits through inflation, current inflation may rise. If at a later time the public starts believing that the government will eventually introduce an effective fiscal adjustment programme to lower the deficit, inflationary expectations may adjust downward and current inflation may fall.

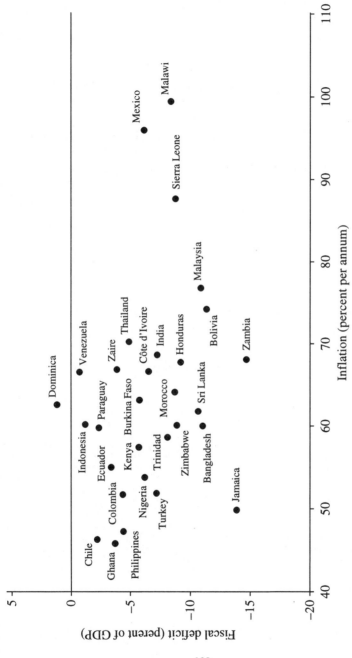

Source: Easterly and Schmidt-Hebbel (1993) and IMF, *International Financial Statistics*

Figure 6.1   Inflation and budget deficits in developing countries (consolidated public sector: 1970–88 average)

139

This shows that there is considerable scope for controversy over the suggestion that inflation in developing countries is a fiscal phenomenon. However, Chapter 7 will show that there is overwhelming empirical evidence on the theoretical view that high inflation in developing countries is essentially a monetary phenomenon (that is, it is caused by an excess money supply originating from either the demand or the supply side of the money market).

Budget Deficits and the Real Interest Rate

In general, budget deficits affect both real interest rates and the structure of financial markets. When budget deficits are financed by borrowing from the public, interest rates may rise unless controlled. This may happen for two reasons. First, the public's confidence in the sustainability of fiscal stance is

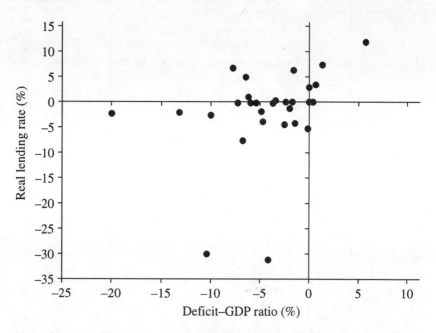

Note: Countries – Rwanda, Sierra Leone, India, Nicaragua, Zambia, Ghana, Cameroon, Egypt, Myanmar, Indonesia, Philippines, Morocco, Guatemala, Papua N. G., Equador, El Salvador, Paraguay, Colombia, Peru, Costa Rica, Thailand, Turkey, Panama, Venezuela, Botswana, Brazil, South Africa, Mauritius, Malaysia, Chile, Uruguay, Greece.

Source: Based on data taken from World Bank, World Development Report, 1996 and IMF, International Financial Statistics Yearbook 1995.

Figure 6.2(a)   Budget deficit and real lending interest rate, 1980

reduced when the level of public debt is increased for persistent budget deficits. This can lower the demand for bonds and raise the interest rate. Second, unless the demand for bonds also increases when there is an increase in the supply of bonds, the price may fall and cause a rise in the interest rate.

Figures 6.2(a)–(e) plot data for budget deficits/surplus and the real interest rates for 32 developing countries. They do not show any strong link between budget deficits/surplus and real interest rates for the years 1980 and 1994. Data reported in Table 6.2 for Asian developing countries also do not show any strong association between budget deficits and the real interest rates during the 1970s and 1980s. As indicated earlier the nominal interest rates in developing countries were controlled by the government until recently, even though they had experienced high and variable inflation. This caused sharp fluctuations in real interest rates. As budget deficits do not have a clear and instantaneous impact on inflation, it is difficult to establish a short-run relationship between budget deficits and real interest rates.

In addition to the effect (if any) on real interest rates, large budget deficits in developing countries have an impact on the structure of financial markets. In general when interest rates are controlled, budget deficits financed by forced selling of Treasury bonds to captive financial institutions impose

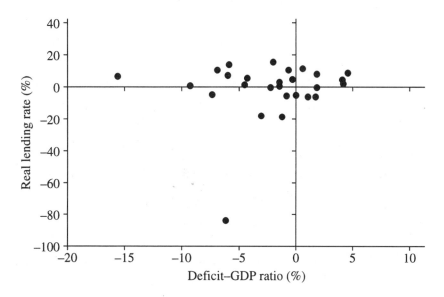

Note and Source: As Figure 6.2(a).

Figure 6.2(b)   Budget deficit and real lending interest rate, 1994

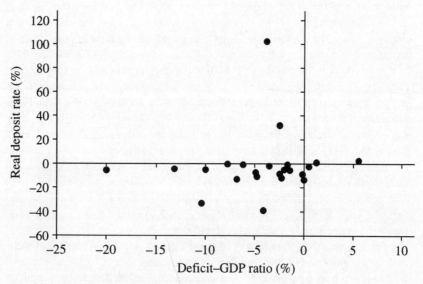

Note and Source: As Figure 6.2(a).

Figure 6.2(c)   Budget deficit and real deposit interest rate, 1980

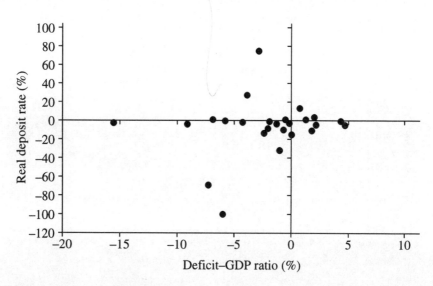

Note and Source: As Figure 6.2(a).

Figure 6.2(d)   Budget deficit and real deposit interest rate, 1994

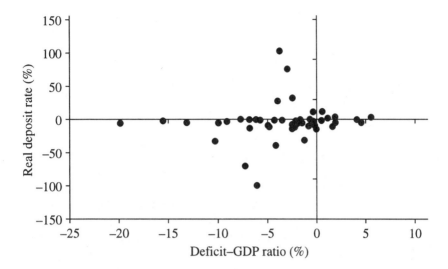

Note and Source: As of Figure 6.2(a).

Figure 6.2(e)   *Budget deficit and real deposit interest rate, 1980 and 1994*

Table 6.2   *Budget deficits and real deposit rates of interest in selected Asian developing countries during the 1970s and 1980s*

	Budget deficit (–)/surplus(+)		Real deposit rates of interest (%)	
	1979–84	1984–89	1975–81	1982–88
Bangladesh	–6.9	–6.2	–3.2	2.3
India	–4.2	–5.3	0.1	1.1
Indonesia	–4.0	–5.7	–5.8	7.6
Korea	–2.2	–0.3	–2.6	5.1
Malaysia	–14.0	–7.8	1.8	5.4
Nepal	–7.8	–9.5	4.0	3.4
Pakistan	–5.9	–7.0	–1.6	3.0
Philippines	–2.3	–2.7	–0.2	–0.3
Sri Lanka	–15.6	–11.4	0.3	4.1
Taiwan	–0.2	0.1	2.9	5.5
Thailand	–3.5	–1.1	1.5	7.7

Source: Fry (1995:423, 431)

implicit taxes on financial assets, creating a shallow financial system. Although a repressed financial system may generate some revenues for the government, even small budget deficits could be destabilizing. The demand for money is often low and sensitive to inflation in financially repressed economies. If there is a flight from money to real goods due to a rapid expansion of the money supply, this may lead to high inflation. When nominal interest rates are controlled, high inflation lowers the real interest rate and causes financial disintermediation (Agenor and Montiel, 1996; Fry, 1995).

Budget Deficits and Private Saving

There are at least two channels through which budget deficits may affect private saving: disposable income and the real interest rate. A standard Keynesian hypothesis is that consumers increase spending when their current disposable income rises, due to a tax cut for example. The permanent income hypothesis of Milton Friedman, however, asserts that consumers increase spending only when their permanent income rises. A temporary tax cut, which creates budget deficit at a given level of spending, might not raise consumers' spending even although such a tax cut increases consumers' disposable income. The Ricardian equivalence hypothesis claims that consumers react in the same way whether government spending is financed through borrowing or taxes. As consumers can foresee that any tax cut today with increased deficit financed by borrowing is nothing but an increase in taxes in the future, they would save rather than spend any increase in disposable income in anticipation of future tax increases. The share of consumers' spending to disposable income is therefore likely to fall in response to a tax cut with unchanged government spending (Barro, 1974).

Agenor and Montiel (1996) suggest that there is another reason – unrelated to the Ricardian hypothesis – why a tax cut could cause private saving to rise or a government consumption increase could cause private consumption to fall. If there are strict government controls over domestic credits and external capital flows, with government having the first claim on credits, an increase in the deficit (or a fall in government saving) reduces the credit available to the private sector, forcing private saving to rise or consumption to fall. They call this effect the 'direct crowding-out' hypothesis.

The net effect of any budget deficit-induced rise in real interest rate on consumer spending is ambiguous. There are three identifiable effects – substitution effect, income effect and wealth effect. The substitution effect occurs when a rise in the interest rate causes both lenders and borrowers to substitute future consumption for present consumption. On the other hand, for a given level of wealth a rise in the interest rate has an income effect, raising the present consumption of both borrowers and lenders. As the substitution and income effects work in opposite directions, the sum of these effects on present consumption is ambiguous.

The third effect is the wealth effect, which reduces the present discounted value of future income and hence consumption of both borrowers and lenders. The wealth effect hits the borrower hardest. This suggests that the net aggregate impact of any rise in the interest rate also depends on the distribution of lenders and borrowers (Burda and Wyplosz, 1993). In line with such theoretical ambiguities, empirical evidences on the impact of real interest rate on private saving have been inconclusive in developing countries (Agenor and Montiel, 1996).

Fiscal Policies and Private Investment

There are at least three channels through which fiscal policies affect private investment: public investment, budget deficits and the user cost of capital.

When public capital is a close substitute for private capital, an increase in public investment can lower private investment by lowering the rate of return. However public investment could be in activities which do not attract private investment. When there is complementarity between public and private investment, an increase in public investment can raise private investment. See Blejer and Cheasty (1989) for a discussion on the relationship between public and private investment in developing countries.

When the financial sector is repressed and the public sector has preferential access to credits, public investment may crowd out private investment. When interest rates are not regulated, large budget deficits, financed through domestic borrowing, can raise the real interest rate and lower private investment by raising the user cost of capital.

Budget Deficits, Current Account and Real Exchange Rates

Most economists agree that there is a close relationship between budget deficits and current account deficits. As shown in Chapter 3, this relationship can be understood by looking at the following identity derived from national income accounting:

$$Y = C + S + T = C + I + G + X - M \qquad (6.7)$$

where Y is income, C is consumption, S is private saving, T is government taxes, I is private investment, X is exports and M is imports. This can be rewritten as:

$$(M - X) = (I - S) + (G - T) \qquad (6.8)$$

This equation, often called the twin-deficit relationship, suggests that a country's trade deficit $(M - X)$ is equal to the excess of private sector investment over private sector saving $(I - S)$ plus the government budget deficit or surplus $(G - T)$. To obtain the twin-deficit relationship it is assumed that the gap between private sector investment and saving remains unchanged over time, so that any increase (decrease) in the size of budget deficit is translated into an increase (decrease) in trade deficit. The policy implication which follows from such a hypothesis is that a government can lower a trade deficit by lowering its budget deficit. In fact many argue that a reduction in budget deficit is both a necessary and a sufficient condition for an improvement in trade deficit.[6]

Dwyer (1985) suggests that the twin-deficit relationship can be interpreted as an extreme case of the capital inflow hypothesis, which suggests that an increase in the government budget deficit results in an inflow of capital from abroad and thereby attenuates the relationship between budget deficit and the interest rate. Within the framework of open economy Mundell-Fleming models, this implies that an increase in budget deficit increases capital flows from abroad, thereby inducing an appreciation of the real exchange rate and causing a rise in current account deficit.

While the twin-deficit hypothesis asserts that a reduction in budget deficit is both a necessary and a sufficient condition for the reduction in current account deficit, the weak version of the capital inflow hypothesis asserts that, since an exogenous increase in private investment may also result in a strengthening of the domestic currency and a deterioration in the current account, there can be an improvement in the current account deficit by lowering the private sector investment-saving gap without a corresponding improvement in budget deficit. This implies that the twin-deficit hypothesis is highly restrictive and therefore any break in the link between budget deficit and current account deficit may be explained in terms of the surge in private investment or in terms of a fall in private saving.

Whereas there is considerable debate on various theoretical and empirical issues relating to the twin-deficit hypothesis, recent research has focused on the link between persistent budget deficits and balance-of-payments crises in developing countries under any fixed exchange rate system. Although somewhat restrictive the basic model developed by Krugman (1979), reported in the following section, has rich policy implications for developing countries.

Budget Deficits and the Balance-of-Payments Crisis

The monetary approach to balance of payments suggests that monetary disequilibrium is the source of any imbalance. As budget deficits can be a major source of growth of the money supply in developing countries, it is plausible that inflation and balance-of-payments deficits originate from the fiscal sector. This gives rise to the fiscal approach to the balance of payments which has been taken by the IMF. To reduce inflation and balance-of-payments deficits, the IMF suggests the reduction of budget deficits. There is another related matter of concern: that a country which runs persistent budget deficits is unable to maintain a fixed exchange rate system because persistent budget deficits create balance-of-payments crises, forcing the country to adopt a flexible exchange rate system and to experience high inflation. Sachs and Larrain (1993) examined the experiences of Latin American countries in the 1970s and 1980s and substantiated the above contention.

The basic model
Under the fixed exchange rate system any budget deficit that is financed by borrowing from the central bank depletes foreign exchange reserves and, if budget deficits persist, the country eventually runs out of reserves. When foreign exchange reserves fall to a critically low level, the fixed exchange rate regime collapses after a speculative attack in which residents, fearing devaluation and inflation, attempt to convert domestic money into foreign currency or financial assets. Such a phenomenon, experienced by Latin American countries in the late 1970s and early 1980s, is called the balance-of-payments crises (Agenor *et al*, 1992; Krugman, 1979; Sachs and Larrain, 1993). Krugman (1979) shows that the speculative attack on the domestic currency takes place before the central bank would have run out of reserves in the absence of speculation.

The basic model of balance of payments crises is presented below:[7]

$$\ln M_t - \ln P_t = \varepsilon \ln Y_t - \zeta r_t \tag{6.9}$$
$$\ln M_t = \xi \ln Cr_t + (1 - \xi) \ln R_t \tag{6.10}$$
$$d\ln Cr_t = \mu \tag{6.11}$$
$$\ln P_t = \ln e_t \tag{6.12}$$
$$r_t = r^*_t + E_t d\ln e_t \tag{6.13}$$

where ln M is the log of the nominal money, ln P is the log of the price level, ln Y is the log of real income, ln Cr is the log of domestic credit which grows at the rate of μ, ln R is the log of domestic currency value of foreign reserves held by the central bank, ln e is the log of the nominal exchange rate, r^* is the foreign interest rate, r is the domestic interest rate, d is a time derivative, and E is the expectational parameter conditional on information available at time t.

Equation (6.9) defines the demand for real money as a positive function of real income and a negative function of the domestic interest rate. Equation (6.10) is a log-linear approximation of the identity linking the money stock to domestic credit and foreign exchange reserves. Equation (6.11) shows that domestic credit grows at the rate of μ. Equations (6.12) and (6.13) define the purchasing power parity (the foreign price level is normalized to one) and uncovered interest parity.

Under the fixed exchange rate system and perfect capital mobility, the central bank accommodates any change in domestic public demand for foreign currency assets by buying and selling foreign currencies. Assume that r* is constant. Substitute equation (6.13) into equation (6.9). As, under perfect foresight, $E_t dln\ e_t = dln\ e_t$ and assuming that domestic money and foreign bonds are two assets available to domestic residents, equations (6.9) and (6.12) show that a high rate of domestic inflation (or devaluation) leads to a substitution of foreign currency assets. When the demand for money does not grow (that is, assume that $dln\ Y = 0$), the relationship between the growth rate of domestic credit and the loss of foreign exchange reserves is given by:

$$dln\ R = -\mu/\theta \text{ (where } \theta = 1 - \zeta/\zeta) \qquad (6.14)$$

The fixed exchange rate collapses when the prevailing exchange rate ln e_o equals the shadow floating rate ln e, defined as the exchange rate that would prevail if ln R = 0 and the exchange rate were allowed to float freely. The following relation shows the time of collapse of the fixed exchange rate regime:

$$t_c = \theta \ln R_0/\mu - \zeta \qquad (6.15)$$

where ln R_0 is the initial stock of reserves. This shows that the higher the initial stock of reserves, or the lower the rate of credit growth, the longer it would take before the collapse occurs. When there is no speculation, the collapse occurs when reserves run down to zero.

The semi-interest elasticity of demand (ζ) for real money determines the size of downward shift in money demand and reserves when the fixed exchange rate regime collapses and the nominal interest rate jumps to reflect the expected depreciation of the domestic currency. The larger ζ is, the earlier the crises. The stock of reserves just before the attack is given by:

$$\ln R_c = \mu\zeta/\theta \qquad (6.16)$$

The first graph in Figure 6.3 shows the behaviour of reserves, domestic credit and the money supply before and after changes in exchange rate regimes. The second graph shows the behaviour of the exchange rate and the price level. Prior to the collapse at t_c, the money stock is constant but its composition varies. Domestic credit increases at the rate of μ and reserves decline at the

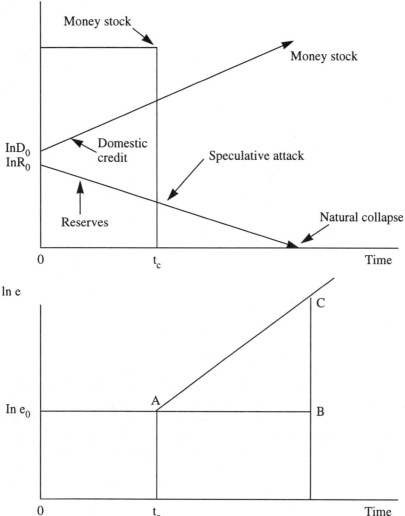

Source: Agenor *et al* (1992)

Figure 6.3   A balance of payments crisis model

rate of μ/θ. When the speculative attack occurs, both reserves and the money stock fall by $\mu\zeta/\theta$. As reserves are exhausted by the attack, the money stock becomes equal to domestic credit in the post-collapse regime. Until the collapse the exchange rate remains at ln e_o. When there is no speculative attack, the path of the exchange rate would be through AB followed by a discrete exchange rate jump BC.

Implications of the model

The main implication arising from the model of balance-of-payments crises is that a fixed exchange rate system is viable only if the fiscal and monetary authorities are able to maintain fiscal-monetary discipline. In countries where there is a lack of fiscal-monetary discipline, exchange rates may act as an anchor for prices (see Chapter 8 for details).

According to the Krugman model, balance-of-payments crises are the equilibrium outcome of maximizing behaviour by rational agents faced with inconsistent monetary and exchange rate policies, rather than the result of exogenous shocks. Although measures such as foreign borrowing and capital controls may temporarily enhance the viability of a fixed exchange rate regime, they may not be able to prevent the ultimate collapse of the regime unless there are fundamental fiscal policy changes.

In general the viability of a fixed exchange rate regime depends on the growth rate of credit and is also affected by the consistency and sustainability of macroeconomic policies. Credibility of a fixed exchange rate regime is important to avoid the balance of payments crises. When rational agents perceive that the authorities' commitment and ability to maintain the fixed exchange rate regime is weak, speculative attacks may occur. Such an attack may take place when the competitiveness of a high inflation country is eroded by adherence to the nominal exchange rate parity. It can reduce the degree of confidence in the existing exchange rate regime and raise expectations about devaluation of the currency. Speculative attacks may therefore be self-fulfilling.

Another implication of the model of balance of payments crises is that under a fixed exchange rate system, a country can avoid inflation from budget deficits as long as foreign exchange reserves are available. Once foreign reserves run out the authorities cannot defend the fixed exchange rate from speculative attacks. Therefore budget deficits would cause inflation after the collapse of the fixed exchange rate system.

Budget Deficits and Economic Growth

Although there are arguments for and against any direct link between budget deficits and economic growth, some policy-makers in developing countries maintain the view that large budget deficits lower economic growth. The view is that large budget deficits create inflation, consequently raising uncertainty and distorting relative prices and resource allocation, which, in turn, lowers private investment and economic growth (Hossain and Chowdhury,

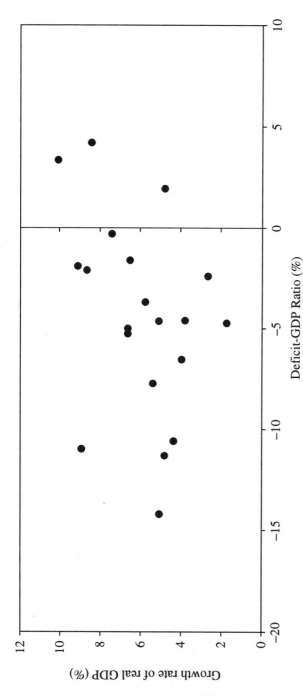

Note: Countries – Hong Kong, South Korea, Singapore, Taiwan, China, Cambodia, Indonesia, Lao, P.D.R., Malaysia, Philippines, Thailand, Vietnam, Bangladesh, Bhutan, India, Maldives, Myanmar, Nepal, Pakistan, Sri Lanka.

Source: Based on data taken from ADB, Asian Development Outlook 1994

Figure 6.4 Budget deficit and real economic growth in developing Asia, 1988–93

1996). Large budget deficits may also increase current account deficits and thus impose a constraint on economic growth.

There is an alternative view that when an economy grows rapidly, large budget deficits may not do much harm. Pakistan is considered to be an example of this as it was able to maintain high economic growth after the mid-1980s despite persistent large budget deficits. However, as recent experience shows, Pakistan faces serious external and internal imbalances owing to unsustainable large budget deficits. Experiences in Latin America also show that the countries which were forced to shift from external to internal financing of deficits because of the debt crisis have shown particularly poor investment and growth performance.

Figure 6.4 shows that low budget deficits in selected Asian developing countries are associated with high economic growth, although this does not imply a one-way causality from the former to the latter.

THE POLITICAL ECONOMY OF BUDGET DEFICITS

The previous section has reviewed the major consequences of budget deficits in developing countries. The question remains: why do developing countries pursue policies which generate persistent budget deficits? This section discusses some plausible hypotheses in a political economy context.

There are three broad overlapping explanations (hypotheses) of deficit financing in developing countries. The first, found in the literature on hyperinflation, maintains that deficit financing through money creation is a deliberate act to create inflation as a device for forced savings. The second view, prominent among the structuralists, is that 'the authorities have imperfect control of the fiscal apparatus and that under these conditions, money creation is the only source of finance' (Dornbusch and Fischer, 1981:330). Tanzi (1982) identifies five structural causes of budget deficits in developing countries. They are the price-inelastic tax system, public sector enterprise performance, increased expenditure for political exigencies or administrative weaknesses, temporary export boom, and worsening of the external terms of trade.

The third and emerging view is the political economy explanation, such as macroeconomic populism (Dornbusch and Edwards, 1990) and macroeconomic opportunism (Hossain and Chowdhury, 1994). The former refers to a situation where a populist government undertakes ambitious programmes and gives priority to distributive objectives, whereas the latter arises when a nondemocratic regime attempts to maintain and legitimize its rule by buying allegiance of political élites of both the left and right. They are reflections of the weakness of the state where the government either caves in to the demands of narrow interest groups or courts interest groups for its survival. In both cases the government underestimates the risk of deficit financing, inflation, external constraint and the reaction of economic agents to aggressive non-market policies.

Healy and Page (1993:284) hold that the degree of political instability in developing countries has a systematic influence on budget deficits and monetizing them:

> The more uncertain are rulers' expectations of the duration of their power, the higher the degree of fiscal and monetary irresponsibility.

Cukierman *et al* (1989) argue that the ruling government has a vested interest in the persistence of an inefficient tax system. The government refrains from reforming the tax system for fear that a more efficient tax system will help an incoming government formed by the opposition. With political uncertainty about the identity of future government, it is optimal for the current government to issue debt because it can transfer resources raised through borrowing to its constituency but it does not have to bear the future costs of debt servicing. A similar idea is shared by Tabellini and Alesina (1990), Alesina and Tabellini (1989, 1990) and Persson and Svensson (1989). They argue that political instability determines the rate of time preference for the society as a whole and hence is relevant to any collective intertemporal decision. Edwards and Tabellini (1991) found strong support for the various political instability hypotheses of fiscal deficits in their study of 21 developing countries.

This discussion reinforces the view that the macroeconomics of budget deficits is intertwined with the state of national politics. In any country where the politicians are not accountable to the public for the consequences of policy decisions, they can get away with policy profligacy or pork-barrel politics without any concern for the welfare of the people. To avoid such a situation, there is a need for development of both economic and political institutions that would improve macroeconomic policy-making. The concluding chapter is devoted exclusively to issues related to the political economy of institutional development in developing countries.

SUMMARY AND CONCLUSION

This chapter has examined the consequences of persistent budget deficits in developing countries. The common perception is that persistent large budget deficits are the root cause of most macroeconomic problems in developing countries. However recent empirical studies show that, as in developed countries, the relationship between budget deficits and any indicator of macroeconomic imbalance is not straightforward; it depends on how budget deficits are financed and for how long. Over reliance on domestic borrowing to finance large budget deficits may mean high real interest rates and falling private investment. Over reliance on foreign borrowing however can cause appreciating real exchange rates, widening current account deficits, unsustainable external indebtedness and dwindling foreign exchange reserves. Over reliance on money creation though may prompt higher inflation. Despite the imprecise nature of the relation, an emerging view is that in developing countries budget deficits should be kept to a level that is consistent with other macroeconomic objectives: controlling inflation, promoting private investment and maintaining external creditworthiness. Although a one-off budget deficit may not create any major problem, a sustained large budget deficit can cause major damage to the economy when it is perceived by investors to be unsustainable.

NOTES

1. In essence, this is the debt circle hypothesis. According to this hypothesis external savings raise domestic investment and economic growth, which in turn stimulates savings and this eventually eliminates foreign debt. Reisen (1996) points out that such a virtuous circle would be complete if it satisfies five conditions. First, external capital flows should augment investment, not consumption. Second, the investment must be efficient. Third, the country must invest in tradables (or trade-related infrastructure). Fourth, there must be an aggressive domestic savings effort. Fifth, capital exporters must be willing to provide stable and predictable flows on terms in line with the recipient country's factor productivity.
2. Tanzi (1994:513) makes the following comment:

   ... especially in developing countries, the public sector, far from being the 'balancing factor' advocated by Keynes, has often been an accomplice – if not the main culprit – in generating major macroeconomic imbalances. This reality must be kept in mind when the government is called on to pursue 'stabilizing' fiscal policies.

3. This discussion follows with Sachs and Larrain (1993).
4. Note that the debt that the Treasury owes to the central bank does not necessarily have to be repaid in a practical sense; it represents a claim by one organ of the government on another.
5. As Fischer (1994:ix) puts it:

   The connection between budget deficits and inflation is evidently complicated: inflation of triple and more digits is always associated with large deficits, but large deficits do not necessarily lead to high inflation.

6. Since the trade account deficit is roughly equal to the net inflow of foreign capital or the net negative foreign investment of domestic residents (I_f) and the government budget deficit equals negative government saving (S_g), the twin-deficit identity can be written as:

$$-I_f = I - S - S_g$$

This can be rewritten as:

$$S + S_g = I + I_f$$

The left hand side of this equation is national saving and the right hand side is national investment. That is, $S = I$ and hence $S_g = I_f$. In terms of the twin-deficit hypothesis, this requires that the term $(S - I)$ remains constant over time.

7. This draws on materials from Agenor *et al* (1992).

7. Money growth, inflation and monetary policy

INTRODUCTION

Chapter 6 examined the consequences of budget deficits on macroeconomic performance in developing countries. One main finding of that chapter is that budget deficits can be a source of inflation if they are persistent rather than temporary and if the government finances them by creating money rather than by issuing bonds to the public. Having analysed some key relations between money growth, inflation and seigniorage/inflation tax, this chapter develops monetary models of inflation for developing countries under both fixed and flexible exchange rate systems. Given that there exists a long-run relationship between money supply growth and inflation, one pertinent question is whether monetary policy should be used as a tool of economic stabilization rather than as an instrument of price stability. This question is analysed by examining the sources and pattern of instability in developing economies.

INFLATION: A MONETARY PHENOMENON

A simple price determination diagram showing aggregate demand and aggregate supply provides a general framework to identify the potential sources of inflation. Such a diagram shows that the price level can change from a shift in either the demand or the supply curve. The factors which can shift the supply curve to the left include negative technology shocks, downward shifts in labour supply and upward-skewed relative cost-shocks. The factors which can shift the aggregate demand curve to the right include an increase in the money stock, a downward shift in money demand and an increase in government spending. There are factors which may simultaneously affect the demand and supply curves (Romer, 1996).

Although both the demand and supply side factors can raise the rate of inflation in the short run, the growth rate of the money supply is often singled out as the determinant of inflation in the long run. The reason is that except the growth of the money supply, all other factors are unable to generate

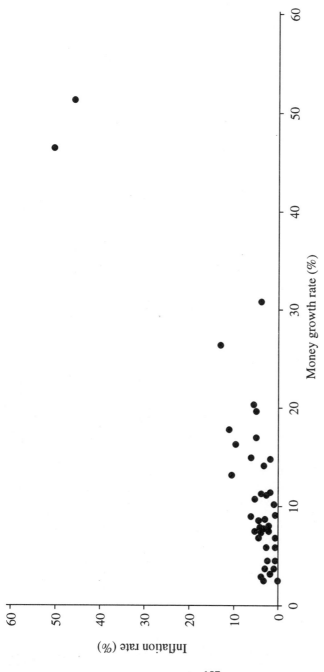

Note: Countries are Australia, Austria, Belgium, Canada, Denmark, Finland, France, Germany, Greece, Iceland, Ireland, Italy, Japan, New Zealand, Norway, Switzerland, United Kingdom, USA, Bolivia, Brazil, Colombia, Costa Rica, Dominican Republic, Ecuador, El Salvador, Guatemala, Haiti, Honduras, Mexico, Panama, Paraguay, Peru, Uruguay, Venezuela, Cyprus, Israel, Jordan, Syria, Bangladesh, India, Nepal, Pakistan, Sri Lanka, Korea South, Malaysia, Philippines, Singapore (from 1965)

Source: Based on data taken from IMF, International Financial Statistics (various issues)

Figure 7.1(a)   Money growth and inflation, 1960–69

157

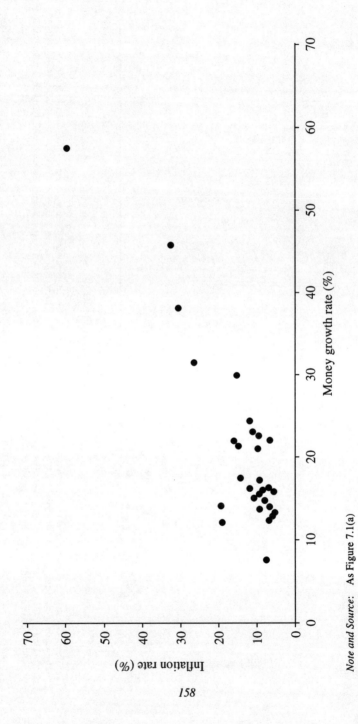

Note and Source: As Figure 7.1(a)

Figure 7.1(b)   Money growth and inflation, 1970–79

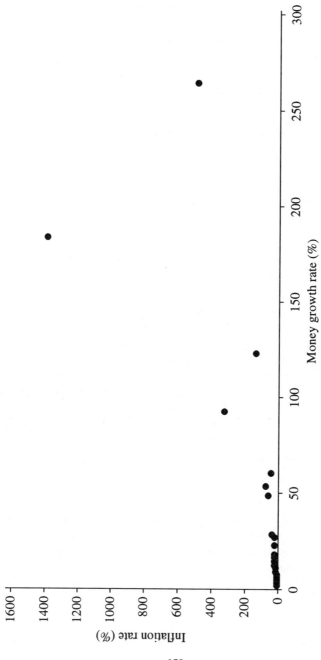

Inflation rate (%)

Money growth rate (%)

Note and Source: As Figure 7.1(a)

Figure 7.1(c)   Money growth and inflation, 1980–89

persistent inflation in the absence of accommodating money supply growth (Mishkin, 1995).

Figures 7.1(a)–(c) show the relationship between narrow money supply growth and inflation in 18 developed and 36 developing countries for three sample periods. Without implying causality, they exhibit a link between money supply growth and inflation, especially in developing economies.

Derivation of the Money Growth-Inflation Relationship

The basic relationship between money supply growth and inflation can be developed by invoking the following money market equilibrium condition:

$$M/P = m(Y,r) \tag{7.1}$$

where M is the money stock, P is the price level, and $m(\bullet)$ is the demand for real balances which is an increasing function of real income (Y) and a decreasing function of the nominal interest rate (r). From equation (7.1), the price level can be shown as:

$$P = M/m(Y,r) \tag{7.2}$$

This equation suggests that, assuming that the income elasticity of demand for real money balances is unity, the price level will double over some period of time without any change in money supply if the demand for money halves owing to a decline in real income and/or a rise in the nominal interest rate. Although such an event is unlikely, there is evidence of doubling of the money supply either over several years in a moderate inflation or over a few days at the height of hyperinflation (Mishkin, 1995; Sachs and Larrain, 1993; Romer, 1996). This is an explanation of why money supply growth is considered a plausible cause of high inflation.

From equation (7.2), the following model of inflation can be derived:

$$\pi = \mu - \eta_m \, g_y + \eta_r \, g_r \tag{7.3}$$

where π is the rate of inflation, μ is the growth rate of the money supply (on money base), η_m is the income elasticity of demand for money, g_y is the growth rate of real income or output, η_r is the semi-elasticity of demand for money with respect to the interest rate, and g_r is equal to Δr.

Equation (7.3) captures the essence of a monetary model of inflation. However this model is not complete in a practical sense unless there is a plausible explanation for monetary expansion. In the inflation literature, one explanation is provided by invoking the idea of monetary expansion as a source of government revenue.

MONEY CREATION AS A SOURCE OF GOVERNMENT REVENUE

Historically, money creation has been an important source of government revenue in poor countries.[1] The fact that government retains the monopoly to print money to pay for its spending (the expansion of money supply) can be considered a part of public finance – sometimes called inflationary finance. The scope for, and nature of, inflationary finance in poor countries was eloquently described by Keynes (1923:37) in the 1920s:

> A government can live for a long time... by printing paper money. That is to say, it can by this means secure the command over real resources, resources just as real as those obtained by taxation. The method is condemned, but its efficacy, up to a point, must be admitted... so long as the public use money at all, the government can continue to raise resources by inflation... What is raised by printing notes is just as much taken from the public as is a beer duty or an income tax. What a government spends the public pays for. There is no such thing as an uncovered deficit.

The analytical basis of inflationary finance in contemporary developing economies and its scope are elaborated further here, starting with a distinction between seigniorage and inflation tax.

Seigniorage and the Inflation Tax[2]

Seigniorage consists of the amount of real resources appropriated by the government by means of money base creation. With the stock of money base denoted by MB and the price level by P, seigniorage S_r is defined as:

$$S_r = dMB/P = \mu m = dm + \pi m \tag{7.4}$$

where $\mu = dMB/MB$ is the growth rate of the money base, dm is the change in real money balances (m), and π is the rate of inflation. This relationship shows a number of key points:

1. The first expression in this equation defines seigniorage as the change in the monetary base divided by the price level.
2. The second expression defines total seigniorage as the product of the rates of growth of nominal monetary base and real balances held by the public. In the public finance literature μ is often referred to as the tax rate

and m, which equals the demand for real balances (when money market is at equilibrium), as the tax base.

3. The third expression expresses the value of resources extracted by the government as the sum of the increase in the real stock of money balances (dm) and the change in the real money stock due to inflation that would have occurred with a constant nominal stock (πm). This last component represents the inflation tax I_{tax} (equal to πm), so that S_r is equal to I_{tax} + dm. This shows that in a stationary state (where dm equals zero), seigniorage is equal to inflation tax. To the extent that money creation causes inflation, thereby affecting the real value of nominal assets, seigniorage is viewed as a tax on private agents' domestic currency holdings.

Relationship Between Money Supply Growth and Seigniorage[3]

As defined earlier, assume that real money balances depend negatively on the nominal interest rate and positively on real income or output. The seigniorage equation (7.4) can be rewritten as:

$$S_r = \mu m(\bullet) = \mu m(r, Y) = \mu m(rr_c + \pi^e, Y) \qquad (7.5)$$

where r is equal to $rr_c + \pi^e$, in which rr_c denotes the constant real interest rate and π^e is the expected inflation rate.

In the steady state, if the growth rate of real output is assumed to be zero and actual and expected inflation are equal, the rate of inflation will equal the rate of money growth. This will give the following expression for seigniorage:

$$S_r = \mu m(rr_c + \mu, Y_c) \qquad (7.6)$$

where Y_c is the constant level of real output. This equation shows that seigniorage equals the money supply growth rate times real money balances. Here the money supply growth rate is analogous to the (tax) rate at which real money balances (tax base) are taxed. However, an increase in the money supply growth rate may not necessarily raise the size of seigniorage. This can be shown algebraically:

$$dS_r/d\mu = m(rr_c + \mu, Y_c) + \mu m_\mu (rr_c + \mu, Y_c) \qquad (7.7)$$

where m_μ denotes the derivative of m(...) with respect to μ. This equation shows the response of seigniorage to an increase in the money supply growth rate.

Whether seigniorage will increase or decrease in response to an increase in the money supply growth rate depends on the behaviour of each of the two terms of the right-hand side of equation (7.7). It is to be noted that although the first term of the right-hand side of equation (7.7) is positive, the second term is negative because an increase in the money supply growth rate lowers the demand for real money balances by raising the rate of inflation. The second term approaches zero as μ approaches zero. Since $m(rr_c + \mu, Y_c)$ is strictly positive, it follows from equation (7.7) that $dS_r/d\mu$ is positive for sufficiently low values of μ. However if μ becomes extremely large, the second expression, which is negative, may dominate and cause a decline in seigniorage with an increase in the money supply growth rate. In other words, there is an inverted U-shaped relationship between money supply growth and seigniorage. This is sometimes called the inflation-tax or seigniorage Laffer curve (see Figure 7.2).

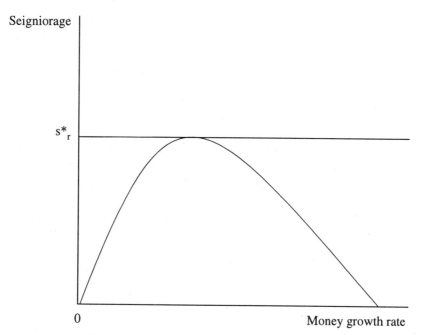

Figure 7.2 Money growth rate and seigniorage

INFLATIONARY FINANCE IN DEVELOPING COUNTRIES[4]

An important branch of the money-growth literature has been concerned with the role of inflationary finance – that is, financing of budget deficits through money creation – in economic growth in developing countries. The original insight into inflationary finance came from the time of the Roman Empire (Gillis *et al*, 1992). However it caught the imagination of policy-makers in developing countries only in the 1950s and 1960s.

Money creation generates forced savings through a rise in inflation which will either redistribute income from classes with low propensities to save to classes with high propensities to save (Thirlwall, 1989), or transfer income from the holders of money to the government through inflation tax. The theoretical framework of the income distribution link between monetary expansion, inflation and economic growth has been provided by Kalecki (1976), Kaldor (1955–56) and Robinson (1962), while the inflationary tax link has been formally developed by Mundell (1965, 1971).

Inflation Tax Revenue

The classic work by Cagan (1956) shows that there is a steady-state rate of inflation at which the government can maximize its inflation tax revenue. In the steady-state the revenue from inflation, R^π (or the size of seigniorage), equals the stock of real balances (m) times the rate of money supply growth (μ). However when the economy grows at the rate g_y, the yield from inflation tax equals the stock of real balances multiplied by the sum of the growth rate of nominal money and the rate of growth of output times the income elasticity of demand for money (η_m) – that is, $m(\mu + \eta_m g_y)$ (Friedman, 1971).

In the Cagan hyperinflation model in which money demand depends on expected inflation, the revenue maximizing rate of inflation (π^*) is given by the inverse of the semi-elasticity (η_r) of demand for real money, so that:

$$\pi^* = 1/\eta_r \tag{7.8}$$

However since in the general model real income is another determinant of money demand, the revenue maximizing rate of inflation in a growing economy (π^{**}) is given by the inverse of the semi-elasticity of demand for money minus the income elasticity of demand for money times the growth rate of real income, so that

$$\pi^{**} = (1/\eta_r) - \eta_m g_y \tag{7.9}$$

Equation (7.9) can be used to calculate the revenue maximizing rate of inflation in high-inflation developing countries. Khan (1980) estimated the semi-elasticities of demand for real money with respect to expected inflation for eight developing countries and found that the estimates lie between three and five. Substitution of these estimates yields the revenue maximizing rates of inflation of 20 to 33 per cent per annum.

In equation (7.9) however, it is obvious that the revenue maximizing rate of inflation is lower in a growing economy compared with that in a stagnant economy. For example, if it is assumed that the economy grows at the rate of 4 per cent per annum and the income elasticity of demand for real money is two, as found by Khan (1980), the revenue maximizing rates of inflation will be somewhere between 12 and 25 per cent per annum.

Tanzi (1989) looked at the issue from the perspective of the net contribution of inflation to total government revenues. He suggests that the debate on inflationary finance should include the adverse effect of inflation on the conventional tax system, so that the net effect of inflation on total government revenue can be used as a criterion for deciding whether inflationary finance is economically justifiable.

As mentioned in Chapter 6, Tanzi found that one common feature of developing countries is that their tax systems are income inelastic and have a long collection lag, implying that the real value of tax revenue declines with inflation. Even in the case of a unitary elasticity of the tax system but a long tax collection lag, the real value of tax revenue may decline with inflation. Assuming a unit elastic tax system, Tanzi used the following formula to calculate the effect of inflation on the ratio of tax revenue to income (or tax burden):

$$T^{\pi} = T_0/(1 + \pi)^{\xi/12} \tag{7.10}$$

where T^{π} is the ratio of tax revenue to income when annual inflation is π, To is the ratio of tax revenue to income when inflation is zero and ξ is the collection lag in months.

As indicated earlier, in a growing economy the revenue from deficit financing (or inflation tax revenue) is given by:

$$R^{\pi} = (\pi + \eta_m g_y) \, m \tag{7.11}$$

Therefore total government revenue (conventional tax revenue plus inflation tax revenue) is given by:

$$TR^{\pi} = R^{\pi} + T^{\pi} \tag{7.12}$$

Taking the derivative of TR^π with respect to π and setting it equal to zero yields a value of π that maximizes total government revenue.

Figure 7.3 shows that inflation tax revenue (curve OA) is zero at zero inflation and reaches the maximum level when inflation is π^* (point E_0). Conventional tax revenue is at a maximum when inflation is zero (point B) but it declines with inflation (curve BC). Total revenue (the horizontal sum of inflation tax revenue and conventional tax revenue as shown in curve BD) is at a maximum at the point E_1 when inflation is π^{**}. Note that at the rate of inflation π^{**}, even though inflation tax revenue is $OR^{\pi^{**}}$, the net contribution of inflation tax revenue to total government revenue is only BF.

Therefore it is found that since the ratio of tax revenue to income falls with inflation, while inflation tax revenue rises with inflation up to a point, total government revenue reaches the maximum level at a rate of inflation which is lower than the rate of inflation at which inflation tax revenue alone is maximized.

Recall that in a growing economy the revenue maximizing rate of inflation lies between 12 and 25 per cent per annum. However when the adverse effect

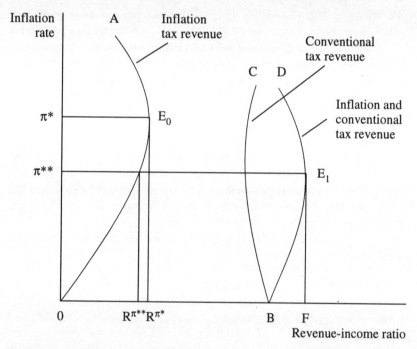

Source: Tanzi (1989)

Figure 7.3   Inflation, tax revenue and inflationary finance

of inflation on the conventional tax system is taken into account, the revenue maximizing rate of inflation is likely to be at a much lower level. This led Tanzi to draw the following conclusion:

> [T]he existence of lags in tax collection implies that government gains from the pursuit of inflationary finance are likely to be lower than has commonly been assumed. If the lags are long and the initial tax burden is high, the loss in revenue may be substantial and may neutralize any gain coming from central bank financing of the deficit. This is an argument against inflationary finance that is quite different from the traditional one based exclusively on welfare-cost considerations of alternative sources of revenue.
>
> (Tanzi, 1989:226–27)

Estimates of Seigniorage and Inflation Tax, 1980–91

Table 7.1 shows data for the average size of both seigniorage and inflation tax in developed and developing countries for the period 1980 to 1991. It is found that the size of both seigniorage and inflation tax is significantly higher in developing countries, particularly in Latin America, than in developed countries. Table 7.1 also shows that, unlike Latin America, the rapidly growing Asian developing countries relied less on inflation tax as a source of revenue. Based on the development experiences of Asian and Latin American developing countries, a consensus view is now emerging that inflation is a dangerous means of economic growth. This contrasts with the early structuralist view that there is a positive association between inflation and economic growth and that inflation is an inevitable price to pay for high economic growth. In a recent article De Gregorio (1993) provides theoretical arguments for, and empirical evidence on, the deleterious effects of high inflation on the rate of investment and on the productivity of investment. In fact most economists now claim that price stability, meaning a very low and steady inflation, is a basic requirement for sustained economic growth. This leads to the view that the main role of monetary policy is to ensure price stability.

Figures 7.4 (a)–(e) plot the data for both seigniorage and inflation tax against the rates of inflation for the countries in Table 7.1. The graphs do not show a strong positive link between the size of seigniorage or inflation tax and the inflation rate. Instead it is found that the lower the rate of inflation, the higher the size of seigniorage and/or inflation tax. This is consistent with the idea that the size of inflation tax decreases with the rate of inflation once the latter reaches a critical rate, which may not be high in a growing economy.

Cagan (1956) and Sachs and Larrain (1993) suggest that for most countries seigniorage at the peak of the Laffer curve is about 10 per cent of GDP. Using plausible parameter values, Romer (1996) shows that raising 2 per cent of

Table 7.1   Seigniorage and the inflation tax, 1980–91

Average over period	Inflation (%)	Seigniorage (% of government revenue)	Seigniorage (% of GDP)	Inflation Tax (% of GDP)
Industrial countries				
Belgium	4.6	0.3	0.1	1.1
Canada	6.3	1.1	0.2	0.8
France	7.4	0.9	0.4	1.8
Germany	2.9	1.6	0.5	0.5
Italy	10.5	5.9	1.6	4.0
Japan	2.6	5.4	0.6	0.8
United Kingdom	7.5	0.6	0.2	1.7
United States	5.4	1.8	0.4	0.9
Developing countries				
Africa				
Burundi	7.3	4.5	0.6	0.9
Cameroon	9.4	3.0	0.6	1.2
Gabon	6.6	1.6	0.2	0.6
Kenya	12.7	4.6	1.0	1.8
Lesotho	13.9	7.3	2.5	2.9
Morocco	7.6	5.8	1.9	2.6
Nigeria	20.9	6.9	1.7	3.4
Somalia	48.6	na	2.1	12.4
Asia				
India	9.5	14.7	2.0	1.5
Indonesia	9.4	4.5	0.9	1.0
Malaysia	3.6	4.8	1.4	0.7
Pakistan	7.8	13.4	2.3	2.2
Philippines	15.3	10.0	1.4	1.2
Singapore	2.9	5.2	1.6	0.7
Sri Lanka	13.5	8.1	1.6	1.7
Thailand	5.8	5.9	1.0	0.6
Latin America				
Bolivia	1155.8	111.6	5.0	91.5
Brazil	547.9	11.0	3.8	14.2
Chile	21.8	40.9	10.7	1.5
Colombia	24.5	24.8	2.9	3.0
Jamaica	19.1	10.0	3.2	3.0
Mexico	61.7	25.0	3.8	4.7
Peru	1058.7	65.3	6.9	110.4
Venezuela	25.5	7.9	1.9	4.0

Notes: Seigniorage is measured in terms of the increase in base money stock as a percentage of total government revenue or GDP. Inflation is measured as the annual rate of change in the consumer price index. The inflation tax is measured as: $\pi_t M_{t-1}/\text{GDP}$.
na = not available

Source: Agenor and Montiel (1996).

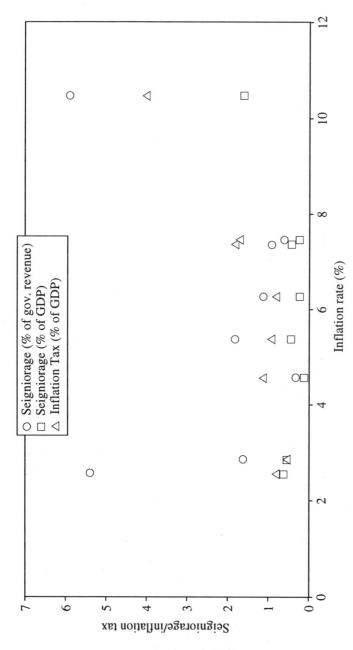

Note: Countries – Belgium, Canada, France, Germany, Italy, Japan, UK, USA

Source: Based on data obtained from Agenor and Montiel (1996)

Figure 7.4(a) Seigniorage, inflation tax and inflation rate in industrial countries, 1980–91

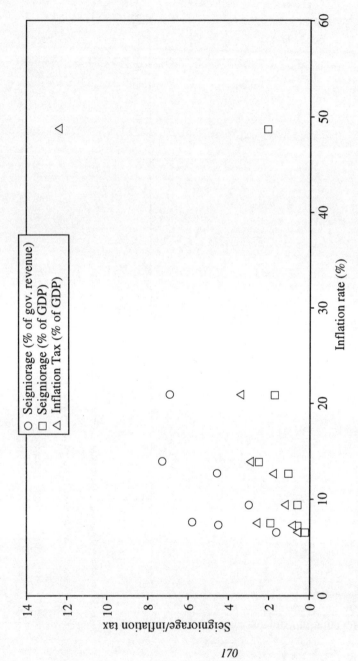

Note: Countries – Burundi, Cameroon, Gabon, Kenya, Lesotho, Morocco, Nigeria, Somalia

Source: As Figure 7.4(a)

Figure 7.4(b) Seigniorage, inflation tax and inflation rate in African countries, 1980–91

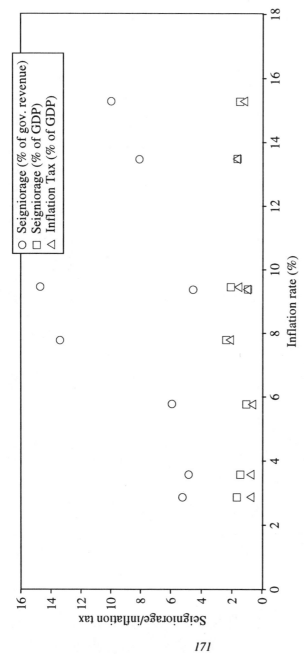

Note: Countries – India, Indonesia, Malaysia, Pakistan, Philippines, Singapore, Sri Lanka, Thailand

Source: As Figure 7.4(a)

Figure 7.4(c)   Seigniorage, inflation tax and inflation rate in Asian countries, 1980–91

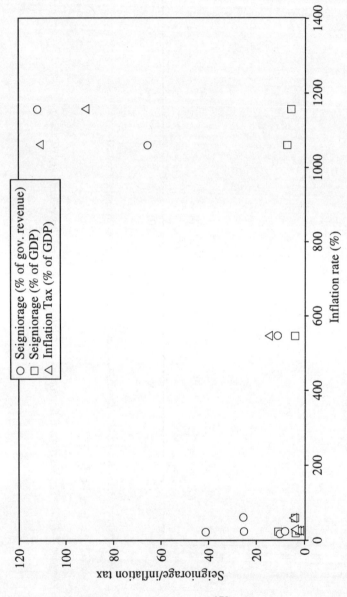

Note: Countries – Bolivia, Brazil, Chile, Colombia, Jamaica, Mexico, Peru, Venezuela

Source: As Figure 7.4(a)

Figure 7.4(d) Seigniorage, inflation tax and inflation rate in Latin American countries, 1980–91

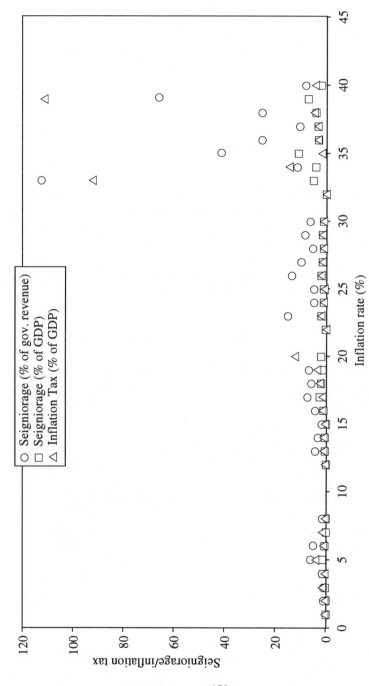

Source: As Figure 7.4(a)

Figure 7.4(e)   Seigniorage, inflation tax and inflation rate in all countries, 1980–91

GDP from seigniorage requires μ equal to 0.24, raising 5 per cent of GDP requires μ equal to 0.70, and raising 8 per cent requires μ equal to 1.42. This suggests that the need for even a moderate size of seigniorage can give rise to substantial inflation and that a large seigniorage need is likely to produce high inflation. A similar message is given by Mundell (1971). The Latin American experience validates this point.

MONETARY MODELS OF INFLATION UNDER THE FIXED AND FLEXIBLE EXCHANGE RATE SYSTEMS[5]

Despite the generalized floating of major currencies since the early 1970s, most developing countries have been operating under adjustable fixed exchange rate arrangements. These countries have also been subjected to credit rules of one form or another under IMF conditionality as a result of the problems they have experienced with current account deficits.

Under a fixed exchange rate system the stock of money supply is endogenously determined. In such a system there is no clear relationship between money supply growth and inflation. For example any expansion of bank credit that creates excess money supply will create balance of payments deficits. The reduction in money base owing to an increase in balance of payments deficits will lower money supply and exert a downward pressure on inflation.

This section develops monetary models of inflation under both fixed and flexible exchange rates systems. The model developed under a flexible exchange rate system could be the basis of the conduct of monetary policy for price stability.

A Traded-Nontraded Goods Model of Inflation under a Fixed Exchange Rate System

Assume that the goods transacted in an open economy can be divided into traded and nontraded goods. The domestic prices of transacted goods (P_t) can then be defined as the weighted average of the prices of traded (PT_t) and nontraded goods (PNT_t). The price level identity can be specified in the following logarithmic form

$$\ln P_t = \phi \ln PT_t + (1 - \phi) \ln PNT_t \qquad (7.13)$$

where ϕ is the share of traded goods in total expenditure. For simplicity assume that ϕ is constant.

For a small open economy the prices of tradable goods in foreign currency are exogenously determined in the international market. From the purchasing power parity proposition, it can be expressed as

$$\ln PT_t = \ln e_t + \ln PT_t^f \qquad (7.14)$$

where e is the exchange rate of domestic currency per unit of foreign currency, and PT^f is the price of tradable goods in foreign currency.

Equation (7.14) suggests that the prices of tradable goods in domestic currency may change because of changes in both the exchange rate of domestic currency and the prices of tradable goods in foreign currency. When the exchange rate is fixed, PT is exogenously determined in a small economy. In contrast, when there is a flexible exchange rate system PT would depend on changes in the exchange rate, even though PT^f is exogenously determined.

The prices of nontradable goods are determined by domestic demand for and supply of nontradable goods, implying that equilibrium prices are established to clear the nontradable goods market. Assume that the prices of nontradable goods change in response to a discrepancy between the log of actual real money balances at the beginning of a period ($\ln m_{t-1}$) and the log of real money balances that individuals desire to hold at the end of a period ($\ln m^d_t$), such that

$$\ln PNT_t - \ln PNT_{t-1} = \gamma \,(\ln m_{t-1} - \ln m^d_t) + u_t \qquad (7.15)$$

where m equals M/P (M is the nominal money supply and P is the price level), γ is the coefficient of adjustment whose value is expected to lie between zero and unity, and u is a random error term. Equation (7.15) shows that only a proportion (γ) of the logarithmic difference between the desired and actual real money balances is eliminated within the period *t*-1 and *t*.

Take the first-order logarithmic difference of equations (7.13) and (7.14) as follows:

$$\ln (P_t/P_{t-1}) = \phi \ln (PT_t/PT_{t-1}) + (1 - \phi) \ln (PNT_t/PNT_{t-1}) \qquad (7.16)$$

$$\ln (PT_t/PT_{t-1}) = \ln (e_t/e_{t-1}) + \ln (PT^f_t/PT^f_{t-1}) \qquad (7.17)$$

Substituting equations (7.15) and (7.17) into equation (7.16) and rearranging terms yields the following equation:

$$\ln (P_t/P_{t-1}) = \phi \,[(\ln (e_t/e_{t-1}) + \ln (PT^f_t/PT^f_{t-1})] \\ + (1 - \phi)\gamma \,(\ln m_{t-1} - \ln m^d_t) + (1 - \phi) \, u_t \qquad (7.18)$$

Specify the desired demand for real money balances as follows:

$$\ln m^d_t = \beta_0 + \beta_1 \ln Y_t - \beta_2 \ln r_t - \beta_3 \ln \pi^e \qquad (7.19)$$

where Y is real income, π^e is expected inflation, r is the nominal interest rate and β^s are structural parameters. As expected inflation is unobservable, it is assumed to be approximate to one period forward actual inflation (that is, π^e_t equals π_{t+1}). Substitution of equation (7.19) into equation (7.18) and the use of π^e_t equal to π_{t+1} would yield:

$$\begin{aligned}\ln (P_t/P_{t-1}) = &- (1 - \phi) \, \gamma\beta_0 + \phi \, [\ln (e_t/e_{t-1}) + \ln (PT^f_t/PT^f_{t-1})] \\ &+ (1 - \phi)\gamma \ln m_{t-1} - (1 - \phi)\gamma\beta_1 \ln Y_t + (1 - \phi)\gamma\beta_2 \ln r_t \\ &+ (1 - \phi)\gamma\beta_3 \ln \pi_{t+1} + (1 - \phi) \, u_t \qquad (7.20)\end{aligned}$$

Equation (7.20) is an estimable regression model of inflation for a developing country. It shows that domestic inflation is linked to the rate of devaluation of the domestic currency, changes in the prices of tradable goods in foreign currency, real income, the interest rate, expected inflation and one period lagged real money supply.

Under a fixed exchange rate system the growth rate of central bank credit is a monetary policy variable. Equation (7.20) shows the effect of credit growth on inflation. For example an expansion of central bank credit, if not accompanied by an increase in money demand, will increase the size of excess money supply for two reasons. First, it will increase the money supply at a given level of foreign exchange reserves. Second, it will lower the demand for money if an increase in credit growth raises expected inflation. An increase in excess money supply leads to an excess demand for goods and services. Given that the prices of traded goods are determined internationally, an excess demand for goods and services would increase the prices of nontraded goods and through them the general price level. However, as any increase in domestic expenditure falls partly on traded goods, there would be trade deficits which would lower foreign exchange reserves and the money supply. Any reduction in money supply would exert downward pressure on the price level, suggesting that even though the expansion of bank credit might increase domestic inflation above world inflation, such an inflation would converge to world inflation in the long run.

Money Growth and Inflation under a Flexible Exchange Rate System

The argument that the main objective of monetary policy should be price stability rather than the lowering of unemployment and/or promoting economic growth is based on the assumption that there is a one-to-one relationship between money supply growth and inflation in the long run. Although under a fixed exchange rate system the relationship between money supply growth and inflation is not well-defined, this is not the case under a flexible exchange rate system. Under a flexible exchange rate system there is an unambiguous relationship between money supply growth and inflation.

The model

A model is developed below to show that inflation in the long run converges to the money supply growth rate.

Assume that the money demand function takes the following form:

$$m^d = Y^{\eta_m} e^{-\eta_r r} \tag{7.21}$$

where m^d is the demand for real money balances, Y is real income, r is the nominal interest rate, η_m is the income elasticity of demand for money, and η_r is the semi-interest elasticity of demand for money.

Assume that the government runs budget deficits and finances them by creating money, such that:

$$\hat{M} = P(def) \tag{7.22}$$

where P is the price level, def is the real budget deficit, M is the stock of money supply and $\hat{M}$ is dM/dt.

Following Krugman (1979), assume that the government adjusts its expenditure so as to keep the budget deficit a constant fraction of the money supply, such that:

$$\hat{M} = P(def) = \lambda_o M \tag{7.23}$$

Equilibrium in the money market requires that the demand for and supply of real money are equal:

$$m^d = m^s = M/P \tag{7.24}$$

where m^s is the real money supply.

The flow equilibrium in the money market requires that a change in the demand for real money is associated with an equal change in the supply of real money, such that:

$$dm^d/dt = dm^s/dt = dm/dt \tag{7.25}$$

By using the notation $\hat{M}$ equal to dM/dt and $(dP/dt)(1/P)$ equal to π, dm/dt can be written as

$$dm/dt = \hat{M}/P - m\pi \tag{7.26}$$

Since $\hat{M}/P = \lambda_o m$, equation (7.26) can be written as:

$$dm/dt = (\lambda_o - \pi)m \tag{7.27}$$

This shows that the growth rate of real money balances $(dm/dt)(1/m)$ is inversely linked with the rate of inflation and that in the steady state (when dm/dt equals 0), λ_o is equal to π.

Adjustment to disequilibrium in the money market

There can be disequilibrium in the money market as a result of any policy induced (or exogenous) shocks that affect the demand for or supply of real money. Monetarists assume that monetary disequilibrium originates from the supply side of money. Assume that the money market is in equilibrium but the monetary authority decides to raise the money growth rate from λ_o to λ_1.

Although neither the money nor the goods market adjusts instantaneously, the adjustment of the money market is quicker than that of the goods market (Dornbusch, 1976). For analytical simplicity, assume that any disequilibrium in the money market adjusts through the partial adjustment mechanism, such that:

$$(dm/dt)(1/m) = \gamma(\ln m^d - \ln m) \tag{7.28}$$

where γ is the coefficient of adjustment which takes a value between zero and unity.

Since $(dm/dt)(1/m)$ is equal to $\lambda - \pi$, equation (7.28) can be written as:

$$\pi = \lambda - \gamma(\ln m^d - \ln m) \tag{7.29}$$

This describes the dynamic behaviour of inflation when there is a disequilibrium in the money market. It shows that π will exceed λ if there is excess supply of money (or excess demand for goods and services). From an equilibrium situation when the growth rate of the money supply is increased from λ_o to λ_1, it will create an excess money supply or an excess demand for goods and will accelerate inflation.

Intertemporal equilibrium inflation in developing economies

Most developing economies are considered to be prone to inflation. As the aim of monetary policy is essentially to maintain price stability, the question is whether monetary targeting can stabilize inflation. It is shown below that a fixed money supply growth rule can ensure an intertemporal stability in inflation. However it presupposes that the country follows a flexible exchange rate system and there exists a stable money demand function.

For analytical simplicity the demand for money is specified here as a function of expected inflation alone. (This is the case of a highly inflationary economy where real income can be considered constant.) Expected inflation in such an economy acts as a better proxy for the opportunity cost of holding money because the interest rates are not market determined.

Assuming that actual inflation approximates expected inflation, the money demand function is specified as

$$\ln m^d = \varepsilon\, \pi \qquad (7.30)$$

Substitute equation (7.30) in the money market adjustment function (7.28) and write it in the following form:

$$\pi = \lambda - \gamma\varepsilon\,\pi - \gamma \ln m \qquad (7.31)$$

Take the time derivative of equation (7.31) and, after simplification, this will take the following form (it is assumed that $d\lambda/dt = 0$):

$$d\pi/dt + z\pi = z\lambda \qquad (7.32)$$

where $z = (\gamma/1 - \gamma\varepsilon)$. This is a non-homogeneous linear differential equation. The solution of this equation is given by:

$$\pi(t) = [\pi(0) - \lambda]e^{-zt} + \lambda \qquad (7.33)$$

This gives a dynamically stable inflation, provided that z is positive. Given that γ and ε are positive, z will be positive if $\gamma\varepsilon < 1$. That is, the e^{-zt} term in the complementary function of the solution tends to zero as t tends to infinity. It implies that when the actual rate of inflation deviates from the equilibrium rate of inflation given by λ, the actual rate of inflation moves towards the equilibrium rate as time passes. This is shown in the phase diagram in Figure (7.5).

Given that the differential equation (7.32) is of the form $dy/dt = f(y)$, it is possible to plot $d\pi/dt$ against π. The slope of the phase line is given by 'z' which implies that the phase line slopes downward. That is, $\pi(t)$ converges to

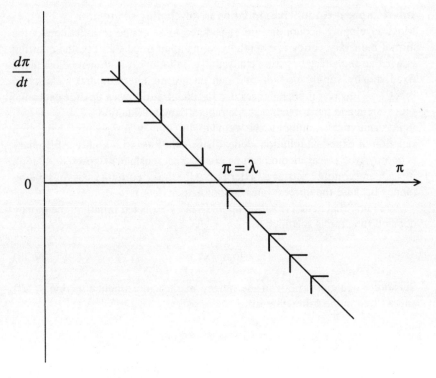

Figure 7.5   A phase diagram of inflation

equilibrium because, starting from a non-equilibrium position, the convergence of $\pi(t)$ hinges on the prospect that e^{-zt} tends to zero as t tends to
infinity. This is clearly the case. Therefore it is possible to say that inflation in
the long run would converge to the rate of money supply growth. However, if
'z' is negative (that is, $\gamma\varepsilon > 1$), inflation will diverge from equilibrium. Such a
situation arises when the demand for real money balances falls proportion-
ately more than the rise in the rate of inflation.

MONETARY POLICY AS A TOOL OF STABILIZATION[6]

It was shown earlier that there is a long-run relationship between money
supply growth and inflation under a flexible exchange rate system. Recent
studies suggest that the money demand function in developing countries is
largely stable (Hossain and Chowdhury, 1996). This leads to the view that the
goal of monetary policy should be to maintain price stability. Although there
is an emerging consensus on this view, in the past the primary objective of

monetary policy in developing countries has been to promote economic growth through inflationary means, interest rate ceilings and directed credit programmes. The theoretical and empirical literature on money, inflation and economic growth shows that the empirical relationship between inflation and economic growth is more complex than is theoretically perceived. The literature on inflationary finance reveals that monetary expansion to finance public investment is a hazardous means of economic growth and that large repressions of the financial sector severely retard economic growth. Therefore activist monetary policy, either in the form of inflationary financing or financial repression (subsidized directed credit) is more likely to hinder economic growth. The lacklustre growth performance of most Latin American countries since the 1950s in an environment of macroeconomic instability indicates that a high and unstable inflation retards economic growth. On the other hand, a relatively low and stable inflation has played a positive role in economic growth in the newly industrializing economies of Asia during the past two decades or so (Chowdhury and Islam, 1993; Hossain and Chowdhury, 1996).

Although the role of macroeconomic stability in economic growth is understood, there is a controversy as to whether monetary policy should be used as a tool of economic stabilization in developing countries. The experience of many developing countries shows that activist monetary policy may itself become a source of macroeconomic instability.

In general the issue of the role of monetary policy and its relative efficacy has its origin in the monetarist-Keynesian debate that started with the publication of Keynes's *The General Theory*. This debate has largely been concentrated on developed economies and did not receive much attention in developing economies. The reason for this is that whereas in developed countries instability in output or employment originates primarily from the demand side, in developing countries such an instability originates mostly from the supply side and neither fiscal nor monetary policy is effective in smoothing out fluctuations in output arising from the supply shock. Here follows an elaboration of this contention.

Demand Shocks and Stabilization

There are two pertinent questions about economic stabilization in developing countries. First, how prevalent are demand shocks to developing economies? Second, how sensitive are developing economies to demand shocks? In general, Keynesians believe that demand shocks are rampant and tend to persist, while monetarists suggest that demand shocks are infrequent and not persistent.

Demand disturbances in a market economy may originate from a number of sources, including private expenditure demand shocks (such as a shift in private consumption or investment spending) and sharp changes in both budget deficits and net exports. In the early literature the debate on private sector instability centred on the question of how unstable is consumption in developing countries? The Keynesian consumption function states that the level of consumption expenditure depends on current disposable income and on an autonomous component. It implies that any shift in the autonomous consumption component because of changes in consumer confidence or optimism may create instability in consumption expenditure. The Keynesian consumption function was later found theoretically inadequate and inconsistent with actual observations. It was superseded by Friedman's permanent income hypothesis and by Modigliani's life cycle hypothesis. Friedman's permanent income hypothesis suggests that consumption expenditure depends on permanent income. Modigliani's life cycle hypothesis goes one step further and suggests that consumers tend to stabilize their consumption expenditures over their lifetimes. Thus these forward-looking consumption theories imply that consumption expenditure is stable. A broad consensus has now emerged that consumption expenditure on non-durable goods and services is stable, although the expenditure on durable goods is procyclical. An outburst of spending on durable goods is one likely source of instability in the private economy (Abel, 1990).

How unstable is consumption expenditure in developing countries? It depends on two main factors: first, whether current or permanent income is the determinant of consumption expenditure and second, the share of durable goods in total consumption expenditure. Gersovitz (1988:389) has reviewed the literature on consumption behaviour in developing countries. He writes:

> the general sense of the literature on developing countries is that a permanent, or lifetime, notion of income...is an appropriate determinant of consumption, rather than current income.

Nevertheless, current income has a role in consumption expenditure in developing countries. The high incidence of absolute poverty is one reason why current income is closely linked with consumption expenditure. Such a link becomes stronger when underdeveloped credit markets create liquidity constraints for various categories of consumers. The presence of liquidity constraints raises the value of the short-run marginal propensity to consume from what is implied by the permanent income-life cycle hypothesis. Consumption expenditure on durable goods is procyclical in developing countries. However the share of consumption expenditure on durable goods (monetized component) appears low in developing countries. Most poor people simply cannot afford to buy many durable consumer goods and most rural households produce various durable goods for their own use rather than purchase (Gersovitz, 1988).

Investment is the second component of private expenditure. Unlike consumption expenditure, investment expenditure is relatively unstable. The Keynesians suggest that investment spending is autonomous, although it depends on business confidence or optimism. In contrast monetarists suggest that private investment expenditure is as stable as consumption expenditure and can be expressed as a function of the cost of borrowing or the real loan rate of interest.

There is a lack of consensus on factors which determine the rate of private investment in developing countries. The debate is centred on the question of whether the real loan rate of interest has an effect on the rate of private investment in developing countries, as the neoclassical theory suggests. Empirical studies, such as Blejer and Khan (1984), Greene and Villanueva (1991), Khan and Reinhart (1990), Sundararajan and Thakur (1980) and Tun Wai and Wong (1982), suggest that the real interest rate, the inflation rate and economic growth are the primary determinants of private investment in developing countries. Therefore the argument that private investment is autonomous or dependent on non-economic factors does not appear to be valid in developing countries. However it does not necessarily imply that the investment function is highly stable. The question is whether any variation in the rate of private investment can generate instability in the private economy. As the share of investment in private expenditure is small in most developing countries, changes in private investment are unlikely to create instability in the private economy. Moreover even if private investment is unstable, when consumption expenditure and investment expenditure are aggregated the resulting private expenditure function may remain stable.

Although the early literature on demand shocks focused on fluctuations of private consumption and investment spending arising from domestic sources, there has been a shift in focus towards international sources of instability. As noted in Chapter 2, in an open economy with a large external sector, autonomous changes in net exports can become a source of demand instability. As most developing economies are heavily linked with industrialized economies, any demand shocks to industrialized economies may affect the incomes and expenditures of developing countries. For example, the sharp rise in interest rates in the industrialized countries in the early 1980s was one of the principal factors that caused a debt crisis in many developing countries. The resultant payment difficulties were responsible for recessions in debt-ridden countries. Sharp changes in the terms of trade are also considered to be another external source of demand disturbance to developing economies. Most of the developing countries, being net importers of oil, faced serious terms of trade shocks in the 1970s following two sharp oil price rises.

In sum, the possibility of demand shocks arising from the domestic source in developing countries is not high. Developing countries are more prone to demand shocks from the external source though as they are mostly primary commodity exporters and importers of industrial machinery and oil. However the extent of the impact of demand shocks, be it internal or external, is an empirical issue.

Sensitivity of the Economy to Demand Shocks

How sensitive the economy is to demand shocks depends on the parameter values of key macroeconomic relations, such as the marginal propensity to consume, the interest elasticity of demand for money and the interest sensitivity of investment spending. The higher the value of the marginal propensity to consume, the larger is the degree of economic instability after a demand shock as it works through the multiplier process. The lower the interest sensitivity of investment spending, the lower is the offsetting change in investment from changes in interest rates arising from the initial shock and therefore the greater is the degree of instability. The higher the interest elasticity of demand for money, the higher is the change in excess money supply from changes in interest rates and therefore the greater is the degree of instability (Aghevli *et al*, 1979). Therefore, the sensitivity of a developing economy to demand shocks may be determined by estimating the parameter values of consumption, investment and money demand functions.

Despite the lack of reliable time series data, a large number of studies have investigated the consumption, investment and money demand functions in developing countries during the past few decades. Findings of those studies can be used to determine the degree of sensitivity of developing economies to demand shocks.

The main parameter value of interest in economic stabilization is the marginal propensity to consume. It has been suggested earlier that for reasons of absolute poverty and liquidity constraints, the value of the marginal propensity to consume may be close to unity in some developing countries. Although empirical studies do not confirm this view, the marginal propensity to consume in developing countries is generally found to be higher. Kandil (1991), for example, has found that the mean value of the marginal propensities to consume for 21 developing countries is 0.60 with a minimum value of 0.32, a maximum value of 0.79 and a standard deviation of 0.11. On the other hand, the mean value of the marginal propensities to consume for 18 developed countries has been found to be 0.56 with a minimum value of 0.43, a maximum value of 0.67 and a standard deviation of 0.06.

Another parameter of importance for the conduct of monetary policy is the value of the interest elasticity of demand for money. Empirical studies suggest that the absolute value of the interest sensitivity of demand for money is low in developing countries. For example, Kandil (1991) found that the mean value for selected developing countries is –0.58, compared with –0.66 for selected developed countries. He has also estimated the slopes of the LM curve for selected developed and developing countries and the slope of the curve for developing countries has been found to be steeper.

Kandil's study also shows that investment spending in developing countries is sensitive to the interest rate. In fact he finds 'a higher sensitivity of investment demand to changes in the interest rate' in developing countries compared with that in developed countries.

In sum, although a larger marginal propensity to consume indicates that developing countries are sensitive to demand shocks, the parameter values of the investment and money demand functions suggest otherwise. As a result developing economies are not likely to be highly sensitive to demand shocks and the impact of demand shocks is unlikely to be large. At the same time, whether or not the impact of demand shocks would persist requiring policy interventions depends on the degree of flexibility of relative prices.

Flexibility in Both Wages and the Interest and Exchange Rates

One of the themes of the Latin American structuralist literature is that there are structural rigidities in the product and factor markets which make wages and prices unresponsive to market conditions. As in the Keynesian model, the structural rigidities of wages and prices may prevent the product and factor markets from clearing after the demand or supply shocks. However most empirical studies do not support that wages and prices in developing countries are rigid and they find that agricultural wages and prices are particularly flexible in those countries. The idea that agricultural real wages in developing countries are flexible contrasts with the implication of the traditional subsistence and nutrition-based efficiency wage theories that agricultural real wages are stable at a subsistence or an efficiency level. A number of empirical studies for developing countries, such as Bangladesh, Egypt and India, provide evidence that agricultural real wages show substantial variations and fluctuate during the peak and slack agricultural seasons. Market forces play a role in agricultural real wage determination in developing countries (Ahmed, 1981; Bardhan, K., 1977; Bardhan, P., 1979; Hansen, 1969; Hossain, 1989; Lal, 1984; Rosenzweig, 1980; Squire, 1981). However unlike agricultural wages, there are downward nominal wage rigidities in the manufacturing and public service sectors in developing countries. Organized unions, minimum wage laws, and the difficulties in hiring and firing of public sector workers create such wage rigidities (Amin, 1982). There are no wage rigidities however in the informal private manufacturing and services sectors as wages in these sectors are determined by market forces (Hossain, 1989).

Table 7.2 shows that more than 60 per cent of the labour force in low-income developing countries are employed in agriculture and the share of agriculture in total output is more than 30 per cent in these countries. The agricultural sector thus bears the burden of adjustment of the economy to any random shocks.

Besides the flexibility of wages, the flexibilities of real interest and exchange rates are important in the adjustment of the economy towards equilibrium after any demand shocks. The nominal interest rates in many developing countries are still institutionally determined and are often not adjusted in response to money market conditions. Nevertheless the real interest rates are flexible because of the flexibility of prices.

Table 7.3 reports the summary measures of the real deposit rates of interest for selected developing countries for the period 1975 to 1987. It shows that the real deposit rates of interest in developing countries are highly flexible. This is reflected in the high value of the coefficient of variation of the real interest rate in most developing countries in the sample.

In an open economy aggregate demand is linked with the real effective exchange rate. A depreciation of the real exchange rate improves the competitiveness of exportable goods and induces a switch in domestic spending towards domestically produced goods. Although most developing countries follow a pegged exchange rates system, the real exchange rates of their currencies fluctuate, sometimes sharply. For example Table 7.4 shows that the real effective exchange rate in Asian developing countries is reasonably flexible and has exhibited a smooth trend of depreciation since the early 1980s.

In sum, developing countries are less prone to demand shocks and these shocks are unlikely to be large. Furthermore, given the flexibility of real wage rates, real interest rates and exchange rates, it is possible that any demand shocks to these economies would be adjusted through price mechanisms so that there may not be any need for active stabilization by the government.

Supply Shocks and Inflation: The Role of Monetary Policy

Although demand shocks are not so prevalent in developing countries, they frequently experience supply shocks originating primarily from the agriculture sector, which features droughts and floods. Agriculture being the dominant sector, any supply shocks to agriculture have macroeconomic consequences. However supply shocks are not restricted to the agricultural sector and may originate also from the external sector. As noted in Chapter 2,

Table 7.2   Sectoral distribution of both output and the labour force in developing countries

	Output (1994)			Labour Force (1990)	
	Agriculture (%)	Industry (%)	Services (%)	Agriculture (%)	Industry (%)
Low-income economies					
Rwanda	51	9	40	92	3
Ethiopia	57	10	33	86	2
Tanzania	57	17	26	84	5
Burundi	53	18	29	92	3
Uganda	49	14	37	85	5
Nepal	44	21	35	94	0
Vietnam	28	30	43	71	14
Bangladesh	30	18	52	65	16
Kenya	29	17	54	80	7
Nigeria	43	32	25	43	7
India	30	28	42	64	16
Ghana	46	16	39	59	13
Pakistan	25	25	50	52	19
China	21	47	32	72	15
Sri Lanka	24	25	51	48	21
Egypt	20	21	59	40	22
Myanmar	63	9	28	73	10
Middle-income economies					
Indonesia	17	41	42	55	14
Philippines	22	33	45	46	15
Colombia	14	32	54	27	23
Tunisia	15	32	53	28	33
Thailand	10	39	50	64	14
Turkey	16	31	52	53	18
Iran	21	37	42	39	23
Malaysia	14	43	42	27	23
Mexico	8	28	64	28	24
Uruguay	8	23	69	14	27
Korea, Rep.	7	43	50	18	35

Source: World Bank, World Development Report 1996.

Table 7.3   Movements of the real time deposit rate of interest, 1975–87

	Maximum	Minimum	Mean	Coefficient of variation
Argentina	107.3	–74.3	–19.2	2.3
Bangladesh	1.2	–10.2	–3.4	1.1
Bolivia	41.7	–98.3	–25.3	1.7
Brazil	42.7	–46.8	–8.7	2.5
Chile	57.4	–3.5	17.1	1.0
Colombia	15.2	–5.6	6.1	1.1
Costa Rica	17.4	–36.1	2.2	6.6
Ecuador	–0.8	–23.9	–9.7	0.6
Guatemala	9.7	–20.4	–1.3	5.6
India	16.9	–5.0	0.7	8.1
Kenya	7.8	–9.7	–2.4	2.3
Korea	11.0	–7.8	3.6	1.4
Mexico	–4.3	–22.4	–10.2	0.6
Pakistan	7.9	–2.1	2.0	1.6
Peru	–7.5	–83.1	–28.0	0.6
Philippines	–18.4	–24.0	–0.2	39.7
Singapore	8.3	–1.5	3.7	0.8
Sri Lanka	12.3	–8.8	2.1	2.7
Thailand	12.0	–8.9	4.2	1.5
Tunisia	0.7	–8.5	–2.6	0.9
Turkey	14.2	–44.2	–7.6	2.4
Uruguay	23.4	–19.7	0.1	210.2
Venezuela	8.0	–15.9	–3.3	2.2
Zimbabwe	–2.6	–11.8	3.6	1.3

Notes:
+   The real interest rate is defined as: $[(1 + r_t)/(1 + \pi_{t+1})-1]*100$, where r is the nominal deposit rate of interest and π is the rate of inflation, which is computed from the consumer price index. Both the interest and inflation rates are divided by 100 (that is, a 5 per cent interest rate is expressed as 0.05). Following Greene and Villanueva (1991), π_{t+1} is used as a proxy for expected inflation.
++   Coefficient of variation = Standard deviation divided by mean.

Sources: Nominal deposit rates of interest (except for Bangladesh): Greene and Villanueva (1991). Inflation rate: IMF, IFS Yearbook 1993. All data for Bangladesh are taken from Bangladesh Bank, Economic Trends (various issues).

the OPEC oil shocks to non-oil developing economies in the 1970s can also be regarded as a supply shock, as higher import prices reduce the marginal product (in terms of external output) of the domestic resources. To the extent

Table 7.4   Movements of the real effective exchange rate in Asian developing countries, 1981–90

1980 = 100	Maximum	Minimum	Mean	Coefficient of Variation
Bangladesh	97	69	83	0.11
Fiji	108	69	91	0.16
Hong Kong	137	100	115	0.10
India	104	64	89	0.16
Indonesia	113	44	71	0.37
Korea, Rep.	103	74	90	0.11
Malaysia	101	68	86	0.17
Myanmar	162	88	111	0.25
Nepal	114	81	96	0.13
Pakistan	110	57	80	0.25
Papua N.G.	102	81	92	0.08
Philippines	102	81	92	0.08
Singapore	109	87	98	0.08
Sri Lanka	105	75	90	0.13
Taiwan	115	87	101	0.09
Thailand	103	72	86	0.16

Note: +   A fall in the index value indicates a depreciation of the real exchange rate.

Source: Computed from data based on ADB, Asian Development Outlook (various issues).

oil is used as a raw material, the rise in oil price shifts the production function inward.

Because of the nature of agricultural production, supply shocks to agriculture are frequent and random. When agricultural supply shocks are negative, they lower output and employment and raise agricultural prices, food prices in particular. In developing countries food prices are politically sensitive because of their dominance in the cost of living index, especially for urban people. Hence the question of whether the monetary authority should adopt a hands-on or a hands-off policy after a supply shock has a considerable economic and political significance at the national level.

In the literature on inflation in developing countries, crop failure is considered to be a cause of inflation. Food crop failure can increase the general price level when non-food prices are rigid downward. However in the absence of any accommodative monetary expansion such price increases are unlikely to be sustained. Why should the monetary authority then increase the money supply in such a situation when there is a danger of sustained price increases (inflation)? This question was addressed in an early paper by Porter (1961). He argued for monetary expansion after an agricultural supply shock in order to lessen the danger of, rather than to ignite, inflation. According to him, in a developing country any increased price level[7] after a crop failure would remain at the higher level whether or not the monetary authority increases the money supply. He then advocates an expansion of the money supply, otherwise farmers may hoard foodgrain to balance the desired and actual levels of wealthholding as a disequilibrium in their wealth position is created after the price increase. Such an action by farmers may increase the price level further because of the decline in food supply in the open market.

However Porter's arguments are weakened if the normal level of food supply in the market can be maintained from both domestic official stocks and imports. In that case there may not be any significant increase in food prices after a food crop failure. Even if there is an increase in the price level after the crop failure, it is unlikely to generate a self-sustaining inflationary process without the support of expansionary economic policies. The adoption of such policies remains at the discretion of the monetary and fiscal authorities. The question of whether farmers will hoard foodgrain after the food crop failure depends on the expected price of food. It is likely that any expansionary monetary and fiscal policies would increase expected inflation, which, contrary to Porter's view, may induce farmers to hoard more foodgrain rather than less.

Following the tradition of the modern monetary theories of aggregate demand and supply, a theoretical model is developed below to explain the above contention.[8] The two building blocks of the model are the monetary theory of aggregate demand and the expectations-augmented aggregate supply functions.

The monetary theory of aggregate demand shows the relationship between output demand and the price level when the money market is in equilibrium. To derive such a relationship, an aggregate money demand function is specified below.

Theory of money demand

Assume that the demand for money is derived in the same way as the demand for any other durable good. Real money balances are considered a type of real asset, a form of wealth with the additional property of higher liquidity, providing a flow of non-observable services that enter into individuals' utility functions. All the individuals are assumed to maximize their utility functions subject to budget constraints. The demand for real money balances, derived by the utility maximization principle, will then depend on real income and the opportunity cost of holding money instead of other financial and real assets.

Let M^d be the demand for nominal money balances, P the price level, Y the real income or output and π^e the expected inflation. Then the demand for money can be expressed in the following semi-logarithmic form:

$$\ln (M^d/P) = \alpha \ln Y - \beta \, \pi^e \qquad (7.34)$$

where α and β are structural parameters and ln represents the natural logarithm. This shows that the demand for money increases with the increase in real income and decreases with the increase in expected inflation.

Money market equilibrium
Equilibrium in the money market refers to a situation where the demand for real money equals the supply of real money, so that at equilibrium ln (M^d/P) is equal to ln (M^s/P). Any discrepancy between the demand for and supply of money indicates that the money market is in disequilibrium. Any excess money supply (or excess money demand) is expected to spill over to the commodity market. In a closed economy it changes the price level and brings equilibrium in the money market. In a completely open economy where there are no non-traded goods, any disequilibrium in the money market adjusts itself through changes in foreign exchange reserves. When an economy is neither completely closed nor completely open, any disequilibrium in the money market adjusts itself through changes in both the price level and foreign exchange reserves.

An aggregate demand function
The money market equilibrium condition yields the following aggregate demand function:

$$\ln Y = \delta_1 \ln (M^s/P) + \delta_2 \, \pi^e \qquad (7.35)$$

where δ_1 is equal to $1/\alpha$ and δ_2 is equal to β/α. This shows that when M^s and π^e remain constant, the demand for output is inversely related with the price level. The downward sloping demand curve shifts to the right with the increase in both the money supply and expected inflation and shifts to the left with the reduction in both the money supply and expected inflation.

An aggregate supply function
An expectations-augmented aggregate supply function can be specified in the form of a single reduced-form equation:

$$\ln Y_t = \ln Y_{nt} + \gamma_1 \ln (P_t/P^e_t) \qquad (7.36)$$

where Y is measured output, Y_n is natural output (determined by factors such as capital, labour and technology), P is the price level, P^e is the expected price level by workers given the information available at time t, and $\gamma 1$ is the elasticity of output with respect to any discrepancy between the current and expected price levels.

The specified function is called the Lucas supply function, although Gordon (1981) prefers to refer to it as the Friedman supply function. In terms of Friedman's labour supply analysis, the demand for and supply of labour depend on the real wage rate. Employers calculate the real wage rate by evaluating the nominal wage rate in terms of the current price level, but workers calculate the real wage rate by evaluating the nominal wage rate in terms of the expected price level. Therefore employment and output change only if the monetary authority can adopt a policy which moves the actual price level without simultaneously moving the expected price level for workers. According to Milton Friedman it is possible that workers can be fooled temporarily due to imperfect information on their part, but not in the long run. If it is assumed that the price expectations are formed rationally in the sense of Muth (1961) as an unbiased estimator of the actual price level, such output fluctuations do not arise and the aggregate supply curve becomes vertical, its position being determined uniquely by the production function and the conditions of equilibrium in the labour market.

Any supply shock that shifts the production curve downward and the marginal productivity of labour curve leftward would shift the aggregate supply curve leftward. Therefore the leftward shift of the aggregate supply curve is the combined effect of the downward shift of the production curve and the lower level of employment because of the decline in the marginal productivity of labour (Branson, 1989).

An application of the model in a closed economy

In Figure 7.6 the aggregate demand and aggregate supply functions are brought together in order to examine the effects on the price level and output of both a hands-off and a hands-on policy of the monetary authority following a supply shock. The $D_0(\ln M^s_0, \pi^e_0)$ line represents aggregate demand with the given money supply M^s_0 and expected inflation π^e_0. The S_0 line represents aggregate supply which corresponds to a specific production function with equilibrium in the labour market. It actually represents the full capacity output. The ES^o_0 line represents the expectations-augmented aggregate supply and cuts the long run aggregate supply line at the level at which the actual and expected price levels are equal ($\ln P^e_0$ equal to $\ln P_0$). Point A is the initial equilibrium position of the economy with output $\ln Y_0$ and the price level $\ln P_0$.

Assume that the economy unexpectedly experiences a supply shock and the aggregate supply line S_0 shifts to the position S_1, which represents a less

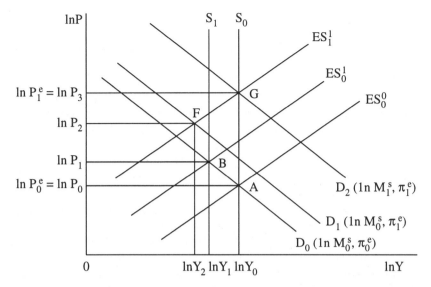

Figure 7.6   The effects on the price level in a closed economy of a hands-off and a hands-on policy by the monetary authority following a supply shock

than full capacity output. As the supply shock is unexpected, the expected price level will remain at $\ln P^e_0$ and the ES^0_0 line will shift to the position ES^1_0. The subscript 0 in ES^1_0 indicates the level of demand represented by $D_0(\ln M^s_0, \pi^e_0)$ and the superscript 1 indicates that the aggregate supply line has unexpectedly moved to the position S_1. After the supply shock the economy will settle at the temporary equilibrium position B with output $\ln Y_1$ and price level $\ln P_1$.

Assume that the supply shock discussed here is a negative agricultural supply shock. Such shocks are random and do not usually persist. Therefore it is expected that after the one-period supply shock is over, there will be normal production in the next period. This will shift the aggregate supply line S_1 rightward to settle at the original position S_0. When that happens, the ES^1_0 line will move to the original position ES^0_0 and the price level will fall from $\ln P_1$ to $\ln P_0$. This shows that the impact of any agricultural supply shock on the price level will be temporary if the monetary authority does not intervene and if there is no change in price expectations.

A complex situation may arise however if there is a policy intervention by the monetary authority. If the economic agents change their price expectations after the supply shock, any policy intervention by the monetary authority will create a complex and uncertain situation. Consider the case where the expected price level increases from ln P^e_0 to ln P^e_1. The ES^o_0 line will then shift to the position ES^1_1. Since the demand for money depends on expected inflation, an increase in the expected price level will shift the aggregate demand line rightward to the position $D_1(\ln M^s_0, \pi^e_1)$. Changes in the expected price level thus shift both the aggregate demand and aggregate supply curves. Given the expected price level ln P^e_1, the temporary equilibrium position of the economy is not B but F with the price level ln P_2 and output ln Y_2.

However F does not represent a stable equilibrium because the actual and expected price levels are not equal. Whether the economy will remain at position F or move towards position A after normal production during the next period will depend on how economic agents form their price expectations. Any action by the monetary authority after the supply shock may provide some vital information which may influence economic agents in forming their price expectations. Even the monetary authority's behaviour in the past in such circumstances could become the guide to economic agents in forming their price expectations. If the norm is such that the monetary authority adopts a hands-off policy following the supply shock, it is possible that the one-off increase in the price level will fall from the peak level after normal production during the next period. When the expected price level falls, wealthholders will substitute money for goods which will shift the aggregate demand curve to the left. The expectations-augmented supply curve is also likely to shift to the right after the normal production. The economy may then return to the original position A.

In contrast if the monetary authority increases the money supply after the supply shock, the aggregate demand curve will shift to a further right position, say $D_2(\ln M^s_1, \pi^e_1)$, which will increase the price level to ln P_3. If the expected price level remains at ln P^e_1, G may be a stable equilibrium because at this point ln P_3 is equal to ln P^e_1. However if the monetary expansion becomes a source of price expectations, the aggregate supply curve may shift to the left and cause a further increase in the price level.

An application of the model in an open economy
The model discussed above can be extended to the case of an open economy under both fixed and flexible exchange rate systems. For simplicity, ignore the international trade in financial assets and capital flows so that the capital account in the balance of payments disappears.

The balance of payments and the monetary sector
In an open economy the national income identity can be written as

$$GNP = C + I + G + X - M \qquad (7.37)$$

where GNP is gross national product, C is consumption spending, I is investment spending, G is government spending, X is exports and M is imports. All variables are at constant prices. Total spending or absorption by domestic residents can be expressed as:

$$A = C + I + G \tag{7.38}$$

Equations (7.37) and (7.38) give:

$$A = GNP - X + M \tag{7.39}$$

Following the monetary approach to the balance of payments theory, the absorption function can be specified as

$$A = GNP + \varepsilon(M^s/P - M^d/P) \tag{7.40}$$

where ε is the adjustment coefficient of monetary disequilibrium ($M^s/P - M^d/P$), whose value lies between zero and unity. Equations (7.39) and (7.40) yield:

$$M - X = \varepsilon(M^s/P - M^d/P) \tag{7.41}$$

Taking the exponent of both sides in equation (7.34) yields:

$$M^d/P = \exp(\alpha \ln Y - \beta \pi^e) \tag{7.42}$$

where exp denotes the exponential operator. Substitution of equation (7.42) into equation (7.41) yields

$$M - X = \varepsilon(M^s/P - \exp(\alpha \ln Y - \beta \pi^e)) \tag{7.43}$$

This shows that the trade balance deteriorates with the increase in both the money supply and expected inflation and that it improves with the increase in income.

Supply shock and inflation under the fixed exchange rate system

In an open economy the effect of supply shock on the price level can be examined by taking into account the possibility that any change in either fiscal or trade deficits due to a supply shock will change the money supply. However whether the net effect of a supply shock on the money supply will be positive or negative will depend on the possibility of any increase in the money supply from increased fiscal deficits exceeding any decline in the money supply from the reduction in foreign exchange reserves due to increased trade deficits.

Consider the case where there is a decline in the money supply because of the reduction in foreign exchange reserves at a given level of central bank credit. In Figure 7.7 the decline in the money supply shifts the aggregate demand curve to $D_3(\ln M^s_2, \pi^e_0)$. The temporary equilibrium is at B^1 with the price level $\ln P^1_1$ rather than $\ln P_1$ and the income level $\ln Y^1_1$ rather than $\ln Y_1$. This shows that in an open economy the decline in output is larger than that in a closed economy.

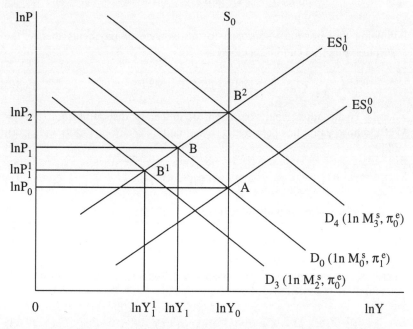

Figure 7.7   The effects on the price level in an open economy of a hands-off and a hands-on policy by the monetary authority following a supply shock

Given that the government revenue is dependent on income, the supply shock which reduces income may lower the government revenue and increase the size of fiscal deficit at a given level of government expenditure. When the government finances fiscal deficits by borrowing from the banking system, it increases the level of the central bank credit component of the money base at a given level of foreign exchange reserves. Assume that such an increase in the money base (or money supply) shifts the aggregate demand curve to the position $D_4(\ln M^s_3, \pi^e_0)$.

As indicated earlier, the net effect of supply shocks on the money supply is determined by the combined effect of the reduction in foreign exchange reserves and any increase in the central bank credit because of monetization of fiscal deficits. Therefore the aggregate demand curve is likely to lie somewhere between $D_3(\ln M^s_2, \pi^e_0)$ and $D_4(\ln M^s_3, \pi^e_0)$. This shows that even if the government does not increase the money supply, the supply shock has a net effect on the money supply, the direction of which cannot be predicted a priori. The movement of the price level will depend on the movement of the money supply. When such an uncertainty is associated with changes in price expectations, the monetary authority may create complex forces by adopting an active monetary policy, the effect of which on the price level cannot be predicted a priori.

Supply shock and inflation under the flexible exchange rate system
Consider the following aggregate demand function:

$$Y = \tau [b_0 + b_1 TB(R) - b_2 rr] \qquad (7.44)$$

where Y is real output, b_0 is autonomous expenditure, TB is the trade balance, R is the real effective exchange rate defined as R equal to $e.P^f/P_d$ where e is the nominal exchange rate of the domestic currency, P^f is the foreign price level, P_d is the domestic price level, and rr is the real interest rate.

This shows that, given the real interest rate, the demand for domestic output is dependent on the real effective exchange rate. A depreciation of the real exchange rate makes the domestic exportable goods competitive in the world market and induces a switch of domestic demand from imports to domestic goods. In contrast an appreciation of the real exchange rate makes the domestic exportable goods uncompetitive in the world market and induces a switch of domestic demand from domestic goods to foreign goods. In the lower part of Figure 7.8, the relationship between the real exchange rate and output is shown as an upward sloping curve.

Assume that the negative supply shock shifts the supply curve EAS^0_0 to EAS^1_0. It increases the price level from P_0 to P_1 and the real exchange rate appreciates from R_0 to R_1. The appreciation of the real exchange rate is the result of the increase in the price level due to the supply shock, which has not been associated with an instantaneous depreciation of the currency. However at the price level P_1 the real wage rate (W/P equal to w) has declined because the nominal wage rate has remained unchanged (W_0) due to, say, short-term wage contracts. The fall in the real wage rate from w_0 (equal to W_0/P_0) to w_1 (equal to W_0/P_1) will increase employment and output and the economy will move from E_1 to E_0 alongside a depreciation of the real exchange rate as the price level declines.

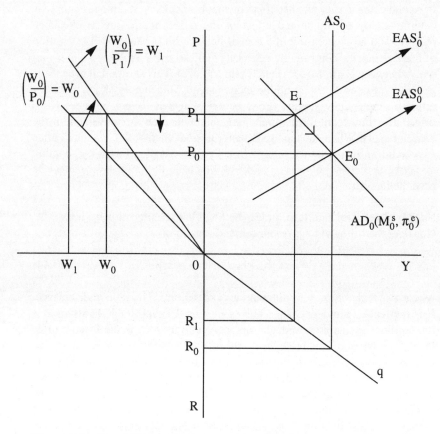

*Figure 7.8   The adjustment of an economy following an adverse supply
            shock under a floating exchange rate system*

The adjustment process discussed above rules out any active government
intervention in the form of monetary policy. An alternative to automatic
adjustment is the adoption of an expansionary monetary policy to expedite
the adjustment process so that the adverse costs of supply shocks are mini-
mized. However any expansion of the money supply will shift the demand
curve rightward and ignite inflation because of the expectations-induced leftward shift of the supply curve and the rightward shift of the demand curve.
Therefore if inflation is a concern to policy-makers, any accommodating
monetary policy would be undesirable after the supply shock.

SUMMARY AND CONCLUSION

This chapter has examined the relationship between money supply growth and inflation. It is found that, although there is no strong relationship between budget deficits and inflation, there is both theoretical and empirical support in favour of a strong relationship between money supply growth and inflation and this relationship is pronounced in developing countries. Having examined some key relationships among money growth, inflation and seigniorage/ inflation tax, this chapter has developed monetary models of inflation under both fixed and flexible exchange rates systems and examined the role of monetary policy in stabilization in developing countries. In the context of the latter the question addressed is whether monetary policy should be, and can be, used for the stabilization of developing economies. A review of the sources of demand disturbances suggests that although there are possibilities of demand disturbances in developing economies originating from both domestic and foreign sources, they are unlikely to be rampant and persistent. The parameter values of the consumption, investment and money demand functions also suggest that developing economies are not highly sensitive to demand shocks. Indeed as the real wage rate and the real interest and exchange rates in developing countries are flexible, it is possible that any demand shocks to developing economies would be adjusted through the price mechanism and there may not be a need for active stabilization by the government. Although demand shocks are not prevalent in developing countries, they frequently experience supply shocks originating from the agricultural sector. However agricultural supply shocks are random and they do not persist.

The question of whether the monetary authority should adopt a hands-on or a hands-off policy has been analysed by applying a model. It is found that the conduct of active monetary policy after a negative supply shock has the danger of igniting inflation. Therefore when the danger of inflation is real after a negative supply shock, the monetary authority may even think of adopting a contractionary monetary policy to dampen inflationary expectations (Barro, 1981; Rivera-Batiz and Rivera-Batiz, 1985).

Given that there exists a relationship between money supply growth and inflation, it is argued that the aim of monetary policy should be to maintain price stability rather than output stabilization. The question is whether monetary targeting can stabilize inflation. It is shown that a money supply growth rule can ensure intertemporal stability in inflation, provided that the country follows a flexible exchange rate system and that there exists a stable money demand function.

NOTES

1. Many developed countries also occasionally resort to money creation as a source of government revenue.
2. There is a subtle difference between inflation tax and seigniorage. Inflation tax refers to capital losses by moneyholders as a result of inflation. Inflation tax revenue (R^{π}) is measured as R^{π} equal to πm, where π is the inflation rate and m is the stock of real money. Seigniorage (S_r) is the revenue collected by the government by exercising its monopoly power to print money. It is measured by the purchasing power of the money which is created and put into circulation in a given period, that is S_r is equal to μm, where μ is the growth rate of nominal money. At the steady state, since the rate of inflation equals the growth rate of nominal money, inflation tax revenue equals the size of seigniorage (Sachs and Larrain, 1993). The rest of the discussion in this section follows with Agenor and Montiel (1996).
3. This discussion follows with Romer (1996).
4. This section draws materials from Hossain and Chowdhury (1996).
5. This section draws materials from Hossain and Chowdhury (1996).
6. This section draws materials from Hossain and Chowdhury (1996).
7. A crop failure will raise the food price and can raise the price level if non-food prices remain unchanged or rise due to people's anticipation of the government's expansionary policies.
8. This section draws materials from Hossain and Chowdhury (1996).

8.   Exchange rate policy

INTRODUCTION

The exchange rate (the price of foreign currency in terms of domestic currency) is one of the most important prices in an open economy. It links the domestic economy with the rest of the world through both the goods and assets markets.[1] Until the 1980s most developing countries maintained multiple exchange rates and controlled foreign exchange to achieve both economic and non-economic objectives. The costs of multiple exchange rate regimes were enormous in terms of resource misallocation, rent seeking, corruption and budget problems (Dornbusch and Kuenzler, 1993).

As indicated in Chapters 2 and 6, the role of the exchange rate in economic management has increased since the generalized floating of the exchange rates of major currencies in 1973. Since then there has been a rapid financial integration of developed and developing economies. This has created both opportunities and challenges for developing countries. Developing countries can now reap the benefits of greater trade opportunities and access to world capital markets, provided that they judiciously use exchange rates as an important instrument of macroeconomic management. This requires the choice of an exchange rate system and involves complex economic and non-economic issues.

After the generalized floating of the exchange rates in 1973, most developing countries opted for an adjustable fixed exchange rate system of one form or other. Since then a large number of developing countries have moved away from a fixed exchange rate system to a more flexible system. Some countries whose currencies were pegged to a single hard currency (for example the US dollar and the British pound sterling) have switched to a composite basket of hard currencies. Some of them have opted for managed floating and even an independently floating exchange rate system (see Table 2.2). This reveals that, instead of reacting passively to fluctuations in the exchange rates of major currencies, developing countries have increased their reliance on flexible exchange rate arrangements under which exchange rates are adjusted frequently or determined by market forces.

There are at least three reasons for the developing countries' switch from fixed to flexible exchange rate arrangements. First, as inflation rates in many developing countries continued to remain at high levels during the 1980s, they allowed their currencies to depreciate to restore external competitiveness. This was part of the general shift in economic policies in developing countries from inward-looking to export-oriented industrialization. Second, the switch from pegging to a flexible exchange rate arrangement was intended to minimize the adverse effects of fluctuations in the exchange rates of major currencies. Third, the move was politically convenient to most governments of developing countries. Aghevli *et al* (1991:3) aptly put it as follows:

> ...given the political stigma attached to devaluation under a pegged regime, an increasing number of countries have found it expedient to adopt a more flexible arrangement for adjusting the exchange rate on the basis of an undisclosed basket of currencies. Such an arrangement enables the authorities to take advantage of the fluctuations in major currencies to camouflage an effective depreciation of their exchange rate, thus avoiding the political repercussions of an announced devaluation.

Although the growing adoption of a flexible exchange rate arrangement by developing countries is a positive development, there has been some criticism of such a policy because it might have caused high inflation in some developing countries through currency depreciation. In a report Aghevli *et al* (1991:13) show that:

> the inflation performance of the countries that have operated under a fixed exchange rate regime has been, on the whole, superior to that of the group operating under more flexible arrangement.

Although this does not necessarily mean that depreciation of the exchange rate causes inflation[2], some IMF Executive Board members have been arguing for fixed exchange rate arrangements for developing countries in the belief that such an arrangement would impose fiscal and monetary discipline and act as nominal anchors (Edwards, 1993b). Their argument is that the adoption of a fixed exchange rate system will induce a government not to undertake the policy of inflationary finance and thereby promote price stability. However the adoption of a fixed exchange rate system does not necessarily lead to low inflation. A fixed exchange rate system which is not backed by strong commitment may be time-inconsistent and hence may lack credibility. In fact, any exchange rate policy in which the government has a discretion to change the nominal exchange rate can lead to high inflation.

In general a fixed exchange rate system reinforces fiscal and monetary discipline in countries which already have a reputation for stability. In countries where such a reputation does not exist, a fixed exchange rate system does not necessarily create fiscal and monetary discipline. In essence the fixed exchange rate system as a contributor to fiscal and monetary discipline is most suitable for countries which need it the least (Edwards, 1993b). It will be argued later that in high inflationary economies, it is desirable to remove government's discretionary power over the exchange rate by fixing it to a stable currency and then leave the exchange rate matters to a currency board independent of the executive branch of the government. This argument is akin to arguments for central bank independence, which are designed to enhance the credibility of government's monetary policy.

THE EXCHANGE RATE AS A PRICE SIGNAL – IS THERE ANY SCOPE FOR MANAGING IT?

In a market economy, prices convey information about the terms on which goods, services and assets are traded and the terms on which purchasing power (income or wealth) can be used to buy them. When markets are efficient, prices reflect all available information. Financial markets are treated as efficient markets, although some studies have reported statistical evidence of deviations from efficiency. Even if prices do not always embody or convey perfect information, they are not 'noise' if market forces, rather than official decrees, determine prices. This is an explanation of why economists in general assign an important role to prices in the efficient allocation of resources. If it is accepted that prices contain valuable information that allocates resources in a market economy, the management of such prices by an outside body is somewhat contradictory. Nevertheless many prominent economists advocate managing exchange rates, even though exchange rates are key prices in an open economy. As the generalized floating has allegedly caused excess volatility in exchange rates, Kenen (1988:19,20,22,42) has provided some economic arguments for exchange rate management:

> Those who 'produce' exchange rates in the foreign-exchange market are differently motivated from those who 'consume' them in the markets for goods, services, and long-term assets. Furthermore, exchange rates are very flexible, like other asset prices, whereas goods prices are sticky, so that nominal and real exchange rates move together.... the stickiness of goods prices that makes the exchange-rate regime important. When nominal exchange rates affect real rates, they also affect economic activity – its level, location, and composition.... The core of the case for exchange-rate management is the sad but simple fact that policies and markets are imperfect and interact in costly ways under floating rates... floating exchange rates have been more costly than expected because they have produced large changes in real exchange rates, which have in turn produced large changes in output and trade patterns and intensified protectionism.

These are rather forceful arguments against any floating exchange rate system but they are not new. Kenen's recent arguments for exchange rate management are a reiteration of the conventional view that market determined exchange rates are prone to excess volatility which can damage the real economy. Recall that this was precisely the reason behind the adoption of the fixed exchange rate system under the Bretton Woods Agreement in 1944. At that time, Nurkse (1944:210–211) wrote about three disadvantages of the flexible exchange rate system:

> In the first place, they create an element of risk which tends to discourage international trade. The risk may be covered by 'hedging' operations where a forward exchange market exists; but such insurance, if obtainable at all, is obtainable only at a price and therefore generally adds to the cost of trading... Secondly, as a means of adjusting the balance of payments, exchange fluctuations involve constant shifts of labour and other resources between production for the home market and production for export. Such shifts may be costly and disturbing; they tend to create frictional unemployment, and are obviously wasteful if the exchange-market conditions that call for them are temporary... Thirdly, ... fluctuating exchanges cannot always be relied upon to promote adjustment. Any considerable or continuous movement of the exchange rate is liable to generate anticipations of a further movement in the same direction, thus giving rise to speculative capital transfers of a disequilibrating kind... Self-aggravating movements of this kind, instead of promoting adjustment in the balance of payments, are apt to intensify any initial disequilibrium and to produce what may be called 'explosive' conditions of instability.

Proponents of fixed exchange rates for developing countries have an additional argument that, as exchange markets in developing countries are thin, market determined exchange rates are most likely to fluctuate excessively and thereby adversely affect the real economy. Apparently this is a valid argument against a floating exchange rate system. However proponents of a flexible exchange rate system challenge such a view by making the point that the alleged excess volatility of the exchange rates is not a phenomenon which could be found only in underdeveloped exchange markets. They add that in a comparison of the volatility in one system with the wasteful resource allocation in the other, why should one conclude that volatility is the worse evil? Importantly, any excess volatility of the exchange rates in developing countries could be the result of macroeconomic policy mismanagement rather than the characteristic of a flexible exchange rate system. If there is monetary and fiscal policy discipline and if economic fundamentals, such as the terms of trade, vary little, speculation could be easy and stabilizing. In contrast if economic policies respond to both internal and external shocks and speculators start guessing policy-makers' responses, the economy is unlikely to have a stable anchor and any levels of wages, prices and exchange rates are equally plausible. This will create volatility not only in the exchange rates but also in wages and prices and thereby interfere with economic performance. In essence the debate is not merely whether a flexible exchange rate system

creates excessive fluctuations in the exchange rates; there are more fundamental issues related to the conduct of macroeconomic policy in developing
countries. This led Quirk (1995:43) to remark that: 'Variability is not always
a bad thing; in many cases, it represents desirable [economic] adjustments'.

As mentioned in Chapter 2, Dornbusch and Kuenzler (1993:120) have
suggested a compromise solution in the debate on the fixed versus flexible
exchange rate. According to them a developing country may adopt a system
of dual exchange rates: an official fixed rate that applies to most trade transactions and a financial or free rate at which all other transactions take place.
Their argument for such a system is as follows:

> The chief benefit of a dual-rate system is avoiding situations in which transitory
> shocks in the capital account significantly affect the exchange rate and hence
> prices and wages. Such a situation might be one in which a temporary event (say,
> political uncertainty or uncertainty about future oil prices) leads to capital flight
> and then the need to devalue the exchange rate. If the exchange rate and prices and
> wages come to be driven by portfolio holders' expectations and the price and
> wage adjustments lead to expectations of further depreciation, the economy easily
> loses the anchor of nominal stability. If capital flows are potentially unstable and
> wages and prices are extremely responsive to movements in the nominal exchange
> rate, and if controlling capital flows is nearly impossible, then dual rates are
> probably the only modus vivendi.

APPROACHES TO EXCHANGE RATE POLICY[3]

There are two broad approaches to the conduct of exchange rate policy in
developing countries: the real targets approach and the nominal anchor approach. In the real targets approach the nominal exchange rate is a policy
instrument distinct from domestic monetary and fiscal policies. This instrument can be varied to attain real objectives along the lines suggested by the
internal-external balance model. For example, as discussed in Chapter 3 the
Swan-Salter model suggests that when a country faces a current account
deficit, the real exchange rate needs depreciating, along with an appropriate
reduction in absorption, to correct it. This approach is Keynesian in spirit.
The government is trusted to make use of the exchange rate and other policies.

Recall that this approach hinges on three main assumptions. First, nominal
wages and prices of non-tradables are sluggish. This will cause a reduction in
real wages in terms of tradables after nominal devaluation and thereby cause
a real devaluation. Second, real devaluations have significant real effects (for
example, increase in net exports). Third, the economy is subject to real
shocks, originating domestically or externally, which differ from the shocks
faced by its trading partners.

The nominal anchor approach suggests that a country's exchange rate should be firmly and credibly fixed to the currency of a low-inflation country, so that the low inflation will, in effect, be imported. It constrains domestic monetary policy, restrains governments and sends out credible signals to private agents about prospects of inflation. An implication is that, if the signals are clear and credible, the real economy will adjust appropriately to any shocks, including anti-inflationary exchange rate policy. Within this approach, to maintain competitiveness the exchange rate leads rather than follows other nominal variables, such as domestic price and wage inflation. Thus this approach is essentially a version of monetarism, namely international monetarism.

For this approach to be successful there are four requirements. First, there should be a firm commitment to maintain the exchange rate so that it brings about discipline in credit creation, especially credit for the public sector. As Corden (1991) puts it, in the nominal-anchor approach the exchange rate leads and fiscal policy (insofar as budget deficits are monetized) follows, whereas in the real-targets approach fiscal policy leads and the exchange rate follows. Second, the exchange rate commitment must be credible in the foreign exchange market. Third, the commitment must be credible in the labour market. Fourth, rigidities in the labour market must not prevent necessary real adjustments (that is, decline in nominal wages relative to trend) in response to adverse shocks that require real devaluations.

There is no general case supporting the real targets approach or the nominal anchor approach to exchange rate policy. There are two major arguments in favour of the nominal anchor approach. First, high inflationary countries (for example, Latin America) should have an anchor against inflation, which would require a nominal anchor approach to exchange rate policy. Second, smaller economies, which have a smaller share of nontradables in total output, may have a lesser ability to bring about real devaluations with nominal devaluations.

Although these two arguments are convincing, there are two points that may strengthen the case for a real targets approach. First, the shocks that most developing countries face (for example the terms of trade) require a real exchange rate devaluation. Second, in the absence of an exchange rate instrument, most developing countries which still have trade restrictions as policy instruments may use them in the event of balance-of-payments crises.

The next section will review the political economy of inflation and make the point that the benefits of a firm and credible fixed exchange rate system are largely restricted to high inflationary developing economies. Most Asian developing countries with low inflation may be better off if they adopt a real targets approach to maintain their external competitiveness. Using the Swan diagram below, it can be shown that if a country keeps the real exchange rate close to its equilibrium real exchange rate, it may conduct an active demand management policy to restore any internal and external imbalance.

The Swan Diagram

In the diagram, shown in Figure 8.1, the IB schedule (which is downward sloping from left to right) represents combinations of the real exchange rate (domestic currency units per unit of foreign currency) and domestic absorption (the sum of consumption, investment and government expenditure) for which the economy is in internal balance, that is, there is full employment with stable prices. To the right of (left of) the IB schedule there is an inflationary (deflationary) pressure on the economy because, for a given real exchange rate, domestic absorption is greater (lower) than what is required to

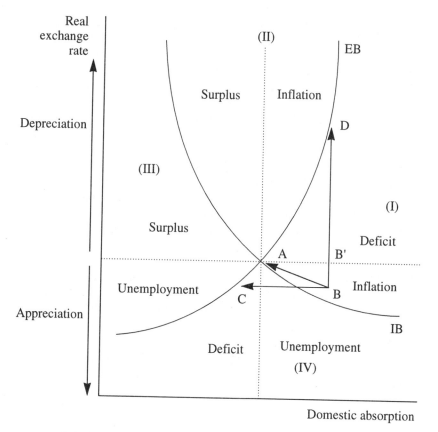

Figure 8.1   The Swan diagram

achieve full employment. The EB schedule, which is upward sloping from left to right, shows combinations of the real exchange rate and domestic absorption for which the economy is in external balance (that is, there is equilibrium in the current account). To the right of (left of) the EB schedule there is a current account deficit (surplus) because, for a given real exchange rate, domestic absorption is greater (lower) than what is required for equilibrium in the current account. The point A where the IB and EB schedules intersect represents both internal and external balance in the economy. All other positions represent disequilibrium or what Swan calls 'four zones of economic unhappiness'.

Assume that a developing economy experiences both inflation and current account deficit problems. This is shown at the point B, the result of, say, an expansionary fiscal policy. Two dotted lines that cross each other at the point A divide the two halves of each zone and suggest the plausible causes of disequilibrium and appropriate policies to correct it.

As the point B is to the right of the IB schedule and lies below the horizontal dotted line, the currency is overvalued and real expenditure is above the level required to bring internal equilibrium. This suggests that in order to bring the economy back to point A, the authorities need to reduce real domestic expenditure and devalue the currency. The use of only one instrument – real exchange rate or domestic expenditure – although it may solve the current account deficit problem, will create unemployment in the case of a large cut in real expenditure, or further inflation in the case of a real devaluation. For example if the authorities maintain the given real exchange rate and try to reduce the current account deficit by cutting back domestic real expenditure, the economy will move toward point C. Although this will solve the current account deficit problem, the economy will be pushed into a recession with resulting unemployment. On the other hand if the authorities do not cut back domestic real expenditure but devalue the currency, the economy will move toward point D. Although this will solve the current account deficit problem, it will create further inflation as the economy moves further away from the IB schedule. Corden (1991) argues that it is wrong in this situation to advocate devaluation without the assurance that adequate fiscal contraction will also take place. Note that where there is any disequilibrium on the dotted lines, the authorities can use a single instrument to achieve both internal and external balance. For example at the disequilibrium point B', the authorities are able to solve both inflation and current account deficit problems by cutting back domestic real expenditure. This shows that as long as the real exchange rate remains close to the equilibrium real exchange rate, the authorities can use expenditure-changing policies to bring both internal and external balance.

THE POLITICAL ECONOMY OF INFLATION

The merit of adopting a firm and credible fixed exchange rate system in developing countries is that the authorities in those countries are tempted to misuse their fiscal and monetary discretion. In the literature this issue is discussed within the perspective of the political economy of inflation. Persson and Tabellini (1990) find that there is a close relationship between the degree of political instability and polarization and the reliance on inflation tax: countries which are politically unstable have a higher proclivity towards inflation (Chapter 7).

Edwards and Tabellini (1991) have devised an index to measure the degree of political instability and they found that Asian nations tend to have a lower degree of political instability compared with that observed in Latin America. Therefore Asian countries have less temptation to misuse their fiscal and monetary discretion and the benefits associated with fixed exchange rates would be smaller in those countries compared with Latin American countries. As Singapore shows, Asian countries may be better off by adopting a system of crawling peg or adjustable fixed rate. In contrast if a country is characterized by political instability and shows a lack of fiscal-monetary discipline, a fixed exchange rate offers a better choice as it may remove the discretion from the monetary authority and that may impose fiscal discipline. As Corden (1991:233) points out, this may also enhance credibility:

> The case in favor of using the exchange rate as the nominal anchor is that it is a very visible, very well-defined anchor, which increases the likelihood that private agents will adjust quickly. It is much more visible, and so more credible, than a money supply or nominal expenditure target or a more general anti-inflation commitment. Its visibility is strengthened when the exchange rate is fixed to a particular currency, such as the dollar, rather than to a basket of currencies.

Thus the key question is credibility. Establishing credibility is difficult in countries where the government has a long history of expansionary policies and high inflation. Aghevli *et al* (1991) suggest that a pegged exchange rate does not necessarily impose financial discipline if the government retains the option of periodically devaluing the currency. To make it costly for the government to engage in expansionary policies, they suggest institutional changes, including the establishment of an independent central bank or a currency union. This has led many Latin American observers to recommend a currency board. There follows a brief discussion on currency boards, which may be an effective way of limiting the discretionary power of government in the making of monetary and fiscal policy.

A currency board is an independent organisation with an exclusive authority to create base money. This is done entirely by the buying and selling of foreign exchange at a fixed rate. The currency board must keep the exchange rate convertible and must back the base money by at least 100 per cent in foreign exchange reserves. Therefore under a currency board system, the money supply is wholly determined by the balance of payments.

Although currency boards were common in colonial territories but fell into disuse when colonial regimes were dismantled, some high inflationary countries (for example Argentina) have used currency boards in recent years as a means of stabilizing their currencies and of bringing monetary and fiscal discipline. For example one of the important conditions is that there will be no lending by the currency board to the government. With a pure currency board arrangement, the authorities also have no freedom to influence interest rates through open market operations. In general the interest rates tend to follow those of the peg currency, although the inflation rate somewhat deviates when the peg currency is that of an industrial country and the currency board is for a developing country (Bennett, 1995).

Clearly the currency board is an extreme form of monetary arrangement and it imposes monetary discipline by removing the discretion from the monetary authority, thereby establishing price stability. However there is a trade-off. As pointed out by Drake (1969, 1980), the currency board system will have a contractionary bias since the money supply cannot expand in step with growing domestic production. This problem does not arise if there is a secular growth of external reserves through a trade surplus and/or net capital inflows. In essence, given the restrictive nature, currency boards are particularly appropriate for high inflationary developing countries as they may be effective in bringing monetary and fiscal discipline.

MAINTAINING COMPETITIVENESS

As indicated earlier, although fiscal and monetary policy discipline is important and it must be maintained, the prime goal of developing countries should be to maintain external competitiveness as part of their drive for outward-oriented industrialization. This section discusses the issues related to the conduct of a real exchange rate policy for the purpose of maintaining international competitiveness.

There is overwhelming evidence that a persistent real exchange rate overvaluation can cause major damage to a country's real economy. Dornbusch (1993a) suggests that one should add Fischer's (1987) rule: 'don't overvalue the exchange rate' with Harberger's (1984) 'thirteen rules' for good economic policy management. Pfeffermann (1985), in the context of developing countries, has outlined the following seven propositions that highlight the principal consequences of overvaluation of the exchange rate. According to him, overvalued exchange rates:

1. undermine exports,
2. harm agriculture,
3. stimulate imports,
4. destabilize the capital account and often precipitate debt crisis,
5. breed protection against imports,
6. do not help curb inflation and
7. promote rent-seeking economies.

This shows the importance of attaining and maintaining a competitive real exchange rate which is consistent with an open and liberal trade regime. If an economy is not highly inflationary and there are checks and balances in maintaining prudent monetary and fiscal policies, one can argue for a real exchange rate rule under which the nominal exchange rate is adjusted continuously and automatically so as to maintain the real exchange rate close to its equilibrium level. The major benefit of such a rule is to prevent the emergence of large and sustained misalignments of relative prices and thereby avoid an external imbalance. The difficulty in adopting such a rule is the determination of the equilibrium real exchange rate, which is sensitive to domestic and external shocks, both temporary and permanent, to the economy (Edwards, 1989). It is argued that in view of the frequency and severity of both external and internal shocks to which many developing economies are frequently subjected, the pursuit of real exchange rate targets could involve the risk of high inflation and macroeconomic instability.

This concern provides some justification for retaining a role for the exchange rate as a nominal anchor by requiring that at least some of the burden of adjustment in the real exchange rate be borne by changes in the domestic price level brought about through restrictive financial policies, rather than by an automatic adjustment in the nominal exchange rate (Aghevli, Khan and Montiel, 1991). Intal (1992) shows that most of the Asian and Pacific economies have successfully adjusted their nominal exchange rates with complementary fiscal and monetary policies during the period 1975 to 1990. In fact the Swan diagram shows that as long as the real exchange rate remains close to the equilibrium real exchange rate, the authorities can use expenditure-changing policies to bring about both internal and external balance.

SUMMARY AND CONCLUSION

This chapter has reviewed key issues in exchange rate policy in developing countries. Since the mid-1980s most developing countries have faced major macroeconomic problems such as high inflation, large current account deficits and slow economic growth, and have been actively using an exchange rate policy, along with fiscal and monetary policies, to achieve both internal and external balance. This is reflected in the fact that since the mid-1980s most developing countries have switched from a fixed to a more flexible exchange rate arrangement. Although such a switch might have caused an acceleration of inflation in some countries, it has allowed those countries to adjust their exchange rates to improve the current account balance position. In general the growing adoption of a flexible exchange rate arrangement has been a positive development. Some doubts remain however whether a flexible exchange rate policy is appropriate for high inflationary countries. The brief discussion on the political economy of inflation suggests that high inflation is linked with political instability and a pegged or fixed exchange rate system does not necessarily lead to fiscal discipline and price stability. The government needs to establish credibility, which is difficult in high inflationary countries unless there are institutional changes to bring monetary-fiscal discipline. There are suggestions that the establishment of a currency board may create credibility.

Having highlighted the difficulties in establishing credibility and achieving price stability in high inflationary countries, this chapter has found that there is a growing consensus that, as a persistently overvalued exchange rate policy can cause major damage to any economy whether it is a fixed or adjustable exchange rate system, the suggested policy rule should be to avoid a cumulative overvaluation through a policy of devaluation that keeps the real exchange rate closely aligned with its fundamentals. In fact by examining the advantages and disadvantages of exchange rate policy in developing countries, Corden (1991:240–241) has made the following recommendations:

> First, in general, the real-targets approach to exchange rate policy is the right one. The exchange rate should follow rather than lead, taking into account the various shocks or changes in other variables – notably fiscal policy, trade policy and terms of trade changes. Second, exchange rate policy should be associated with an appropriate non-inflationary monetary policy.... Third, because of capital mobility, delayed exchange rate adjustments must be avoided; if the rate needs to be changed, it should be done quickly. Fourth, there is some role for the nominal-anchor approach for two groups of countries, which are at opposite extremes of the inflation scale. One group includes countries that have long-established fixed exchange rate systems (with occasional devaluations) and relatively non-inflationary records. These countries may be well advised to stay with such a system, since their commitment will be credible. ... At the other extreme are countries with a

history of high inflation that are ready to stabilize by radically shifting their policies and making the necessary commitment. These countries may find a fixed exchange rate (or an active crawling peg) a valuable anchor in helping to constrain government monetary policies and in achieving credibility with the markets (including the labor market).

NOTES

1. In the goods market the exchange rate is the link between domestic and world prices of tradable goods. For example PT is equal to e PT^f, where PT is the price of tradable goods in the domestic market, 'e' is units of domestic currency per unit of foreign currency, and PT^f is the price of tradable goods in the world market. This shows that, given the price of tradable goods in the world market, the price of those goods in the domestic market is proportionally linked with the exchange rate. This linkage can be formalized in terms of the real exchange rate, defined according to the purchasing power parity approach as R equal to e P^f/P^d, where P^f is the foreign price level and P^d is the domestic price level. The real exchange rate is interpreted as one measure of competitiveness as it shows the price of domestic goods in terms of foreign goods. With an appreciation (depreciation) of the real exchange rate the prices of domestic goods in terms of foreign goods rise (fall) and this weakens (improves) the competitiveness of the domestic economy.

   In addition to the goods market, domestic and foreign asset markets are linked through the exchange rate. This can be expressed by showing a link between the domestic and foreign interest rates: r_d is equal to $r_f + x$, where r_d is the domestic currency interest rate, r_f is the foreign currency interest rate, and x is the expected rate of depreciation of domestic currency. In the absence of controls over capital mobility, domestic investors compare the rates of return on domestic and foreign currency denominated assets and choose the one which is relatively attractive. For example if $r_d > r_f + x$, domestic currency denominated assets would be competitive. If this condition did not hold, then domestic investors would prefer to hold foreign currency denominated assets. When the rate of return on domestic assets remains persistently lower than that of foreign assets, the result could be capital flight and loss of resources for investment. For further discussion see Dornbusch and Kuenzler (1993).

2. Exchange rate changes do not have a permanent effect on the inflation rate but cause temporary changes. Once the exchange rate of the currency stops appreciating or depreciating, its direct effect on domestic inflation tends towards zero. Hafer (1989) argues that the depreciation of the exchange rate and the acceleration of inflation may be the manifestation of the same thing, namely the rise in the growth rate of the money supply.

3. This discussion is based on Corden (1991, 1993).

4. Corden (1991) points out that although a nominal exchange rate commitment imposes a constraint on an expansionary fiscal-monetary policy, there are two ways governments may try to evade this constraint, albeit temporarily. First, governments may impose tight import restrictions. Second, governments may run down reserves and/or finance current account deficits with foreign borrowing.

9. The political economy of macroeconomic management: the need for institutional change

INTRODUCTION

The central puzzle of human history is to account for the widely divergent paths of historical change. How have societies diverged? What accounts for their widely disparate performance characteristics? ... Although we do observe some convergence ... the gap between rich and poor nations, between developed and underdeveloped nations, is as wide today as it ever was and perhaps a great deal wider than ever before. What explains the divergence? And perhaps equally important, what conditions either lead to further divergences or produce convergence?
North (1990:6–7)

The above questions have two implications in the context of the present volume. First, what macroeconomic policy mix is conducive to economic growth? Second, why do governments of some countries adopt the optimal policy mix and others do not? The previous chapters have addressed the first question with regard to open developing economies. One consistent theme that emerged is that the growth of real income and the overall macroeconomic stability – both internal and external – are mutually interdependent and both form an integral part of an adequate, consistently sustained process of economic development. The simple policy rules that follow are:

1. Prolonged and pronounced inflationary deficit financing must be excluded as a deliberate instrument of growth.
2. Monetary policy should be directed to price stability and should not be used for short-term output stabilization.
3. Adjustment to external shocks requires both absorption and production responses and must not be delayed.
4. The exchange rate must not be misaligned or over-valued for a prolonged period.

This concluding chapter will attempt to address the second question, that is, what distinguishes the countries that succeeded by following the optimal policy mix from those which did not. Perhaps it is useful at this juncture to refer to the experience of the successful countries of Asia. Clearly the vast majority of developing economies have failed to lift their economic growth and living standard compared with a small group of Asian economies which excelled. In just over two decades the dynamic Asian economies were able to catch up their former colonial masters while others stagnated. Two distinguishing economic features of these successful economies stand out: (1) openness or 'neutral' trade regime and (2) active government intervention.

The neoclassical economists (for example Balassa, 1968; Bhagwati, 1978; Krueger, 1978; Little, 1979) emphasize the role of openness. On the other hand there is a body of literature (for example Amsden, 1989, 1982; Lee, 1992; Sachs, 1987; Wade, 1990) which emphasizes the role active government intervention played in achieving late industrialization. While both have some elements of truth, overemphasis of one or the other misses important issues. For example the neoclassical economists are not at ease with the coexistence of high import protection with export orientation and active government non-price interventions with market-oriented policies in some of these economies. On the other hand the 'statists'' explanation of why state interventions did not go fatally wrong in these economies as in other developing countries depends crucially on the state being 'strong'. More fundamentally though, they cannot explain how a 'strong' state emerges and why some strong dictators (such as Marcos or Idi Amin) did not maintain macroeconomic stability and wrecked their economies. One important shortcoming of both explanations is an inadequate focus on institutions. None of these approaches takes into account the formal and informal constraints and rigidities in which policymaking occurs. This chapter reflects on institutional frameworks that are likely to induce the optimal macroeconomic policy response by the government.

INSTITUTIONS AND ORGANIZATIONS

Nobel Laureate economist Douglass North (1990:4) defines institutions as 'any form of constraint that human beings devise to shape human interactions'. They are designed to reduce uncertainty. Institutions can be both formal and informal. The institution of property rights is an example of formal constraints while a whole gamut of socio-religious and cultural norms define informal constraints or codes of behaviour on human interactions. For institutions to be meaningful there must be strict enforcement. That is, violation of rules and codes of behaviour must attract costly and credible sanctions.

North (1990, 1995) also distinguishes institutions from organizations. According to North (1995:23) 'Organizations are players: groups of individuals bound by a common purpose to achieve objectives. They include political bodies (political parties, the senate, a city council, a regulatory agency), social bodies (churches, clubs, athletic associations), and educational bodies (schools, colleges, vocational training centres)'. Organizations 'provide structure to human interaction' (North, 1990:4). They are created in response to the opportunity set defined by both formal and informal rules of behaviour or institutions. The two great organizations that human beings developed are markets and governments. Markets are composed of such organizations (players) as consumers, employers' associations, labour unions, regulatory agencies, etc. Interactions within markets are generally governed by informal rules, reinforced by formal property rights. On the other hand the organizational branches of government (such as the Parliament, local councils or regulatory bodies) are predominantly guided by formal rules, supplemented by informal norms.

Although organizations are created in response to institutional constraints, they are interlinked and influence each other. In the absence of appropriate institutions, organizations can fail in the sense that the outcome of human interactions within that organization is socially non-optimal. For example it is well known that if property rights are not well defined, markets can fail. Macroeconomic imbalances such as unemployment or stagnation are examples of market failures. The organization of government is created to provide formal constraints in order to prevent market failures. For example, the Parliament enacts laws to define property rights or to achieve full employment. Central banks are created, among other things, for the prudential regulation of the banking market. Thus government interventions are seen as necessary for the rectification of market failures. However it can be argued that government interventions such as the minimum wage legislation or the existence of strong interest group organizations such as trade unions are themselves the sources of market failures such as unemployment.

In the context of developing countries, government interventions are traditionally justified on the grounds of markets' inability to generate socially desirable income distribution and investment. Thus the predominant paradigm in the 1950s and 1960s was the primacy of governments over markets. However it was not realized that paradoxically the supremacy of governments and market interventions can sow the seeds of 'government failures'. Large government budget deficits and the consequent high inflation and external imbalance are examples of government failures.

SOURCES OF GOVERNMENT FAILURES

At least four sources of government failures can be identified:

1. lack of administrative capacity,

2.   overzealous government rules and regulations,
3.   rent-seeking behaviour and
4.   inefficient political cycles.

Most developing countries are not endowed with a large pool of skilled administrators or bureaucrats. In addition, the lack of sufficient training can lead to a limited capacity to interpret and enforce rules and regulations.

Even when there is an élite bureaucracy, it cannot be assumed that state officials, who as private citizens maximize their own welfare, would behave in the interests of the nation inside the public office. Quite often the predatory behaviour of state officials can lead to a degree of state intervention that is in excess of the socially optimal level. Thus cascading regulations can be found whose usefulness is not clear even to regulators. They only serve as instruments of corruption by officials and rent-seeking activities of the private sector. In the words of North (1990: 110):

> If organizations – firms, trade unions, farm groups, political parties and congressional committees, to name a few – devote their efforts to *unproductive activity*, the institutional constraints have provided the incentive structure for such activity. Third World countries are poor because the institutional constraints define a set of payoffs to political/economic activity that do not encourage productive activity.

The preoccupation of market's inability to generate equitable income distribution and adequate employment quite often conflates the distinction between social and economic objectives. Public sector enterprises (PSEs) are thus not required to operate on strict commercial principles as long as they achieve 'social objectives'. The conflicting social and economic objectives can potentially lead to a lack of accountability and a 'soft budget constraint'. The bailing out of loss-making PSEs is one of the main reasons for the persistence of large government budget deficits. This also allows the management to hide inefficiency/incompetence and corruption and political patronage. Bardhan (1988:221) paints a vivid picture of such events in India:

> ... the deliberate promotion of trade unions affiliated to the ruling political party has often led to damaging union rivalries and irresponsible 'economism.' Overstaffing, 'featherbedding,' fake payrolls, absenteeism in regular hours, working only for 'overtime' payments and other irregularities are condoned, if not actively encouraged, by trade unions and their political bosses, who cite flagrant cases of corruption, political patronage and cronyism at the top in many public enterprises. Irresponsibilities at the managerial, technical and worker levels thus feed on each other, creating a general atmosphere of demoralization and parasitism on the state. Plundering of public sector produced goods by agents of influential politicians in collaboration with public enterprise staff, private contractors and the criminal underworld is also far too common. Thus, a regime of clientelist machine politics, fostered by a flabby and heterogeneous dominant coalition pre-

occupied with an anarchical grabbing of public resources, has choked off efficient management and utilization of capital in the public sector.

Next we focus on the issue of macroeconomic performance in the presence of inefficient political cycles which arise from either vote-maximizing behaviour of politicians or legitimacy crisis of the regime. According to 'opportunistic' models, the policymakers maximize their probability of re-election only, or the probability of 'survival' in office (see Nordhaus, 1975; Lindbeck, 1976). In 'partisan' models, political parties in office follow policies which are favourable to their constituencies (see Hibbs, 1977). Both kinds of models of political cycles are relevant for developing countries.

Let us begin with countries which have some form of democracy. The partisan models are most applicable to such countries. If these countries are characterized by a high degree of political polarization, dominated by left-wing politics, then distributional considerations are likely to get preference over strict economic rationalism. The policy framework that emerges can be categorized as 'macroeconomic populism'. Dornbusch and Edwards (1990) describe macroeconomic populism as a set of policies which emphasize reactivation, redistribution of income and restructuring of the economy. However populist economic policies result in large government budget deficits, high inflation and unsustainable external imbalance, so that they hurt the very section of the populace who were supposed to be favoured in the first place. Thus the disillusion results in the replacement of the populist regime with right wing regimes which attempt to reverse the populist policy framework. This often means very conservative economic policy with considerable costs.

Thus there is a positive relationship between political and social polarization and the variability of macroeconomic policies. In the words of Alesina (1992:17):

> These macroeconomic policy cycles often introduce a very large variance and unpredictability in expectations of future policies. Such uncertainty is likely to be associated with poor economic performance by making long run planning more difficult. Recent results ... suggest links between the degree of political uncertainty and instability and the level of investments and growth in large samples of countries.

The opportunistic model is more appropriate to countries with dictators. When dictators suffer from the legitimacy crisis and are in danger of being overthrown, they adopt opportunistic policies. One main feature of such policies is 'favour-buying' and large military expenditure which results in large budget deficits. Thus the end result of both macroeconomic populism and opportunism is the same – large budget deficits, high inflation and balance of payments crises.

The situation becomes worse if the dictator is convinced that the overthrow of the regime is imminent and his time horizon in office is very short. The collapsing dictator will do 'anything' and responsible macroeconomic management will be secondary to his political and physical survival (Alesina, 1992). As the time in office gets shorter, the dictator may simply choose to steal the country's wealth for his personal and friends' gain (Marcos of the Philippines and Mobutu of Zaire are clear examples). This means that new democracies often face very difficult economic problems.

The Nature of State and Macroeconomic Performance

The preceding discussion shows that a state can be either strong or weak. A weak state is one where government failures are large and widespread. Furthermore there is no correspondence between the types of government and the nature of a state. Government failures can be rampant in both democracies and dictatorships. Hence one can find weak states in both democracies and dictatorial regimes.

Table 9.1 provides a typology of states. It shows that when a democratic or a dictatorial government is strong *vis-à-vis* its relations with the private sector (market), then the state can be characterized as a 'developmental' or 'technocratic' state. The economic policy framework can be classified as 'state capitalism', which includes a strong public sector operating under strict commercial principles. These economies display superior macroeconomic performance. When a democratic or dictatorial government is weak, one obtains either a regulatory or an oligarchic state where rent seeking and cronyism is rampant, resulting in inferior macroeconomic performance.

Table 9.1   Political system and the nature of state

	Strong State	Weak State
Democratic Government	Developmental State (State capitalism)	Regulatory State (Rent seeking)
Dictatorial/Patrimonial Government	Technocratic State (State capitalism)	Oligarchic State (Booty capitalism)

Note: The outcome is in the parenthesis.

Source: Adapted from Hutchcroft (1994)

Table 9.2 draws on the experience of Asian countries and classifies the nature of these states. As can be seen from Table 9.2 the macroeconomic

Table 9.2   Classification of Asian states

	Political system	Nature of state	State involvement in economy	Macroeconomic performance
Malaysia, Singapore	Semi-democracies	Strong state, developmental	Large public sector, venture capital	High growth, low inflation and sustainable external account
South Korea, Taiwan	Dictatorial/ transitional democracies	Strong state, technocratic	Strong planning agencies, industry policy	High growth, low inflation and sustainable external account
India	Democracy	Weak state	Large public sector, government controls and repression	Low growth, repressed inflation, unsustainable external account
Philippines	Dictatorial/ transitional democracies	Weak state, patrimonial	State patronization of cronies	Low growth, high inflation and unsustainable external account

performance of weak states, whether democracies or dictatorial, is inferior to strong states for the reasons explained in the preceding section. Figure 9.1 is a flow chart that summarises the nexus between the weak state and macroeconomic performance. This shows that both populist (under democracies) and opportunist (under dictatorial regimes) policies are characterized by large budget deficits financed by money creation. The end result of both is macroeconomic crisis. Thus the key to macroeconomic stability lies in ensuring responsible government budget.

THE NEED FOR INSTITUTIONAL CHANGE

The above typology of political system-state-economic performance nexus reveals that there can be various combinations of the nature of state and political system and each combination would create a particular form of economic system. As there is no one-to-one relationship between the political system and the nature of state, it is somewhat naive to assume that an authoritarian system will automatically produce a 'strong state'. Whether a

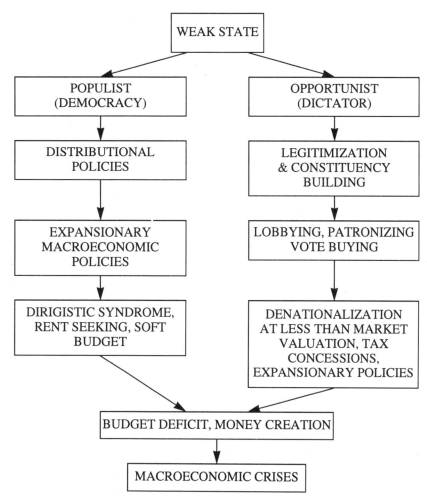

Figure 9.1   Weak state and macroeconomic performance

state is going to be strong or weak depends much on its historical, cultural, and geopolitical factors. Given the nature of human fallibility it is safer to advocate a democratic system, as the alternative to 'bourgeois democracy', as Kohli (1988:5) points out, is not likely to be revolutionary socialism but counter-revolutionary authoritarianism that carries a much higher risk akin to 'putting all one's eggs in one basket'. However since a democratic system is vulnerable to both rent- seeking and pork-barrel politics, one cannot exaggerate the importance of institution building. Importantly, as Bardhan (1988:214) points out in the context of India where poverty is massive and inequality in income and wealth is perverse, a democratic system has the danger of being rejected by the people for an alternative:

> ... a country where the ideal of equal access of all to some basic political rights clearly conflicts with what may have been history's most elaborate and well-entrenched ideological system of legitimizing social inequality, one would think that the tendency for the body politic to reject the foreign transplant would be rather strong. Moreover, faced with such massive and excruciating poverty, people are apt to be impatient with the slow processes of democracy and to find arguments for alternative systems compelling.

In the 1970s and 1980s when the damage due to government failures became well known, the response was a wholesale assault on the government both from outside and within. At the intellectual front the challenge was mounted by the rational expectations revolution and the political charge was led by the Thatcher-Reagan axis. At the international level the assault on big government came from the IMF and the World Bank. This rejection of government and the reliance on free market philosophy was described by Killick (1988) as a 'reaction too far'. Stiglitz (1990) has summarized the debate between *laissez-faire* and the role of the government and argued that in the presence of asymmetric information there is a role for government.

Thus in the presence of imperfect political climate and market imperfections, there is a need for building institutions that will minimize both market and government failures. Three important organizational branches of government that affect macroeconomic policy configurations are the bureaucracy, the central bank and the parliament. The experience of East Asian newly industrializing economies shows that a strong and élite bureaucracy can prevent governments from adopting expansionary populist or opportunist policies by exposing their economic costs (World Bank, 1993). Thus the creation of a strong administrative capacity is one of the founding blocs of a 'good state' (Dornbusch, 1993b). Therefore institutional change must start with administrative reform. It is paramount that a meritocratic civil bureaucracy recruited through a highly competitive examination is ensured. This must be boosted with the provision of a high quality training programme to enhance the administrative capacity.

The above also points to the need to keep the size of government small. The government should intervene only when there is a clearly defined market failure and concentrate on areas where it has a clear advantage, such as the maintenance of law and order, the enforcement of property rights and the provision of infrastructure. At this juncture it is worth emphasizing the role of the state in establishing the rule of law. In many developing countries the legal system is not only archaic but also has a judiciary which is not independent of the executive branch of the government. This compounds the market failure as politicians interfere with the operation of the private sector. Thus administrative reform must be supplemented by reform of the legal system. Once the property rights are clearly defined and enforced by an independent judiciary, the area where government interventions are genuinely required becomes limited.

Where government interventions are necessary, market based instruments (price) should be given priority over quantitative restrictions as a general principle. There is also a need for rules to be simplified and the objectives of such rules to be made clear. For example if a fine is designed with the objective of law enforcement, it should not be mixed up with the government's revenue earning aims. Furthermore the government departments must have clear demarcation of functions and should not have both social and economic objectives, which are often conflicting. This will enhance accountability and transparency and thereby remove the root cause of inefficiencies in public sector enterprises. When an organization is given multiple and often conflicting objectives, there will obviously be trade-offs. However how this trade-off is weighed often remains vague. When one takes into account the constitution of the board of directors and the compliance requirement of government directives, there is little doubt that short-run political objectives always dominate. The multiplicity of conflicting objectives also allows the authority to pursue its own aim and hide any failure in one respect against achievement in another. In other words this is a recipe for incompetence and the avoidance of accountability.

In mature democracies governments remain accountable to the parliament and the budgetary process goes through strict scrutiny. Unfortunately this organizational branch of government is also weak in many developing countries. Thus political reforms are necessary to develop an accountable and responsive political system that creates an economically aware and technically trained political/bureaucratic élite for the management of the economy. Although a development-minded, authoritarian political regime may have certain advantages over democracy in promoting economic growth during the early stages of development,[1] it can breed social and political instability in an underdeveloped society which goes through social and political upheavals. As mentioned earlier there is also no guarantee that in an authoritarian regime the autocratic leader would be developmentalist as in Taiwan, Singapore and South Korea, or 'a great thief' as Mobutu was in Zaire, Marcos was in the Philippines and Ershad was in Bangladesh. What is important for development is the relative autonomy or insulation of the state against the ravages of both rent-seeking groups and pork-barrel politics by decision-makers: authoritarianism is neither necessary nor sufficient for such insulation of the state (Bardhan, 1990,1993).

A competitive, democratic political system under well-defined rules and norms can accommodate the political aspirations of the people. However it may remain exposed to rent-seeking and pork-barrel politics unless the role of the private sector *vis-à-vis* public sector is sufficiently increased in economic activity. If the economy is adequately deregulated and opened up, the scope of patronage by both politicians and bureaucrats in a market-driven economic system will be limited. Politics may then become a relatively less attractive profession in an economic sense and the state may be insulated from rent-seeking groups if price distortions are eliminated. Under a competitive, rather than a dynastic, political system, quality political leaders are likely to replace 'agitation mongers' who thrive on chaotic street politics rather than in the high offices of governance. As Huff (1995) finds for East Asia, insofar as economic development is concerned, there are no substitutes for economic and political leaders who have personal integrity, a high level of formal education and an extensive training in economics.

Finally, the political reform should attempt to prevent the emergence of a coalition government or a situation where minority parties hold the balance of power. A coalition government is often found to delay adjustments as it is difficult to achieve agreement among partners on how to stabilize the economy. As Alesina (1992:28) noted:

> Coalition governments are more often observed in parliamentary democracies with proportional representation. Therefore the institution of proportionality may not be conducive to swift fiscal reform when they are needed.

If a situation does arise where minority parties hold the balance of power there is the danger of a 'war of attrition' as each party waits for the other to concede. This happens as the cost of delay to each party is a private information. This sort of situation can be avoided in two ways. First, the cost of delay must be made explicit and herein lies the importance of an economically literate élite bureaucracy. Second, some institutional mechanism should be devised whereby the gainers compensate the losers.

In the macroeconomic policymaking arena, the reform must begin with the central bank. The evidence shows that an independent central bank with a clear mandate for price stability enhances macroeconomic performance (Alesina and Summers, 1993; Cukierman *et al*, 1992). Therefore the central bank's legislation should be amended to give a mandate to control inflation only rather than a host of conflicting objectives. This is in line with what has been proposed above in order to enhance accountability and transparency of government departments. However as a lender of last resort, it is held that the central bank will have to cave in and monetize debt if the government remains irresponsible. This 'war of attrition' may lead to considerable political instability and larger fiscal imbalance (Alesina, 1992).

Therefore the credibility of government's fiscal and monetary policy lies ultimately in the accountability and transparency of the budgetary process. Here lies the importance of an independent fiscal board (IFB). The IFB must have sufficient power to review government expenditure programmes and all new initiatives must be cleared by it.[2] The idea of an IFB is akin to an independent judiciary. Just as an independent judicial system monitors political interference with institutions for greater political efficiency, an IFB will ensure that the budgetary process is not influenced by political considerations and will enhance efficiency in macroeconomic management. An IFB is a superior arrangement than a 'fiscal constitution' restricting the government to a balanced budget. Such a constitutionally binding arrangement could be unnecessarily debilitating. An IFB should work closely with an independent central bank in order to avoid any co-ordination problem between fiscal and monetary policies.[3]

At this juncture it is pertinent to reflect on the currency board system which has been attracting attention in recent times. The interest in currency boards arose from the need to stabilize countries with a history of high inflation and large budget deficits. The currency board arrangement is an extreme form of fixed exchange rate system where the domestic currency is pegged with a strong and stable foreign currency. As mentioned in Chapter 8, the arrangement restricts governments' ability to conduct monetary and fiscal policies. It is more restrictive than either an independent central bank or an IFB would entail and hence has costs. However as the experience of Argentina and Estonia shows, in countries suffering from hyperinflation or where financial stability is not yet well established, the benefits of currency boards clearly outweigh the costs. Once the financial and macroeconomic stability is achieved and consolidated, countries could relax the arrangement and consider institutional arrangements such as an IFB.

In a country where politicians have little respect for either constitution or institutions and which is prone to *coups d'état*, what guarantee is there that the arrangements suggested above would prevail? Here lies the importance of trade and financial liberalization. As expounded in Chapter 1, the experience of highly successful economies of East and South East Asia shows that the pursuit of export-oriented, rather than inward-looking, industrialization policies can act as an external constraint on the mismanagement of the economy. In an open economy both the recognition and reaction lags are shorter. In other words the macroeconomic mistakes quickly become clearer as the inflation rate accelerates and the exchange rate is overvalued (recognition lag), and governments cannot remain complacent as competitiveness declines (reaction lag). Large and persistent budget deficits can fuel the expectations of accelerating inflation and create balance of payments and exchange rate crises that lead to an eventual sharp devaluation of domestic currency. The fear of large depreciations of currency may cause massive capital flights, exacerbating the exchange rate crises. Most military dictators try to avoid exchange rate crises and capital flights as they deepen their legitimacy crisis. Incidentally, macroeconomic stability and economic growth are powerful weapons that legitimize the dictatorial regimes.

The external constraint is reinforced when there is a well developed financial sector. The financial sector is generally averse to inflation as it generates economic uncertainties. Thus a well developed and well functioning financial sector can act as a strong anti-inflationary lobby and constrain the government (politicians) which would otherwise attempt to either maximize votes or legitimize the regime. A liberalized financial sector is expected to enhance financial development. Thus both financial and trade liberalization must go hand in hand.

In sum, institution buildings, administrative and constitutional reforms along with liberalization of the economy are all essential ingredients for a sustained improvement in macroeconomic performance.

NOTES

1. For a review of the theoretical arguments and empirical studies on political regimes and economic growth, see Prezeworski and Limongi (1993). The emerging consensus view is that neither democracy nor authoritarianism per se is superior to the other in fostering economic growth.
2. Reforms are necessary in the areas of fiscal deficit accounting practice and methods of deficit financing. A broad and meaningful definition of fiscal deficit should be followed, which must include the revenue and expenditure of public sector enterprises, otherwise fiscal deficit, as normally measured, may at times understate the inflationary impact of the public sector on the economy as a whole (Tanzi, 1982). Accurate and detailed information on the sources of deficit financing should also be consistently published so that their effects on the different aspects of the economy can be examined. In most developing countries, the present system is not only vague but also suspicious in the sense that neither a clear-cut definition of fiscal deficit nor information about the sources of deficit financing is readily available (Hossain, 1994).
3. It is often suggested that countries which are characterized by large fiscal deficits and high inflation should follow a fixed exchange rate system. They can achieve monetary discipline by pegging the currency to a stable or a basket of currencies. This acts as a nominal anchor and can be used to persuade political leaders to restrain their propensity to deficit financing and macroeconomic populism. The institutional arrangement of a currency board can impose a strict commitment to a fixed exchange rate. See chapter 8 for details.

Bibliography

Abel, A.B. (1990), 'Consumption and Investment', in B. Friedman and F.H. Hahn (eds), *Handbook of Monetary Economics*, Amsterdam: North-Holland.

Agenor, P., J. Bhandari and R. Flood (1992), 'Speculative Attacks and Models of Balance of Payments Crises', *IMF Staff Papers*, **39**(2): 357–394.

Agenor, P.R. and P.J. Montiel (1996), *Development Macroeconomics*, Princeton, New Jersey: Princeton University Press.

Aghevli, B., M. Khan, P. Narvekar and B. Short (1979), 'Monetary Policy in Selected Asian Countries', *IMF Staff Papers*, **26**:775–824.

Aghevli, B., M. Khan and P. Montiel (1991), 'Exchange Rate Policy in Developing Countries: Some Analytical Issues', *IMF Occasional Paper No. 78*, Washington, DC: International Monetary Fund.

Ahmed, I. (1981), 'Wage Determination in Bangladesh Agriculture', *Oxford Economic Papers*, **33**(2):298–322.

Alesina, A. (1992), 'Political Models of Macroeconomic Policy and Fiscal Reform', *Policy Research Working Paper No. WPS 970*, Washington, DC: World Bank.

Alesina, A. and G. Tabellini (1989), 'External Debt, Capital Flights and Political Risk', *Journal of International Economics*, **104**:325–345.

Alesina, A. and G. Tabellini (1990), 'A Political Theory of Fiscal Deficits and Government Debt', *Review of Economic Studies*, **57**:403–414.

Alesina, A. and L. Summers (1993), 'Central Bank Independence and Macroeconomic Performance', *Journal of Money, Credit and Banking*, **25**:151–162.

Amin, A.T.M.N. (1982), 'An Analysis of Labor Force and Industrial Organization of the Informal Sector in Dacca', Unpublished PhD Thesis, Department of Economics, University of Manitoba, Canada.

Amsden, A. (1989), 'Asia's Next Giant: South Korea and Late Industrialization', New York: Oxford University Press.

Areskoug, K. (1973), 'Foreign Capital Utilization and Economic Policies in Developing Countries', *Review of Economics and Statistics*, **55**:182–189.

Argy, V. (1994), *International Macroeconomics: Theory and Policy*, London and New York: Routledge.

Argy, V. and M.G. Porter (1972), 'The Forward Exchange Market and the

Effects of Domestic and External Disturbances Under Alternative Exchange Rate Systems', *IMF Staff Papers*, **19** (November):503–532.

Arndt, H.W. (1987), *Economic Development: The History of an Idea*, Chicago: Chicago University Press.

Asian Development Bank (ADB) (various years), *Asian Development Outlook*, Manila: ADB.

Balassa, B. (1968), *Economic Growth, Trade and the Balance of Payments in Developing Countries, 1960–65*, Washington, DC: World Bank.

Balassa, B. and F. McCarthy (1984), 'Adjustment Policies in Developing Countries: An Update 1979–83', *World Bank Working Paper 675*, Washington, DC: World Bank.

Bangladesh Bank (various issues), *Economic Trends*, Dhaka: Bangladesh Bank.

Baran, P. (1957), *The Political Economy of Growth*, New York: Monthly Review Press.

Bardhan, K. (1977), 'Rural Employment, Wages and Labour Markets in India: A Survey of Research, Part I, Part II, and Part III', *Economic and Political Weekly*, **12**(26):A34–48, **12**(27):1062–74, **12**(28):1108–18.

Bardhan, P. (1979), 'Wages and Unemployment in a Poor Agrarian Economy: A Theoretical and Empirical Analysis', *Journal of Political Economy*, **87**(3):479–500.

Bardhan, P. (1988), 'Dominant Proprietary Classes and India's Democracy', in A. Kohli (ed.), *India's Democracy*, Princeton, NJ: Princeton University Press.

Bardhan, P. (1990), 'Symposium on the State and Economic Development', *Journal of Economic Perspectives*, **4**(3):3–7.

Bardhan, P. (1993), 'Symposium on Democracy and Development', *Journal of Economic Perspectives*, **7**(3):45–49.

Barro, R.J. (1974), 'Are Government Bonds Net Wealth?', *Journal of Political Economy*, **82** (November):1095–1117.

Barro, R.J. (1981), 'Rational Expectations and the Role of Monetary Policy', in R. Lucas and T. Sargent (eds), *Rational Expectations and Econometric Practice*, London: Allen and Unwin.

Bauer, P.T. (1981), *Equality, Third World and Economic Delusion*, Cambridge, Massachusetts: Harvard University Press.

Bauer, P. and B. Yamey (1992), 'Foreign Aid: What Is at Stake?', in D. Lal (ed.), *Development Economics* (Volume IV), Aldershot, UK and Brookfield, US: Edward Elgar.

Bennett, A.G.G. (1995), 'Currency Boards: Issues and Experiences', *Finance and Development*, September:39–42.

Bhagwati, J. (1978), *Foreign Trade Regimes and Economic Development: Anatomy and Consequences of Exchange Control Regimes*, Cambridge, MA: Ballinger.

Bhagwati, J. and T. Srinivasan (1975), *Foreign Trade Regimes and Economic Development: India*, New York: NBER.

Bhalla, S. (1982), 'The Transmission of Inflation into Developing Economies', in W. Cline and Associates (eds), *World Inflation and the Developing Countries*, Washington, DC: Brookings Institution.

Blejer, M. and A. Cheasty (1989), 'Fiscal Policy and Mobilization of Savings for Growth', in Blejer, M. and K. Chu (eds), *Fiscal Policy, Stabilization and Growth in Developing Countries*, Washington, DC: IMF.

Blejer, M. and M. Khan (1984), 'Government Policy and Private Investment in Developing Countries', *IMF Staff Papers*, 31:379–403.

Borensztein, E. (1989), 'The Effect of External Debt on Investment', *Finance and Development*, September:17–23.

Branson, W.H. (1989), *Macroeconomic Theory and Policy*, New York: Harper and Row.

Bruno, M. (1993), 'Monetary Policy Rules in a Small Open Economy', in R. Dornbusch (ed.), *Policymaking in the Open Economy: Concepts and Case Studies in Economic Performance*, New York: Oxford University Press.

Bruno, M. and J. Sachs (1985), *Economics of Worldwide Stagflation*, Oxford: Blackwell.

Burda, M. and C. Wyplosz (1993), *Macroeconomics: A European Text*, New York: Oxford University Press.

Burki, S.J. and R.L. Ayres (1986), 'A Fresh Look at Development Aid', *Finance and Development*, March:6–10.

Cagan, P. (1956), 'The Monetary Dynamics of Hyperinflation', in M. Friedman (ed.), *Studies in the Quantity Theory of Money*, Chicago: University of Chicago Press.

Calvo, G.A., L. Leiderman and C.M. Reinhart (1996), 'Inflows of Capital to Developing Countries in the 1990s', *Journal of Economic Perspectives*, 10(2):123–139.

Cardoso, E.A. and R. Dornbusch (1989), 'Foreign Private Capital Flows', in H.B. Chenery and T.N. Srinivasan (eds), *Handbook of Development Economics* (Volume II), Amsterdam: Elsevier Science Publishers.

Carroll, C. and D.N. Weil (1994), 'Saving and Growth: A Reinterpretation', *Carnegie-Rochester Conference Series on Public Policy*, 40 (June):133–192.

Cassen, R. (1986), 'The Effectiveness of Aid', *Finance and Development*, March:11–14.

Cassen, R. and Associates (1987), *Does Aid Work?*, Oxford: Oxford University Press.

Chenery, H.B. and M. Bruno (1962), 'Development Alternatives in an Open Economy: The Case of Israel', *Economic Journal*, 72:79–103.

Chenery, H.B. and A. Strout (1966), 'Foreign Assistance and Economic Development', *American Economic Review*, **56**:679–733.

Chenery, H.B. and P. Eckstein (1970), 'Development Alternatives for Latin America', *Journal of Political Economy*, **78**:966–1006.

Chenery, H.B. and M. Syrquin (1975), *Patterns of Development*, Oxford: Oxford University Press.

Chowdhury, A. (1996), 'Macroeconomic Management in East Asian Newly Industrialising Economies', in B. Kapur *et al* (eds), *Trade, Development and the Asia-Pacific*, Singapore: Prentice-Hall.

Chowdhury, A. and I. Islam (1993), *The Newly Industrialising Economies of East Asia*, London and New York: Routledge.

Corbo, V. and J. de Melo (1987), 'Lessons from Southern Cone Policy Reforms', *World Bank Research Observer*, **2**:111–142.

Corbo, V. and L. Hernandez (1996), 'Macroeconomic Adjustment to Capital Inflows: Lessons from Recent Latin American and East Asian Experience', *World Bank Research Observer*, **11**(1):61–85.

Corden, M. (1984), 'Macroeconomic Targets and Instruments for a Small Open Economy', *Singapore Economic Review*, **24**(2): 24–37.

Corden M. (1987), 'Relevance for Developing Countries of Recent Development in Macroeconomic Theory', *World Bank Research Observer*, **2**(2): 171–88.

Corden, W.M. (1981), *Inflation, Exchange Rate and the World Economy*, Oxford: Oxford University Press.

Corden, W.M. (1991), 'Exchange Rate Policy in Developing Countries', in J. de Melo and A. Sapir (eds), *Trade Theory and Economic Reform: North, South and East*, Oxford: Basil Blackwell.

Corden, W.M. (1993), 'Exchange Rate Policies for Developing Countries', *Economic Journal*, **103** (January):198–207.

Cuddington, J. (1986), 'Capital Flight: Estimates, Issues and Explanations', *Princeton Studies in International Finance No. 58*, Princeton: Princeton University.

Cukierman, A., S. Edwards and G. Tabellini (1989), 'Seigniorage and Political Instability', *NBER Working Paper No. 31999*, Cambridge, Mass.: NBER.

Cukierman, A., S.B. Webb and B. Neyapti (1992), 'Measuring the Independence of Central Banks and its Effects on Policy Outcomes', *World Bank Economic Review*, **6**(1):353–398.

Dean, J.W. (1996), 'Recent Capital Flows to Asia/Pacific Countries: Tradeoffs and Dilemmas', *Journal of the Asia-Pacific Economy*, **1**(3):287–318.

Deepler, M. and M. Williamson (1987), 'Capital Flight: Concepts, Measurement and Issues', in *Staff Studies for the World Economic Outlook*, Washington, DC: Institute for International Economics.

De Gregorio, J. (1993), 'Inflation, Taxation and Long-Run Growth', *Journal of Monetary Economics*, **31**(2):271–298.

Diaz Alejandro, C.F. (1983), 'Stories of the 1930s for the 1980s', in P. Aspe Armella, R. Dornbusch and M. Obstfeld (eds), *Financial Policies and the World Capital Market: The Problem of Latin American Countries*, Chicago: University of Chicago Press.

Domar, E. (1946), 'Capital Expansion, Rate of Growth, and Employment', *Econometrica*, **14** (April):137–147.

Domar, E. (1947), 'Expansion and Employment', *American Economic Review*, **37**:34–55.

Dooley, M. (1986), 'Country-Specific Risk Premiums, Capital Flight and Net Investment Income Payments in Selected Developing Countries', (Mimeo), Washington, DC: IMF.

Dooley, M., E. Fernandez-Arias and K. Kletzer (1996), 'Is Debt Crisis History? Recent Private Capital Inflows to Developing Countries', *World Bank Economic Review*, **10**(1):27–50.

Dornbusch, R. (1976), 'Expectations and Exchange Rate Dynamics', *Journal of Political Economy*, **84**:1161–1176.

Dornbusch, R. (1980), *Open Economy Macroeconomics*, New York: Basic Books.

Dornbusch, R. (1983), 'Exchange Rate Economics: Where Do We Stand?', in J.S. Bhandari and B.H. Putnam (eds), *Economic Interdependence and Flexible Exchange Rates*, Cambridge, Mass.: MIT Press.

Dornbusch, R. (1984), 'External Debt, Budget Deficits and Disequilibrium Exchange Rates', *NBER Working Paper No.4*, Cambridge, Mass: NBER.

Dornbusch, R. (1993a), 'Introduction', in *Policymaking in the Open Economy*, New York: Oxford University Press for the World Bank.

Dornbusch, R. (1993b), *Stabilization, Debt, and Reform: Policy Analysis for Developing Countries*, New York: Harvester Wheatsheaf.

Dornbusch, R. and S. Fischer (1981), 'Budget Deficits and Inflation', in J. Flanders and A. Razin (eds), *Development in an Inflationary World*, New York: Academic Press.

Dornbusch, R. and S. Edwards (1990), 'The Macroeconomics of Populism in Latin America', *Journal of Development Economics*, **32**:247–277.

Dornbusch, R. and A. Reynoso (1993), 'Financial Factors in Economic Development', in R. Dornbusch (ed.), *Policymaking in the Open Economy: Concepts and Case Studies in Economic Performance*, New York: Oxford University Press: 64–90.

Dornbusch, R. and L.T. Kuenzler (1993), 'Exchange Rate Policy: Options and Issues', in R. Dornbusch (ed.), *Policymaking in the Open Economy*, New York: Oxford University Press for the World Bank.

Dornbusch, R. and S. Fischer (1994), *Macroeconomics*, New York: McGraw Hill.

Drake, P.J. (1969), *Financial Development in Malaysia and Singapore*, Canberra: Australian National University Press.

Drake, P.J. (1980), *Money, Finance and Development*, Oxford: Martin Robertson.

Dwyer, G. (1985), 'Federal Deficits, Interest Rates and Monetary Policy', *Journal of Money, Credit and Banking*, **17**:655–681.

Easterly, W. and K. Schmidt-Hebbel (1993), 'Fiscal Deficits and Macroeconomic Performance in Developing Countries', *World Bank Research Observer*, **8**(2):211–239.

Easterly, W., C.A. Rodriguez and K. Schmidt-Hebbel (eds) (1994), *Public Sector Deficits and Macroeconomic Performance*, New York: Oxford University Press.

Eaton, J. (1989), 'Foreign Public Capital Flows', in H. Chenery and T.N. Srinivasan (eds), *Handbook of Development Economics* (Volume II), Amsterdam: Elsevier Science Publishers.

Edwards, S. (1984), 'The Order of Liberalization of the External Sector in Developing Countries', *Essays in International Finance No.156*, New Jersey: International Finance Section, Princeton University.

Edwards, S. (1989), *Real Exchange Rates, Devaluation and Adjustment: Exchange Rate Policies in Developing Countries*, Cambridge, Mass.: MIT Press.

Edwards, S. (1993a), 'Introductory Presentations: Dollarization in Latin America', in N. Liviatan (ed.), *Proceedings of a Conference on Currency Substitution and Currency Boards, World Bank Discussion Papers 207*, Washington, DC: World Bank.

Edwards, S. (1993b), 'Exchange Rates as Nominal Anchors', *Review of World Economics*, **129**(1):1–32.

Edwards, S. (1994), 'The Political Economy of Inflation and Stabilization in Developing Countries', *Economic Development and Cultural Change*, **42**:235–266.

Edwards, S. and A.C. Edwards (1987), *Monetarism and Liberalization: The Chilean Experiment*, Cambridge, Massachusetts: Ballinger Publishing Company.

Edwards, S. and G. Tabellini (1991), 'Explaining Fiscal Policies and Inflation in Developing Countries', *Journal of International Money and Finance*, **10**:16–48.

El-Erian, M. (1988), 'Currency Substitution in Egypt and the Yemen Arab Republic', *IMF Staff Papers*, **35**:85–103.

Erbe, S. (1985), 'The Flight of Capital from Developing Countries', *Intereconomics*, **20**:268–275.

Ethier, W.J. (1995), *Modern International Economics*, New York: W.W. Norton and Company.

Fernandez-Arias, E. and P.J. Montiel (1996), 'The Surge in Capital Inflows to Developing Countries: An Analytical Overview', *World Bank Economic Review*, **10**(1): 51–77.

Findlay, R. (1973), *International Trade and Development Theory*, New York: Columbia University Press.

Findlay, R. (1984), 'Growth and Development in Trade Models', in R. Jones and P. Kennen (eds), *Handbook of International Economics*, (Volume I), Amsterdam: North-Holland.

Fischer, S. (1987), 'Economic Growth and Economic Policy', in V. Corbo, M. Goldstein and M. Khan (eds), *Growth-Oriented Adjustment Programs*, Washington, DC: IMF and World Bank.

Fischer, S. (1994), 'Foreword', in W. Easterly, C.A. Rodriguez and K. Schmidt-Hebbel (eds), *Public Sector Deficits and Macroeconomic Performance*, New York: Oxford University Press.

Fischer, S. and W. Easterly (1990), 'The Economics of the Government Budget Constraint', *World Bank Research Observer*, **5**(July):127–142.

Friedman, M. (1953), 'The Case for Flexible Exchange Rates', in *Essays in Positive Economics*, Chicago: Chicago University Press.

Friedman, M. (1958), 'Foreign Economic Aid: Means and Objectives', *Yale Review*, **47**:24–38.

Friedman, M. (1971), 'Government Revenue from Inflation', *Journal of Political Economy*, **79**:846–856.

Fry, M. (1991), 'Domestic Resource Mobilization in Developing Asia: Four Policy Issues', *Asian Development Review*, **19**(1):14–39.

Fry, M. (1995), *Money, Interest, and Banking in Economic Development*, (Second Edition), Baltimore: Johns Hopkins University Press.

Gavin, M. (1993), 'Adjusting to a Terms of Trade Shock: Nigeria, 1972–88', in R. Dornbusch (ed.), *Policymaking in the Open Economy: Concepts and Case Studies in Economic Performance*, New York: Oxford University Press.

Gersovitz, M. (1988), 'Saving and Development', in H. Chenery and T. Srinivasan (eds), *Handbook of Development Economics*, (Volume I), Amsterdam: Elsevier Science Publishers.

Gillis, M., D. Perkins, M. Roemer and D. Snodgrass (1992), *Economics of Development*, New York: Norton and Company.

Gooptu, S. (1993), 'Portfolio Investment Flows to Emerging Markets', in S. Claessens and S. Gooptu (eds), *Portfolio Investment in Developing Countries*, Washington, DC: World Bank.

Gordon, R.J. (1981), 'Output Fluctuations and Gradual Price Adjustment', *Journal of Economic Literature*, **19**(July):493–530.

Greene, J. and D. Villanueva (1991), 'Private Investment in Developing Countries', *IMF Staff Papers*, **38**(1):33–58.

Griffin, K.B. (1978), *International Inequality and National Poverty*, London: Macmillan.

Griffin, K.B. and J.L. Enos (1970), 'Foreign Assistance: Objectives and Consequences', *Economic Development and Cultural Change*, **18**:313–327.

Hadjimichael, M.T. and Others (1995), 'Sub-Saharan Africa: Growth, Savings, and Investment, 1986–93', *IMF Occasional Paper No.118*, Washington, DC: IMF.

Hafer, R. (1989), 'Does Dollar Depreciation Cause Inflation?', Federal Reserve Bank of St. Louis, *Economic Review*, July/August.

Hansen, B. (1969), 'Employment and Wages in Rural Egypt', *American Economic Review*, **59**(3):298–313.

Hanson, J. and J. de Melo (1985), 'External Shocks, Financial Reforms and Stabilization Attempts in Uruguay During 1974–83', *World Development*, **13**(8): 917–939.

Haque, N., D. Mathieson and S. Sharma (1997), 'Causes of Capital Inflows and Policy Responses to Them', *Finance and Development*, March:3–6.

Harberger, A.C. (1984), 'Economic Growth and Economic Policy', in *World Economic Growth*, San Francisco: Institute for Contemporary Studies.

Harrod, R. (1939), 'An Essay in Dynamic Theory', *Economic Journal*, **49**:14–33.

Healy, J. and S. Page (1993), 'The Use of Monetary Policy', in S. Page (ed.), *Monetary Policy in Developing Countries*, London and New York: Routledge.

Hibbs, D. (1977), 'Political Parties and Macroeconomic Policy', *American Political Science Review*, **7** (December): 1467–1487.

Hogendorn, J.S. (1992), *Economic Development*, New York: HarperCollins.

Hossain, A. (1989), 'Inflation, Economic Growth and the Balance of Payments: A Macroeconometric Study 1974–85', PhD Thesis, La Trobe University, Australia.

Hossain, A. (1994), 'Financial Innovation, Financial Deregulation and the Stability of the Australian Short-Run Narrow Money Demand Function', *Economic Notes*, **23**(3):410–437.

Hossain, A. and A. Chowdhury (1994), 'Monetary Policy', in H. Zafarullah, M. Taslim and A. Chowdhury (eds), *Policy Issues in Bangladesh*, New Delhi: South Asian Publishers.

Hossain, A. and A. Chowdhury (1996), *Monetary and Financial Policies in Developing Countries: Growth and Stabilisation*, London and New York: Routledge.

Huff, W.G. (1995), 'The Developmental State, Government and Singapore's

Economic Development Since 1960', *World Development*, **23**(8):1421–1438.

Hutchcroft, P. (1994), 'Booty Capitalism: Business, Government Relations in the Philippines', in A. MacIntyre (ed.), *Business and Government in Industrialising Asia*, Sydney: Allen and Unwin.

Intal, Jr, P.S. (1992), 'Real Exchange Rates, Price Competitiveness and Structural Adjustment in Asian and Pacific Economies', *Asian Development Review*, **10**(2):86–123.

International Monetary Fund (various issues), *International Financial Statistics Yearbook* plus *Monthly Issues*, Washington, DC: IMF.

International Monetary Fund (1973), *IMF Annual Report 1973*, Washington, DC: IMF.

International Monetary Fund (1995a), *World Economic Outlook*, (May), Washington, DC: IMF.

International Monetary Fund (1995b), *International Capital Markets: Developments, Prospects, and Policy Issues*, (August), Washington, DC: IMF.

Islam, I. and A. Chowdhury (1997), *Asia-Pacific Economies – A Survey*, London: Routledge.

Iyoha, M. (1973), 'Inflation and "Openness" in Less Developed Economies: A Cross-Country Analysis', *Economic Development and Cultural Change*, **22**(1):31–37.

Johnson, H. (1958), 'Towards a General Theory of Balance of Payments', in *International Trade and Economic Growth*, London: Allen and Unwin.

Joshi, V. and I. Little (1994), *India: Macroeconomics and Political Economy*, Washington, DC: World Bank.

Kaldor, N. (1955–56), 'Alternative Theories of Distribution', *Review of Economic Studies*, **23**:83–100.

Kalecki, M. (1976), *Essays on Development Economics*, Brighton, Sussex: Harvester Press.

Kandil, M. (1991), 'Structural Differences Between Developing and Developed Countries: Some Evidence and Implications', *Economic Notes*, **20**(2):254–278.

Kearney, C. (1996), 'International Financial Integration: Measurement and Policy Implications', *Journal of the Asia-Pacific Economies*, **1**(3):347–364.

Kenen, P.B. (1988), *Managing Exchange Rates*, London and New York: Routledge.

Keynes, J.M. (1923), *A Tract on Monetary Reform*, reprinted (1971), London: Royal Economic Society.

Keynes, J.M. (1936), *The General Theory of Employment, Interest and Money*, London: Macmillan.

Khan, M. (1980), 'Monetary Shocks and the Dynamics of Inflation', *IMF Staff Papers*, **27**:250–284.

Khan, M.S. and N.U. Haque (1987), 'Capital Flight from Developing Countries', *Finance and Development*, March: 2–5.

Khan, M.S. and C.M. Reinhart (1990), 'Private Investment and Economic Growth in Developing Countries', *World Development*, **18**:19–27.

Kiguel, M. and L. Leiderman (1993), 'On the Consequences of Sterilized Intervention in Latin America: The Cases of Colombia and Chile', Mimeo, Washington, DC: World Bank.

Killick, T. (1988), *A Reaction Too Far*, London: ODI.

Kirkpatrick, C. and F. Nixson (1977), 'Inflation and "Openness" in Less Developed Countries: A Cross-Country Analysis: Comment', *Economic Development and Cultural Change*, **26**(1):147–152.

Klein, L. (1965), 'What Kind of Macroeconomic Model for Developing Countries?', *Econometric Annual of the Indian Economic Journal*, **13**(3):313–324.

Klein, L. (1978), 'The Supply Side', *American Economic Review*, **68**(March):1–7.

Kohli, A. (1988), 'Introduction: Interpreting India's Democracy: A State-Society Framework', in *India's Democracy*, Princeton, NJ: Princeton University Press.

Krueger, A. (1978), *Foreign Trade Regimes and Economic Development: Liberalization Attempts and Consequences*, New York: NBER.

Krugman, P.R. (1979), 'A Model of Balance of Payments Crises', *Journal of Money, Credit and Banking*, **3**:311–325.

Krugman, P.R. and M. Obstfeld (1989), *International Economics: Theory and Policy*, New York: HarperCollins.

Lal, D. (1984), 'Trends in Real Wages in Rural India 1880–1980', *World Bank Research Paper*, Washington, DC: World Bank.

Lal, D. (1992), 'The Evaluation of Capital Flows', in *Development Economics* (Volume IV), Aldershot, UK and Brookfield, US: Edward Elgar.

Lee, C.H. (1992), 'The Government Financial System and Large Private Enterprises in the Economic Development of South Korea', *World Development*, **20**(2):187–197.

Leipziger, D. and V. Thomas (1993), 'An Overview of Country Experiences', in *Lessons from East Asia Series*, Washington, DC: World Bank.

Lessard, D. and J.J. Williamson (eds.) (1987), *Capital Flight: The Problem and Policy Responses*, Washington, DC: Institute for International Economics.

Levy, V. (1988), 'Aid and Growth in Sub-Saharan Africa: The Recent Experience', *European Economic Review*, **32**:1777–1795.

Lewis, W.A. (1954), 'Economic Development with Unlimited Supplies of Labour', *The Manchester School*, **22**:139–191.

Lewis, W.A. (1955), *Theory of Economic Growth*, London: Allen and Unwin.

Lewis, W.A. (1980), 'Slowing Down of the Engine of Growth', *Economic Journal*, **90**(4):555–564.

Little, I.M.D. (1979), 'An Economic Reconnaissance', in W. Glenson (ed.), *Economic Growth and Structural Change in Taiwan*, Ithaca: Cornell University Press.

Little, I. and J. Mirless (1991), 'Project Appraisal and Planning Twenty Years On', *Proceedings of the World Bank Annual Conference on Development Economics 1990*, Washington, DC: World Bank.

Little, I., R. Cooper, M. Corden and S. Rajapatirana (1993), *Booms, Crisis and Adjustment: The Macroeconomic Experience of Developing Countries*, New York: Oxford University Press.

Mankiw, N.G., D. Romer and D.N. Weil (1992), 'A Contribution to the Empirics of Economic Growth', *Quarterly Journal of Economics*, **107** (May):407–437.

McKinnon, R.I. (1964), 'Foreign Exchange Constraints in Economic Development and Efficient Aid Allocation', *Economic Journal*, **74**:388–409.

McKinnon, R.I. (1973), *Money and Capital in Economic Development*, Washington, DC: Brookings Institution.

McKinnon, R.I. (1981), 'Financial Repression and the Liberalization Problem Within Less Developed Countries', in E. Grassman and E. Lundberg (eds), *The Past and Prospects for the World Economic Order*, London: Macmillan.

McKinnon, R.I. (1982), 'The Order of Economic Liberalization: Lessons from Chile and Argentina', *Carnegie-Rochester Conference Series on Public Policy*, **17**:159–186.

McKinnon, R.I. (1991), *The Order of Economic Liberalization: Financial Control in the Transition to a Market Economy*, Baltimore: Johns Hopkins University Press.

McKinnon, R.I. and H. Pill (1996), 'Credible Liberalizations and International Capital Flows: The "Overborrowing Syndrome"', in T. Ito and A.O. Krueger (eds), *Financial Deregulation and Integration in East Asia*, Chicago: Chicago University Press.

Meade, J. (1951), *The Balance of Payments*, London: Oxford University Press.

Meier, G.M. (1989), *Leading Issues in Economic Development*, New York: Oxford University Press.

Meier, G.M. and R.E. Baldwin (1957), *Economic Development: Theory, History and Policy*, New York: Wiley.

Mirza, H. (1988), 'The New International Economic Order', in M. Brooke and P. Buckley (eds), *Handbook of International Trade*, London: Macmillan.

Mishkin, F. S. (1995), *The Economics of Money, Banking, and Financial Markets*, New York: HarperCollins Publishers.

Moreno, R. (1995), 'Macroeconomic Behavior During Periods of Speculative Pressure or Realignment: Evidence from Pacific Basin Economies', *Economic Review*, Federal Reserve Bank of San Francisco, **3**:3–16.

Mosley, P., J. Hudson and S. Horrell (1987), 'Aid, the Public Sector and the Market in Less Developed Countries', *Economic Journal*, **97**:616–641.

Mundell, R. (1962), 'The Appropriate Use of Monetary and Fiscal Policy for Internal and External Stability', *IMF Staff Papers*, **9** (March):70–79.

Mundell, R. (1963), 'Inflation and Real Interest', *Journal of Political Economy*, **71**:280–283.

Mundell, R. (1965), 'Growth, Stability and Inflationary Finance', *Journal of Political Economy*, **73**:97–109.

Mundell, R. (1968), *International Economics*, New York: Macmillan.

Mundell, R. (1971), *Monetary Theory*, California: Goodyear Publishing Company.

Muth, J.F. (1961), 'Rational Expectations and the Theory of Price Movement', *Econometrica*, **29**(2):315–335.

Naqvi, S.N.H. (1996), 'The Significance of Development Economics', *World Development*, **24**(6):975–987.

Nordhaus, W. (1975), 'The Political Business Cycle', *Review of Economic Studies*, **42**(April): 169–190.

North, D. (1990), *Institutions, Institutional Change and Economic Performance*, Cambridge: Cambridge University Press.

North, D. (1995), 'The New Institutional Economics and Third World Development', in J. Harris, J. Hunter and C. Lewis (eds), *The New Institutional Economics and Third World Development*, London: Routledge.

Nurkse, R. (1944), *International Currency Experience*, Geneva: League of Nations.

Nurkse, R. (1953), *Problems of Capital Formation in Underdeveloped Countries*, Oxford: Blackwell.

Papanek, G.F. (1972), 'The Effect of Aid and Other Resource Transfers on Savings and Growth in Less Developed Countries', *Economic Journal*, **82**:934–950.

Persson, T. and L. Svensson (1989), 'Checks and Balances on the Government Budget', *Quarterly Journal of Economics*, **104**:325–345.

Persson, T. and G. Tabellini (1990), *Macroeconomic Policy, Credibility and Politics*, Harwood: Academic Publishers.

Petrie, P. (1993), 'Common Foundations of East Asian Success', in *Lessons From East Asia Series*, Washington, DC: World Bank.

Pfefferman, G. (1985), 'Overvalued Exchange Rates and Development', *Finance and Development*, March:17–19.

Pilbeam, K. (1992), *International Finance*, London: Macmillan.

Porter, R. (1961), 'The Dangers of Monetary Policy in Agrarian Economies', *Pakistan Development Review*, **1**:59–72.

Prachowny, M.F. (1981), 'Macroeconomic Analysis for Small Open Economies', *Institute for Economic Research, Discussion Paper No.445*, Queens University.

Prezeworski, A. and F. Limongi (1993), 'Political Regimes and Economic Growth', *Journal of Economic Perspectives*, **7**(3):51–69.

Quirk, P.J. (1995), 'Exchange Rate Regimes as Inflation Anchors', *Finance and Development*, March:42–45.

Rahman, A. (1968), 'Foreign Capital and Domestic Savings: A Test of Haavelmo's Hypothesis with Cross-Section Data', *Review of Economics and Statistics*, February:137–138.

Rao, V.K.R.V. (1952), 'Investment, Income and the Multiplier in an Underdeveloped Economy', *Indian Economic Review*, **1**(1):55–67.

Reisen, H. (1996), 'Managing Volatile Capital Inflows: The Experience of the 1990s', *Asian Development Review*, **14**(1):72–96.

Riedel, J. (1994), 'Strategies of Economic Development', in E. Grilli and D. Salvatore (eds), *Economic Development*, London: Greenwood Press.

Rivera-Batiz, F. and L. Rivera-Batiz (1985), *International Finance and Open-Economy Macroeconomics*, New York: Macmillan.

Robinson, J. (1962), 'A Model of Accumulation', in *Essays in the Theory of Economic Growth*, London: Macmillan.

Rodriguez, M.A. (1987), 'Consequences of Capital Flight for Latin America', in D. Lessard and J. Williamson (eds), *Capital Flight and Third World Debt*, Washington, DC: Institute for International Economics.

Romer, D. (1996), *Advanced Macroeconomics*, New York: McGraw-Hill.

Rosenzweig, M. (1980), 'Neoclassical Theory and the Optimizing Peasant: An Econometric Analysis of Market Family Labor Supply in a Developing Country', *Quarterly Journal of Economics*, **94**:31–55.

Rosenzweig, M. (1988), 'Labor Markets in Low-Income Countries', in H.B. Chenery and T. Srinivasan (eds), *Handbook of Development Economics*, **I**, Amsterdam: Elsevier Science Publishers.

Rostow, W.W. (1990), *Theorists of Economic Growth from David Ricardo to the Present*, New York: Oxford University Press.

Royal Institute of International Affairs (1937), *The Problem of International Investment*, London: Oxford University Press.

Sachs, J. (1987), 'Trade and Exchange Rate Policies in Growth-Oriented Adjustment Programs', in V. Corbo, M. Goldstein and M. Khan (eds), *Growth-Oriented Adjustment Programs*, Washington, DC: IMF.

Sachs, J. and F. Larrain (1993), *Macroeconomics in the Global Economy*, New York: Harvester Wheatsheaf.

Salter, W. (1959), 'Internal and External Balance: The Role of Price and Expenditure Effects', *Economic Record*, **35**:226–238.

Sen, A.K. (1983), 'Development: Which Way Now?', *Economic Journal*, **93** (December):745–762.

Shaw, E. (1973), *Financial Deepening in Economic Development*, New York: Oxford University Press.

Spiegel, M. (1995), 'Sterilization of Capital Inflows Through the Banking Sector: Evidence from Asia', *Economic Review*, Federal Reserve Bank of San Francisco, No.3:17–34.

Squire, L. (1981), *Employment Policy in Developing Countries: A Survey of Issues and Evidence*, New York: Oxford University Press.

Stiglitz, J. (1990), *Economic Role of State*, London: Allen and Unwin.

Summers, L. and V. Thomas (1993), 'Recent Lessons of Development', *World Bank Research Observer*, **8**(2):235–257.

Sundararajan, V. and S. Thakur (1980), 'Public Investment, Crowding Out and Growth: A Dynamic Model Applied to India and Korea', *IMF Staff Papers*, **27**:814–855.

Sunkel, O. (1960), 'Inflation in Chile: An Unorthodox Approach', *International Economic Papers*, **10**:107–131.

Swan, T.W. (1956), 'Economic Growth and Capital Accumulation', *Economic Record*, **32**:334–361.

Swan, T.W. (1960), 'Economic Control in a Dependent Economy', *Economic Record*, **36**:51–66.

Tabellini, G. and A. Alesina (1990), 'Voting on the Budget Deficit', *American Economic Review*, **80**:37–49.

Tanzi, V. (1982), 'Fiscal Disequilibrium in Developing Countries', *World Development*, **10**:1069–1082.

Tanzi, V. (1989), 'Lags in Tax Collection and the Case for Inflationary Finance: Theory with Simulations', in M. Blejer and K. Chu (eds), *Fiscal Policy, Stabilization, and Growth in Developing Countries*, Washington, DC: International Monetary Fund.

Tanzi, V. (1994), 'The Political Economy of Fiscal Deficit Reduction', in W. Easterly, C.A. Rodriguez and K. Schmidt-Hebbel (eds), *Public Sector Deficits and Macroeconomic Performance*, New York: Oxford University Press.

Taslim, M.A. and A. Chowdhury (1995), *Macroeconomic Analysis for Australian Students*, Sydney: Prentice-Hall.

Taylor, L. (1983), *Structuralist Macroeconomics*, New York: Basic Books.

Theil, H. (1961), *Economic Forecasts and Policy*, Amsterdam: North-Holland.

Thirlwall, A.P. (1989), *Growth and Development with Special Reference to Developing Economies*, London: Macmillan Education Limited.

Tinbergen, J. (1952), *On the Theory of Economic Policy*, Amsterdam: North-Holland.

Tobin, J. (1965), 'Money and Economic Growth', *Econometrica*, **33**:671–684.

Tobin, J. (1978), 'A Proposal for International Monetary Reform', *Eastern Economic Journal*, **4**:153–159.

Todaro, M. (1994), *Economic Development in the Third World*, New York: Longman.

Triffin, R. (1960), *Gold and the Dollar Crisis*, New Haven: Yale University Press.

Triffin, R. and H. Grubel (1962), 'Adjustment Mechanism to Differential Rates of Monetary Expansion Among the Countries of the European Economic Community', *Review of Economics and Statistics*, **44**, (November):486–491.

Tseng, W. and R. Corker (1991), 'Financial Liberalization, Money Demand, and Monetary Policy in Asian Countries', *IMF Occasional Paper 84*, Washington, DC.

Tun Wai, U. and C. Wong (1982), 'Determinants of Private Investment in Developing Countries', *Journal of Development Studies*, **19**:19–36.

UNCTAD (various issues), *UNCTAD Bulletin*, Geneva: United Nations.

UNDP (1992), *Human Development Report 1992*, New York: Oxford University Press.

Wade, R. (1990), *Governing the Market: Economic Theory and the Role of Government in East Asian Industrialization*, New Jersey: Princeton University Press.

Weisskoph, T.E. (1972), 'The Impact of Foreign Capital Inflow on Domestic Savings in Underdeveloped Countries', *Journal of International Economics*, **2**:25–38.

Whitman, M. (1969), 'Economic Openness and International Financial Flows', *Journal of Money, Credit and Banking*, **1** (November):727–749.

Williamson, O. (1975), *Markets and Hierarchies: Analysis and Antitrust Implications*, New York: Free Press.

World Bank (various years), *World Bank Development Report*, New York: Oxford University Press.

World Bank (various years), *World Tables*, Washington, DC: World Bank.

World Bank (1993), *The East Asian Miracle: Economic Growth and Public Policy*, New York: Oxford University Press.

World Bank (1994), *Adjustment in Africa; Reform, Results, and the Road Ahead*, World Bank Policy Research Report, New York: Oxford University Press.

Index

absorption policies 74–5, 79
accounting identities, absorption
  approach and 50, 74
accumulation of capital 80–81
adjustable fixed exchange rate system
  201
African countries 4, 83
  adjustment program and 95
  capital flight 32
  debt crisis 120–21
  foreign aid 89, 91–2, 96, 115
  seigniorage and inflation tax 168, 170,
    173
  see also individual countries
Agenor, P.R. 125, 137, 144–5, 147, 149,
  168–9
Aghevli, B. 36, 184, 202, 209, 211
agriculture 185–6, 189, 193, 199
aid donors and recipients 86
aid-fatigue 115
Alesina, A. 153, 218–19, 224
Amin, President Idi 215
Argentina 5, 15, 188
  capital flight 124
  capital inflows 83, 91, 98, 109
  currency boards 210, 225
  debt crisis 92, 95, 120, 122
Argy, V. 37, 39, 53, 111
Asia-Pacific countries 6, 29, 56, 110,
  211
Asian countries
  budget deficit 143, 151–2
  capital flight 32, 128
  capital flows 91–2, 97, 102–3, 108
  classification of states 220
  currency trading in 125
  foreign aid programmes 115
  level of political instability 209
  real effective exchange rate 186, 189
  real targets approach exchange rates
    206

seigniorage and inflation tax 167–74,
  171, 173
successful 7, 83, 215
see also individual countries
Australia 83, 86, 91, 94, 145

balance of payments 8, 12–13, 44
  absorption and 9, 49–50
  crisis model 149
  monetary approach 50–52
  monetary sector and 194–5
  problems in Latin America (1970s)
    126, 147
  sterilized 70
  unsustainable budget deficits 127, 225
Balassa, B. 11, 215
Baldwin, R.E. 80, 82
Bangladesh 5, 13, 15, 86, 143, 151, 185,
  187–9
Bardhan, P. 185, 217–18, 221–3
Barro, R.J. 144, 199
basket of hard currencies 14, 29, 201
Bauer, P. 87, 89
Belgium 168–9
Benelux 91
Bhagwiti, J. 3, 215
Bhutan 15, 151
black markets, foreign currency and 125
Bolivia 15, 93, 122, 168, 172–3, 188
bonds 97, 132, 134, 141
boom-bust cycle 6–7
'bourgeois democracy' 221
Brandt Commission 42–3
Brazil
  capital flows 98
  debt crisis 95, 120, 122
  economic performance 5, 15
  gold bond prices (1930s) 93
  real time deposit rate of interest 188
  seigniorage and inflation tax 168,
    172–3

GDP 5–6, 18
monetary policy 15, 187, 189
oil and 24–5, 27
seigniorage and inflation tax 168, 171, 173
Industrial Revolution, meaning of 81
industrialization 2–3, 202, 225
industrialized countries 43, 95, 168–9, 173, 183
inflation 2–3, 7, 21, 115, 129, 168
budget deficits and 135–6, 150
crop failure in developing countries 189–90, 200
developing countries and 139–40, 164–7
effect on conventional tax system 165, 167
exchange rates and 202, 213
financial sector aversion to 226
intertemporal equilibrium 179–80
monetary phenomenon 156–60, 174–80, 199
monetization effect of capital inflows 102, 108
money creation and 1, 135, 154, 164
phase diagram of 180
political economy of 209–10, 212
supply shocks and 186–90
inflation shocks 19, 20–21
inflation tax revenue 164–7
institutional changes 37–44
need for 220–26
institutions, organizations and 215–16
Integrated Programme for Commodities (IPC) 44
internal balance, open economy and 19
internal and external balance 54–5, 79
international commodity agreements (ICA) 44
international competitiveness, inflation rate and 48
International Monetary Fund *see* IMF
International Trade Centre (ITC) 44
International Trade Organisation (ITO) 40
Iran 15, 187
Islam, I. 37, 181
Israel 15, 87, 89
Italy 86, 168–9

Jamaica 15, 168, 172
Japan 86, 168–9
Jordan 15, 86

Kaldor, N. 2, 164
Kalecki, M. 2, 164
Kandil, M. 184–5
Kearney, C. 111, 145
Kenen, P.B. 203–4
Kenya 15, 18, 25, 86, 138, 168, 170, 187–8
Keynes, J.M. 161, 181
Keynesian
consumption function 182
economics 19, 52, 144, 181, 183, 185, 205
Khan, M. 165, 183, 211
Khan, M.S. 125, 127–9, 183
Korea 4–6, 15, 18, 25, 27, 30, 98, 143, 187–9
Krueger, A. 3, 28, 215
Krugman, P.R. 120, 127, 146–7, 150, 177
Kuenzler, L.T. 36, 201, 205

Lao 15, 151
Larrain, F. 118–19, 120–21, 123–4, 147, 160, 167
Latin American countries 4, 152, 185
balance-of-payments crises 147, 174
capital flight 32, 123–4, 126, 128, 131
capital flows and 91, 96–7, 102–3, 108, 131
debt crisis (1930s) 93–4, 118
debt crisis (1980s) 118, 120–22, 152
gold bond prices (1930s) 93
nominal anchor approach exchange rate 206
oil shocks and 95
political instability 209
private foreign capital 115
'quasi-fiscal' cost 29
ratios of debt service to exports 122
seigniorage and inflation tax 167–8, 172–3
unstable inflation and growth 181
see also individual countries
Lesotho 15, 168, 170
Lewis, W.A. 20, 80–82
Little, I. 4, 6–7, 11, 25, 34, 37, 39, 52